Oxford Studies in Philosophy of Law

Volume 3

EDITED BY

JOHN GARDNER
University of Oxford

LESLIE GREEN
University of Oxford

BRIAN LEITER
University of Chicago

CW01425543

OXFORD
UNIVERSITY PRESS

OXFORD
UNIVERSITY PRESS

Great Clarendon Street, Oxford, OX2 6DP,
United Kingdom

Oxford University Press is a department of the University of Oxford.
It furthers the University's objective of excellence in research, scholarship,
and education by publishing worldwide. Oxford is a registered trade mark of
Oxford University Press in the UK and in certain other countries

Published in the United States of America by Oxford University Press
198 Madison Avenue, New York, NY 10016, United States of America

British Library Cataloguing in Publication Data
Data available

Library of Congress Cataloging in Publication Data
Data available

ISBN 978-0-19-882817-4 (hbk.)
978-0-19-882818-1 (pbk.)

Printed and bound by
CPI Group (UK) Ltd, Croydon, CR0 4YY

Oxford Studies in
Philosophy of Law

Contents

List of Contributors

James Edwards is Tutorial Fellow in Law at Worcester College and Lecturer in Law at Brasenose College, University of Oxford.

Stephen Finlay is Professor of Philosophy at the University of Southern California.

Richard Holton is Professor of Philosophy at the University of Cambridge and Fellow of Peterhouse.

Rae Langton is Knightbridge Professor of Philosophy at the University of Cambridge and a Fellow of Newnham College.

Liam Murphy is Herbert Peterfreund Professor of Law and Professor of Philosophy at New York University.

David Plunkett is Assistant Professor of Philosophy at Dartmouth College.

Victor Tadros is Professor of Criminal Law and Legal Theory at the University of Warwick.

Kevin Toh is Senior Lecturer in the Faculty of Laws at University College London.

I

Plan-Attitudes, Plan-Contents, and Bootstrapping: Some Thoughts on the Planning Theory of Law

1. INTRODUCTION

Scott Shapiro calls the theory about the nature of law that he presents in his book *Legality* (2011) "the planning theory of law". And the germ of the theory is contained in his thoughts that laws are plans or plan-like norms, and that legal systems are institutions of social planning (pp. 120, 171). From elaborations on these ideas, Shapiro infers much that is of significance and interest for legal philosophy, including allegedly a vindication of legal positivism.

This paper is a critical assessment of the planning theory of law.[1] Given the limitations of space, I will have to skip over what I deem its many considerable theoretical virtues. The planning theory could be considered a culmination of some dominant trends in contemporary philosophical thinking about the nature of law, the trends that actually unite most participants in the debate, including those belonging to nominally opposing camps. And the problems of the theory that I will identify in this paper are, in my view, symptomatic of those trends. Here, I diagnose those trends in a way that shows why they lead to the problems that I identify, while also discussing some problems specific to the planning theory. Elsewhere, I have been developing an alternative and, what appears to me, better trajectory in legal philosophical thinking

---

[1] This paper was substantially written in 2012–13. There are certain parts of the paper that I would articulate differently now if I were writing it afresh, but I still endorse the broad outlines of the paper. There are also some significant and relevant contributions to the literature that have appeared in the intervening years that I do not discuss here.

Oxford Studies in Philosophy of Law Volume 3. John Gardner, Leslie Green, and Brian Leiter (eds)
This chapter © Kevin Toh 2018. First published in 2018 by Oxford University Press

shorn of those trends. Although the arguments of this paper are in great measure negative, they are meant to have the positive effect of helping the reader to see why that alternative trajectory is worth developing.

I will first point to a distinction that will prove crucial in my assessment of the planning theory of law—namely, the distinction between the psychological attitudes of planning on the one hand and the contents of plans on the other (Section 2). I will go on to argue that, at least on first glance, Shapiro's attempt to vindicate legal positivism by invoking the nature of plans is significantly hampered by his being less than scrupulous about that distinction (Section 3). There are, however, also indications that Shapiro's more considered opinion is that some principle of instrumental rationality requires us to be bound by our plans once we form and do not abandon them, and he seems to be appealing to this principle in trying to bridge the gap between the "existence conditions" of plan-contents and those of plan-attitudes. And Shapiro seems to believe that this way of bridging the gap between plan-attitudes and plan-contents, combined with a conception of laws as plans, will afford a vindication of legal positivism. In several sections that form the torso of this paper (Sections 4–7), I will argue that the assumption, shared by many contemporary legal philosophers, including Shapiro, that there is a need to bridge the gap between some set of conative psychological attitudes and their contents arises from a failure to distinguish among different kinds of legal facts. I will then go on to argue, in closing (Sections 8–9), that, even assuming the need to bridge the aforementioned gap between plan-attitudes and plan-contents, it is quite unlikely that there is a plausible version of any principle of instrumental rationality that would be serviceable for that purpose.

2. ATTITUDES AND CONTENTS

I begin by pointing to a distinction to which Shapiro seems insufficiently attentive. Let us say that I suspect the following about my neighbor Judy:

(1A)   Judy believes that it will rain tomorrow.

It is quite clear that the kind of investigation that I should undertake to determine whether Judy actually has this belief is quite different from the kind of investigation that I should undertake to determine whether

Judy's belief is true—i.e. whether it will rain tomorrow. Both are empirical investigations, but whereas the former would be a psychological investigation, the latter would be a meteorological investigation.[2]

An analogous distinction can be observed when I suspect the following of Judy:

(2A)   Judy believes that drivers ought to refrain from using cellphones.

The contents of the two beliefs referred to in (1A) and (2A) are as follows, respectively:

(1C)   It will rain tomorrow.

(2C)   Drivers ought to refrain from using cellphones.

(1C) is a descriptive content, whereas (2C) is a normative content. According to some metanormative views, an attitude that takes a normative content rather than a descriptive content as its object is not strictly speaking a belief, but something more like a desire. But let me set that issue aside. Whatever the nature of the psychological attitude involved, in determining whether Judy actually has that attitude, once again, I would have to undertake a psychological investigation. On the other hand, to determine whether what she believes—namely, (2C)—is the case, whether it is true or correct, I would have to undertake a normative investigation. I would have to figure out, for example, whether the kinds of risks that cellphone-using drivers impose on themselves and others are worth taking.[3]

As we distinguish between the psychological attitudes of belief (or their desiderative counterparts) on the one hand and their contents on the

---

[2] Of course, there is the possibility that Judy is a local meteorologist, in which case it may make sense for me to figure out what she believes in order to determine what the weather will be like tomorrow. I am neglecting this and similar possibilities in the text.

[3] I have proceeded as if psychological explanations and investigations are non-normative. And I would like to retain this supposition throughout the rest of this paper. There is, of course, an influential strand in the philosophy of psychology that conceives psychological explanations and investigations as partly normative. See e.g. Davidson (1970 & 1974a). I am conjecturing that whatever norms or principles of rationality that constitute psychological facts and that need to be appealed to in psychological explanations, they are, to use Cherniak's (1986) terminology, norms or principles of "minimal" rationality rather than those of "ideal" rationality. It is the latter that we need to invoke in normative investigations that we need to carry out to assess (2C) and its ilk. I cannot defend this conjecture here, but I hope it is sufficiently plausible to entitle me to treat psychological investigations as quite different in kind from the more fully or ideally normative investigations. By "normative" in the text then, I mean "ideally normative", or at least "more than minimally normative".

other, so we should distinguish between the psychological attitudes of planning (or having a plan) on the one hand and their contents on the other. Let us say that I suspect the following of Judy:

(3A)   Judy plans to visit the zoo this Saturday.

Unlike in the cases of (1A) and (2A), there is no "that"-clause in (3A). This syntactic difference, however, does not seem to be of deep theoretical significance for the purposes of this paper. For we can reformulate (3A) as:

(3A′)   Judy plans that she visit the zoo this Saturday.

What follows "that" in (3A′) is the content of Judy's plan. And that content should be distinguished from the psychological attitude of planning that Judy has. In order to talk about both the psychological attitude of planning and the content of such an attitude without inviting unnecessary confusion, it would be helpful to employ hereinafter the terms "plan-attitudes" and "plan-contents".

To determine whether (3A′) is the case—i.e. whether Judy has the above-mentioned plan-attitude—once again, I would have to undertake a psychological investigation. What about the investigation to determine whether Judy's plan-content is the case—i.e. whether it is correct or apt? The nature of this investigation would depend on the nature of the plan-content—whether it is a descriptive content like (1C) or a normative content like (2C). Michael Bratman, from whom Shapiro borrows much of his thinking about plans, reserves the term "plan" to refer to psychological attitudes, and the functionalist characterization that he provides of plans is meant to distinguish these psychological items from other ones like beliefs and desires. Bratman says that these attitudes are larger and less detailed versions of intentions, and he classifies intentions as "pro-attitudes".[4] Despite his theoretical debts to Bratman's work, Shapiro differs from Bratman in his explicit conception of plans as contents, and not psychological attitudes. He says:

By a "plan," I am not referring to the mental state of "having a plan." Intentions are not plans, but rather take plans as their objects. For my purposes, plans are abstract propositional entities that require, permit, or authorize agents to act, or not act, in certain ways under certain conditions.   (2011, p. 127)

---

[4] See Bratman (1987, pp. 15, 28–9). Bratman says early in his book that "[i]ntentions are, so to speak, building blocks of . . . plans; and plans are intentions writ large" (p. 8).

Shapiro further says that plans are a species of norms (pp. 127–9). We can infer that plan-contents, as Shapiro conceives them, are normative rather than descriptive. It follows that the content of Judy's plan could be formulated as follows:

(3C)   Judy ought to visit the zoo this Saturday.

And (3A′) in turn could be reformulated as:

(3A″)   Judy plans that she ought to visit the zoo this Saturday.

Perhaps weaker versions of these theses in terms of "reasons" rather than "ought" would be more accurate. But for now, we can bracket this issue given the way I will be reformulating these theses shortly.

I want to reformulate (3A″) and (3C) further in order to avert a particular misunderstanding that could detain us or trip us up unnecessarily. There is a tendency among some philosophers, especially many legal philosophers, to take any "ought" (or at least any practical "ought") as a moral "ought". Philosophers with such an inclination would read (3A″) as attributing to Judy what necessarily is a moral commitment, and also read (3C) as necessarily a moral content. To avert such readings, the two could be reformulated as:

(3A*)   Judy plans that she is to visit the zoo this Saturday.
(3C*)   Judy is to visit the zoo this Saturday.

These formulations, I hope, retain the sense in which Judy's plan-content is a normative content, without the unwanted implication that necessarily it is a moral content, and the sense in which Judy's plan-attitude is a normative attitude, without the unwanted implication that necessarily it is a moral commitment. To be sure, the locution "is to" is not unambiguous. But to my (albeit non-native) ear, there is a sense of "is to" that is synonymous with "should" or "ought to", without at the same time carrying any moral import as some philosophers think that "should" or "ought to" invariably does.[5] It is that sense that I am invoking in formulating (3A*) and (3C*) as I do.

In any case, given the just-specified nature of plan-contents, it follows that the investigation to determine whether any plan-content is the case

---

[5] Smith (1994, p. 7), for example, distinguishes beliefs and desires in terms of their "directions of fit" by saying that the former psychological states represent how the world is, whereas the latter represent how the world "is to be".

is at least partly a normative investigation, whereas the investigation to determine whether someone has a plan-attitude is a psychological and more generally an empirical investigation.

3. "PLAN POSITIVISM"

At a couple of key junctures in *Legality*, Shapiro says that "plan positivism" is uncontroversially true (2011, pp. 119, 178). The term "plan positivism" is obviously a play on "legal positivism". Early in his book, Shapiro explains legal positivism as the metaphysical thesis that "all legal facts are ultimately determined by social facts alone"—i.e. facts about "what people think, intend, claim, say, and do"—and the accompanying epistemological thesis that investigations to determine what the law is are empirical, and more specifically sociological, investigations (p. 27).[6] In endorsing plan positivism then, Shapiro is endorsing the idea that all "plan facts" are ultimately determined by such "social facts" alone, and the accompanying idea that investigations to determine "what the plan is" are empirical, and more specifically sociological, investigations. He thinks that this last pair of views is uncontroversially true, and in fact the ruling design of *Legality* is to appeal to the allegedly uncontroversial plan positivism and the conception of laws as plans (and plan-like norms) to infer and vindicate legal positivism.

The distinction I made in the preceding section between plan-attitudes and plan-contents, however, should give us pause. What Shapiro says about plan positivism is as follows:

> The proper way to establish the existence of plans...is simply to point to the fact of their adoption and acceptance. Whether I have a plan to go to the store today, or we have a plan to cook dinner together tonight, depends not on the desirability of these plans but simply on whether we have in fact adopted (and not yet rejected) them.   (p. 119)

Here, by speaking of "the existence of a plan", Shapiro seems to be speaking of someone having a plan-attitude, rather than of a plan-content being the case. Now, "positivism" about the existence of plan-attitudes is quite compelling. Whether Judy has a plan to go to the zoo seems to

---

[6] I am here speaking only of legal reasoning strictly so-called. Shapiro draws a distinction between "legal reasoning" and "judicial decision making", and concedes that the latter often involves appeals to normative considerations. See Shapiro (2011, chs. 8–9, esp. pp. 247–8).

be determined fully by social facts, or perhaps more particularly by psychological facts, alone. And an investigation to determine whether Judy has a plan to go to the zoo this Saturday, for example, would be an empirical investigation, and more specifically a psychological one. But what Shapiro needs, to argue eventually for legal positivism, is not plan-*attitude* positivism, but plan-*content* positivism. After all, what could be called "moral judgment positivism" is no less plausible than plan-attitude positivism. In other words, the fact that a person has made or holds a moral judgment would consist entirely of social or psychological facts, and any investigation to determine whether such a fact exists would be a purely empirical investigation. If plan-attitude positivism were sufficient to imply legal positivism, then moral judgment positivism would be sufficient to imply moral positivism as well. Shapiro explicitly rejects moral positivism (p. 118), and presumably this rejection is motivated by his conception of moral positivism as the view that the *content* of morality, not merely the existence of moral judgments or moral practices, is determined ultimately by social facts alone. Likewise, if plan positivism were to give support to legal positivism, the former should not be taken to mean merely that the existence of plan-attitudes, or of any social practices motivated by such attitudes, is determined ultimately by social facts alone, but instead or also that plan-contents are determined ultimately by social facts alone.

The problem for Shapiro is that plan-content positivism is not as obvious or uncontroversial as plan-attitude positivism. As I pointed out in the preceding section, if we conceive plan-contents as normative contents as it seems that we should, and as Shapiro actually seems to do, then the natural position to take is that they are determined at least partly by normative considerations, and it would follow that any investigation to ascertain that they are the case would be at least partly a normative investigation. That is far from positivism as Shapiro characterizes that notion. The worry then is that in deploying the planning theory of law to vindicate legal positivism, Shapiro relies crucially on an equivocation between plan-attitudes and plan-contents, and that this equivocation vitiates his case for legal positivism.

My impression is that at the very least Shapiro draws substantial rhetorical benefits from the aforementioned equivocation between plan-attitudes and plan-contents. But I also believe that he would have something to say in response to the charge of equivocation. Shapiro seems to think that plans are quite special in the sense that whether any plan-content is the case depends solely or at least significantly—that is, much more so than is the case with other kinds of conative attitudes—on whether the corresponding plan-attitude is held (by the person or community that the relevant plan-content refers to).[7] In other words, Shapiro seems to think that plans are special in enabling a sort of *bootstrapping* from the mere having of plan-attitudes to the relevant plan-contents being the case—i.e. from a mere *attitude* positivism to a *content* positivism. This I think is what he is getting at when he says: "Plans are 'positive' entities—they are created via adoption and sustained through acceptance. By contrast, logical and moral norms exist simply by virtue of their ultimate validity" (p. 128). And Shapiro is of the opinion that some principle(s) of instrumental rationality enable such bootstrapping (pp. 123, 416 n.4).

A frustrating feature of *Legality*, however, is that it merely mentions but does not develop or defend this suggestive thesis. What exactly (or even approximately) is the content(s) of the principle(s) of instrumental rationality that connects a person's holding a plan-attitude with the relevant plan-content being the case? How is this normative relation different from analogous relations between other conative attitudes and their contents, respectively? We would need answers to such questions to assess the plausibility of Shapiro's bootstrapping thesis, and also to see whether his case for legal positivism based on plan positivism is any more credible than the ones based on the "positivisms" of other conative psychological attitudes.

I believe, however, that, there is an even more significant gap in Shapiro's reasoning. This has to do with the very motivation for wanting to bootstrap for the purposes of legal philosophy. Shapiro is not alone among contemporary legal philosophers for wanting to establish a bootstrapping relation between certain psychological facts—or more accurately, the existence of a certain social practice among a group of people, which is partly constituted by a certain kind of psychological attitudes on the part of the people—on the one hand, and normative contents on the other. Indeed, Shapiro's planning theory of law is meant to be the latest entrant

---

[7] Notice that a plan-content like (3C*) in Section 2 above refers to the agent who is to do what the plan-content calls for. For simplicity's sake, I shall be assuming throughout this paper that the relevant agent is the one who has the plan-attitude. This assumption is not always apt, but I do not think this issue is material for the purposes of this paper.

in the contest to establish such a relation, and it is meant to solve problems that beset all prior legal philosophical attempts to establish such a relation. As I will point out in Sections 8–9 below, there are reasons to question whether Shapiro succeeds in establishing such a relation and in enabling thereby a bootstrapping of the relevant sort. But there is a more pressing need, I think, to explain and question the need to establish such a relation. And it is to this last task I first turn in the next four sections.

4. VARIETIES OF POSITIVISM

The felt need to establish a bootstrapping relation between a set of conative psychological attitudes and their contents stems from a certain understanding of legal positivism. Once again, Shapiro himself explains legal positivism as the thesis that "all legal facts are ultimately determined by social facts alone"—i.e. facts about "what people think, intend, claim, say, and do" (2011, p. 27). This recently very typical formulation of legal positivism, however, is multiply equivocal. Certain things it could mean are rightly considered commitments or implications of the legal theories that are typically classified as legal positivist; whereas certain other things it could mean are at best only contingently related to such theories, and in my opinion mistakenly demanded of such theories by many contemporary legal philosophers.[8]

Before going on, let me be quite explicit about an issue. Although in what follows I will be speaking of what legal positivist theories are really committed to or imply, and what they are only spuriously or contingently connected with, I am in the end uninterested in regimenting the usage of the label "legal positivism". Some theses that are often associated with legal positivism are warranted because they are commitments or implications of legal theories that are explanatorily successful; whereas other theses are not so warranted by explanatory considerations. Where exactly in the list of these various theses the line between genuine legal positivism and non-genuine legal positivism should be drawn seems unimportant. My concern instead is to show that the aforementioned desire to bootstrap is borne out of commitments, explicit or implicit, by legal philosophers to a set of theses that are not warranted on explanatory grounds. It would

---

[8] Gardner (2001) also has an aim of "unbundling", as its author puts it, genuine commitments of legal positivism from some associations and connections that that view of the nature of law has come to acquire over the years. My specific conclusions, however, are quite different from Gardner's.

follow that *credible* theories about the nature of law, including credible legal positivist theories, should not be committed to such theses.

The equivocal nature of Shapiro's conception of legal positivism stems from ambiguities of "legal facts" and "determines". I shall here concentrate on "legal facts", as the appropriate senses of "determines" would follow to a large extent from the kinds of legal facts that we are concerned with. In order to facilitate the reader's comprehension of the distinctions among various legal facts I have in mind, let me first distinguish among the following types of *moral* facts:[9]

(MF1)   A community has (or is governed by) mores, or a set of moral norms.

(MF2)   Some particular norm is one of a community's mores, or is treated by the members of that community as one of their moral norms.

(MF3)   Some such-and-such is morally the case.

I hope these three moral facts strike the reader as intuitively quite distinct from each other. And we can draw a distinction among analogous statements of legal facts:

(LF1)   A community has (or is governed by) laws, or a set of legal norms.

(LF2)   Some particular norm is one of a community's laws, or is treated by the members or officials of the community as one of their legal norms.[10]

(LF3)   Some such-and-such is legally the case in a community.

It is easy to lose sight of the distinction between (LF2) and (LF3), but the distinction between (MF2) and (MF3) should give us a pause before jumping too quickly to equate (LF2) and (LF3). Both distinctions

---

[9] By speaking of "facts" in the text, my intention is not to prejudge any metaethical or metanormative issues. For all I have said, some form of non-factualism about morality and/or law may be the case, in which case (MF3) and/or (LF3) would not be a "fact" in any robust, non-deflationary sense of "fact". The reader can assume that I am working with a suitably deflationary sense of "fact" in formulating the theses in the text.

[10] Our terminological resources are not what they should be. Notice that the availability of the term "mores" makes the second clause of (MF2) plainly redundant. But the term "laws" has to do double duty when discussing legal matters. It refers to both the norms that are treated as legal norms and the norms that actually are legally the case. The unavailability of a legal analogue of "mores" makes the second clause of (LF2) necessary.

mark the difference between what is treated as the case and what really is the case. My point is that we should be mindful of that difference in law as well as in morality. Many think that the very point or essence of legal positivism is to collapse that distinction, so that if some norm were treated (in some appropriate way) by the members of a community as their law, then that alone would be sufficient for the content of that norm to be legally the case in that community. But H.L.A. Hart is the paradigmatic legal positivist of recent times, and Hart was especially keen to mark out the distinction in question by distinguishing what he called "external legal statements" from what he called "internal legal statements" (1961/94, pp. vi, 89–91, 102–5; cf. Bulygin 1982). The former are made to represent facts of the (LF2) variety; whereas the latter are made to represent the facts of the (LF3) variety.[11] The recent tendency among many legal philosophers to all but ignore the distinction between these two kinds of legal statements has exacerbated the tendency to elide between (LF2) and (LF3).

The tendency among many recent legal philosophers to ignore the distinction among different sorts of legal facts is displayed and also exacerbated by their frequent characterization of Hart as espousing what is called a "practice theory of rules". The term is of Joseph Raz's devising, but the characterization of Hart's position that the term sums up goes back to Ronald Dworkin. Hart conceived laws as a particular kind of rules, and his theory of the nature of law is founded on his conception of rules. According to the practice theory of rules that Raz attributes to Hart, rules *are* practices. Rules in effect consist of, or are constituted by, the psychological and behavioral facts that make up practices.[12] This reading of Hart has proved enormously influential, and quite consequential for the subsequent development of legal philosophy.

---

[11] The sense of "represent" here is meant to be deflationary in the way that the sense of "facts" is, as I observed in note 9 above. If nonfactualism were suitable for (LF3) facts, then the obvious semantics for statements of such facts would be some form of expressivism, according to which such statements are non-representational in the robust, non-deflationary sense of "representational". Indeed, as I argued in Toh (2005), Hart arguably opted for an expressivist analysis of internal legal statements.

[12] See Raz (1975/90, §2.1) for the definitive attribution of this conception of rules to Hart. Raz (p. 205 n.7) cites Dworkin (1972). At one point in that paper, Dworkin characterizes Hart's view as follows:

Duties exist when social rules exist providing for such duties. Such social rules exist when the practice-conditions are met. These practice-conditions are met when the members of a community behave in a certain way; this behavior *constitutes* a social rule, and imposes a duty.   (p. 49)

Many if not most contemporary legal philosophers have adopted both the terminology of "practice theory", and more importantly the conception of Hart's legal theory that the terminology implies.[13] But Hart's actual view was quite a bit different. Hart says that statements stating "existence" of rules may be internal statements by which speakers express their acceptances of the relevant rules, or external statements by which they describe a community members' acceptances of the rules (1961/94, pp. 109–12; cf. p. 291). The talk of the practice theory may be an adequate explanation of "the existence of rules" that the latter kind of statements represent, but it completely overlooks the normative facts that the former kind of statements represent. In sum, the characterization of Hart as espousing and building on a practice theory of rules excises from the picture what is a central element of his position, and has the effect of having him ignore the distinction between (LF1) and (LF2) facts on the one hand and (LF3) facts on the other. And insofar as many contemporary legal philosophers see themselves as following Hart, they too seem to ignore this distinction in their own theorizing about the nature of law.

While conceding a general distinction between (LF2) and (LF3), some may argue that when it comes to the ultimate legal norms, or what Hart calls "rules of recognition", the distinction collapses. In other words, it may be argued that the following two facts are *not* distinct:

(LF2$_R$)   Some particular norm is treated by the members or officials of a community as the rule of recognition of their legal system.

(LF3$_R$)   The rule of recognition of the community's legal system demands or calls for such-and-such.

Hart himself has lent some credence to this position by saying at one point in *The Concept of Law* that "[t]he assertion that [a rule of recognition] exists can only be an external statement of fact" (1961/94, p. 110; cf. 1958, p. 88). Some, including Shapiro (2011, pp. 93–104, esp. p. 413 n.29), make much of this passage and read Hart as here trying to collapse the distinction between (LF2$_R$) and (LF3$_R$). But it is far from clear that

---

[13] See e.g. Greenberg (2006a, p. 126; 2006b, pp. 271–2; 2011, p. 69); Gardner (2008, pp. 66–70; cf. 2012, pp. 280, 283); Leiter (2009, p. 1222); Marmor (2009, p. 156); Shapiro (2011, p. 95); Green (2012, pp. xxi, xxvii).

this last is a considered opinion on Hart's part. In fact, merely two pages later, Hart says:

[W]e need to remember that the ultimate rule of recognition may be regarded from two points of view: one is expressed in the external statement of fact that the rule exists in the actual practice of the system; the other is expressed in the internal statements of validity made by those who use it in the identifying of the law. (1961/94, p. 112)[14]

In any case, Hart's first statement (on p. 110) is at best an ad hoc addendum to his legal theory. Let me explain.

Hart's theory is an explanatory theory meant to account for significant invariable or noncontingent facts about communities governed by laws in such a way as to show law's differences from other means of social regulation such as morality and coercion. Such facts include: (i) the fact that legal systems include some power-conferring norms (as opposed to duty-imposing norms) among laws; (ii) the fact that certain customary norms are legally valid even before being recognized as such by anyone; (iii) the fact that there can be legal limitations on the powers of all legislators; (iv) the fact that laws are amenable to deliberate change; and (v) the fact that legal disputes are amenable to decisive and authoritative resolutions. It is the failure of command theories of law proposed by Jeremy Bentham and John Austin to explain some of these facts, such as (i)–(iii), that prompted Hart to propose an alternative theory. And this alternative theory can be roughly summed up as:

(H)   A community is governed by laws when its members are regu-
      lated in their behavior and practical thought by their accept-
      ances of a set of norms, which set includes some higher-order

---

[14] I believe that there was a complex set of reasons that motivated Hart to make his claim on p. 110 that assertions of the existence of a rule of recognition can only be an external statement of fact, none central to his theory. Most likely, Hart thought that the notion of validity could not appropriately be predicated of rules that are not systematized—either because they do not belong to systems of rules or because they are the rules that validate and are not validated by other rules—and he is over-generalizing from that thought to deny the possibility of internal statements that assert unsystematized rules. Hart also seems to have been much impressed with Wittgenstein's (1921) view that some things, including the rules of logical inference, can only be shown and not said. From time to time, Hart flirts with the idea that rules of recognition can only be shown and not said. See e.g. Hart (1961/94, p. 101). This seems to be one reason why Hart is sometimes reluctant to say that one can outright assert the content of a rule of recognition, rather than merely showing one's acceptance of it in asserting the contents of subordinate legal norms. The first hypothesis is considered a bit further in Toh (2014/15, pp. 343–4).

norms governing the following types of operations of the norms
of the set: (i) revision of the norms of the set; (ii) resolution of
disputes about the norms of the set; and (iii) identification of
the norms that belong to the set.

This is Hart's account of (LF1). His position is that the fact that a community is governed by laws consists of, is determined by, the behavioral and psychological facts that (H) summarizes, and that this conception enables us to account for all the significant explananda that we want to account for. With (H), we also get an account of (LF2$_R$). According to (H), the existence of a legal system in a community requires the members of that community (or their officials more specifically) to employ a norm that sets out the criteria that norms need to meet for them to belong to that community's legal system. And the fact that a particular norm is treated by the members or officials of the community as their rule of recognition consists of, or is determined by, their acceptance of it and their being motivated by it in their identifications of the norms of their legal system.

Now, here is the important question: Does (H) also imply an account of (LF3$_R$)? Does (H) say that the fact that a particular norm *is* the rule of recognition of a community—and not just the fact that that norm *is treated as* the rule of recognition—consists of, or is determined by, the fact that the members or officials of the community accept that norm and are motivated by it in their identifications of the norms of their legal system? Does (H) provide us with first-order legal truths, or the truth- or correctness-makers of first-order legal statements, as well as being a meta-legal theory that informs us of the nature of law? I submit that the answer is "no", or at least that (H) need not be construed so. Notice that (H) is compatible with either option on (LF3$_R$). That is, (H) is compatible with the view that (LF3$_R$) consists of the fact that the people of a community accept a particular norm and are motivated in their law-identifications by that acceptance, and also with the view that (LF3$_R$) consists of something else altogether—e.g. some alternative sets of social facts, some norms, or some combination of social facts and norms. Think again of the moral analogues of the crucial theses. We can resort to certain metaethical views to come up with a moral analogue of (H). According to Allan Gibbard's (1990) influential conception of morality, for example, the norms of morality can be distinguished from other norms by the fact that the norms of morality regulate the emotions of guilt and impartial anger.[15] We can sum up the resulting conditions for the existence of a morality as follows:

> (G)   A community is governed by mores when its members regulate their emotions of guilt and impartial anger by a set of norms, and those emotions of guilt and impartial anger in turn regulate the members' behavior and practical thought.

Like (H), (G) needs to earn its keep by its explanatory work, but we need not here try to assess (G), as we are using it merely as an example. (G) is an account of (MF1), and implies an account of what could be called "(MF2$_R$)". (G) implies that the fact that the members of a community treat some norm as the ultimate norm of morality consists of their acceptance of that norm as the highest norm for regulating the emotions of guilt and impartial anger. But notice that it does not imply that the fact that some norm *is* the ultimate norm of morality consists of the same fact. A community of people may treat, say, the principle of utility as their ultimate moral norm. But that alone would not mean that the ultimate moral norm really is the principle of utility. Clearly, (G) is compatible with alternative accounts of what could be labeled "(MF3$_R$)"; analogously, I am arguing, (H) is compatible with different accounts of (LF3$_R$).

I hope I have gone a fair distance in persuading the reader to see that there are several different senses of "legal facts". And given these several senses, there are correspondingly different senses of "legal positivism". Once again, Shapiro defines legal positivism as the thesis that "all legal facts are ultimately determined by social facts alone"—i.e. facts about "what people think, intend, claim, say, and do" (2011, p. 27). And he further says at one point that "[a] legal fact is a fact about either the existence or the content of a particular legal system" (p. 25). These statements suggest that Shapiro thinks that legal positivism requires all LF-facts we have so far listed as determined solely by social facts. But if my preceding arguments are on the right track, then we have at least one legal theory that is considered a paradigmatic legal positivist theory—namely, the one summarized by (H)—which is not committed to the

---

[15] Although Gibbard is a metaethical expressivist, this conception of morality is detachable from his expressivism. For similar conceptions of morality, see Brandt (1979, ch. 9); Williams (1986, ch. 10); Skorupski (1993). See also Hart (1961/94, ch. 9) for a more rudimentary conception along a similar line.

view that (LF3) and (LF3$_R$) are determined by social facts alone. More important, given that our real goal in devising theories of the nature of law is to explain certain significant noncontingent features of communities with laws, we must wonder why exactly we should try to show that the fact that the law is such-and-such, or that the rule of recognition is such-and-such, is determined by social facts alone. In other words, we must wonder what noncontingent features of communities with laws we end up missing if we fail to establish that (LF3) and (LF3$_R$) are determined by social facts alone.

The fact of the matter is that at one point even Shapiro denies that (LF2$_R$) and (LF3$_R$) are equivalent. He argues that Hart tried to *reduce* (LF3$_R$) to the social facts that amount to (LF2$_R$), and that he failed in this endeavor (pp. 102–4). Shapiro further makes a rather startling claim that Hart committed a "category mistake" in trying to equate rules of recognition, which are norms, with facts about social practices. For the reasons outlined in my foregoing discussion, this strikes me as an unusually and uncharacteristically defective reading of Hart. What is more important here, however, is that although Shapiro deems Hart's attempt to establish a legal positivism of (LF3$_R$) a failure, he thinks that there is a need to establish such a positivism by some other means. It is in place of the reduction that Hart allegedly attempted that Shapiro is offering plan positivism and the crucial bootstrapping that plan positivism supposedly affords. If the social practices that amount to a community's treatment of some norm as their rule of recognition is constituted by the members of that community having plan-attitudes to follow that norm and their being motivated by such attitudes, Shapiro is in effect proposing, then we can conclude that the content of the members' shared plan is the content of the rule of recognition of that community.

5. "THE POSSIBILITY PUZZLE"

We thus have an interim answer to the question of why Shapiro feels compelled to try to establish some sort of a bootstrapping relation between plan-attitudes and plan-contents. It is to vindicate a legal positivism of (LF3), and more specifically of (LF3$_R$). I say "interim" because we so far have little idea of why we should be after such a legal positivism, in addition to the legal positivisms of the (LF1) and (LF2)/(LF2$_R$) varieties. So far, we have in our view no obvious explanandum that we get to explain only by establishing such an additional legal positivism. Shapiro's way of motivating the need to establish a legal positivism of the (LF3)/(LF3$_R$) variety in *Legality* is by way of what he calls "the Possibility Puzzle". In short, Shapiro believes that bootstrapping is necessary to solve the Possibility Puzzle, and thereby explain "the possibility of law", in a satisfactory way. It is to this puzzle I now turn.

Although Shapiro invokes the Possibility Puzzle with the explicit aim of clarifying the relevant legal philosophical dialectic (2011, p. 20), I myself find his expositions of it more obscuring than clarifying. This is especially the case when he first introduces the Puzzle by way of an allegorical sketch in chapter 2 of *Legality*. I must urge the reader to check my subsequent explanation of the Puzzle by consulting the relevant pages of *Legality* himself.[16] Having said that, as far as I can see, the Puzzle has to do with the following question. According to Hartian legal theories like (H), each community governed by laws has a rule of recognition. The question the Puzzle asks is:

(Q0)   In virtue of what is a particular norm the rule of recognition of a community's legal system?

Put another way:

(Q0')   What makes it the case that a particular norm is the rule of recognition of the relevant community's legal system?

Shapiro apparently thinks that this question needs to be answered in a proper way to explain the possibility of law. There are, I believe, actually two dialectical tributaries that converge to give rise to this question as Shapiro understands it. One tributary is Kelsenian; and the other, Dworkinian. Let me first discuss the Kelsenian tributary as that one is more prominently featured in chapter 2 of *Legality* when Shapiro first introduces the Puzzle.[17] The Dworkinian tributary becomes more prominent in chapter 4 where Shapiro critiques Hart's theory.

---

[16] Some of the crucial passages include those in pp. 20, 36–40, 95–6, 107, 115, 178–9.

[17] The Kelsenian source of the Puzzle seems to explain what at first sight may appear a gratuitously Kantian sounding way of putting it in terms of the "possibility" of law or legal authority. Cf. Coleman (2001, p. 74). Kelsen himself was writing at the height of neo-Kantianism in Continental Europe, and liked to articulate his questions and answers in Kantian terms. See e.g. Kelsen (1960, p. 202), quoted in Raz (1974, pp. 132–3).

Many followers of Raz take the question I have just articulated quite seriously,[18] and Raz (1974 & 1977) in turn has traced the problem to Hans Kelsen. Kelsen is supposed to have struggled with this question throughout his long career.[19] There have been two main camps in answering the question, according to Kelsen.[20] Natural law theorists have argued that it is partly in virtue of some moral considerations or facts that a particular norm is the rule of recognition—or "the basic norm", in Kelsen's own terminology[21]—of a legal system. Legal positivists have argued that it is in virtue only of some social facts that a particular norm is the rule of recognition or basic norm of a legal system. The problem with the natural law answer, according to Kelsen, is that it posits moral facts that are metaphysically and epistemologically suspect.[22] Kelsen's objection to the legal positivist answer is motivated by his understanding and appropriation of the Humean *is-ought* gap. Laws, including the basic norm, are norms; and such norms cannot obtain in virtue only of some social facts.[23] Shapiro (2011, pp. 45–9) essentially replicates this last consideration in his exposition of the Possibility Puzzle. Kelsen is supposed to have avoided both sets of pitfalls by a nifty maneuver of characterizing any basic norm as merely "presupposed", rather than fully endorsed.[24] Whatever the merits of that maneuver,[25] Shapiro thinks that

[18] In addition to Shapiro, see e.g. Green (1999); Gardner (2000); Coleman (2001, lecture 7); Marmor (2009, ch. 7).

[19] By saying "supposed", I am not expressing any doubt about the accuracy of Raz's and others' descriptions of Kelsen's works. I am merely registering my own limited familiarity with the Kelsenian oeuvre and the resulting inability to assess their accuracy. And given the notorious difficulty and obscurity of Kelsenian texts and doctrines, worries about the accuracy of any descriptions may be unavoidable. Raz himself prefaces his exposition with qualms about its accuracy. See Raz (1974, p. 122).

[20] See Raz (1977, p. 150); Green (1999, pp. 35–6); Shapiro (2011, pp. 42–4).

[21] As I understand it, the Kelsenian basic norm is not quite equivalent to the Hartian rule of recognition. A basic norm is the earliest in a temporal sequence of fundamental legal norms (or rules of recognition) of a community. I ignore the difference in the two notions for ease of exposition in the text.

[22] The objection seems to be essentially from what Mackie (1977, ch. 1) calls the "queerness" of moral facts. Kelsen also seems to have been motivated by a crude form of moral relativism. See Raz (1974, pp. 130–2).

[23] See Raz (1974, pp. 124–5); Green (1999, pp. 35–6); Marmor (2009, pp. 158–9).

[24] By members of the community governed by the relevant legal system? By those studying the legal system from the outside? I think the official Kelsenian line is the latter, as he is concerned with "legal science". But it is not always clear that Kelsen sticks to that line. See Raz (1974, pp. 140–1).

[25] As I will explain in Section 9 below, Shapiro eventually adopts a version of this Kelsenian move.

a satisfactory solution can be devised by keeping firmly to the allegedly legal positivist camp of thinking that any rule of recognition obtains in virtue only of some social facts. His crucial move is to construe the relevant social facts as social practices made up of plan-attitudes and behavior motivated by such attitudes. Given the special nature of plans, he thinks, "the possibility of law" can be explained without contravening the Humean *is-ought* gap in an illicit way. Presumably, the idea is that some principle(s) of instrumental rationality that enables bootstrapping from the mere holding of plan-attitudes to the relevant plan-contents being the case would enable a licit bridging of the gap.

Despite its distinguished provenance, however, it is far from clear that the Possibility question is a well-formed question. What exactly is being asked for when it is asked in virtue of what a particular norm is the rule of recognition of a community's legal system? There are multiple possibilities, none really happy for Shapiro's purposes, it appears to me. The question could be conceived as an empirical one about etiology, and could be formulated as one of the following:

(Q1) What caused a particular norm to come to be treated as the rule of recognition of a community's legal system?

(Q1′) What causes a particular norm to be treated as the rule of recognition of a community's legal system?

Shapiro's discussion sometimes veers to suggest such a conception of the Possibility question (e.g. 2011, p. 37),[26] but I believe that that is not what he really has in mind. There is nothing puzzling, or at least philosophically puzzling, about such empirical questions. We, or the specialists among us, should be able to gather the pertinent historical, anthropological, sociological, and psychological evidence to make progress in answering such questions.

Alternatively, the Possibility question could be conceived as a metaphysical question as follows:

(Q2) What facts constitute or amount to a community's *treating* a particular norm as the rule of recognition of their legal system?

In other words, what facts constitute or amount to $(LF2_R)$? Here, there is a philosophical problem, and more specifically a metaphysical problem,

---

[26] Gardner & Macklem (2011) appear to do the same in their review of Shapiro's book when they characterize the Possibility Puzzle as a "genealogical problem".

but that problem has been addressed quite satisfactorily by (H); or at least we are entitled to think so insofar as we are unable to identify any crucial explanandum that (H) fails to explain. As pointed out in Section 4, Shapiro at one point explicitly recognizes the distinction between the fact that a particular norm is treated as a rule of recognition by the members of a community and the fact that a particular norm is the rule of recognition of that community—that is, between (LF2$_R$) and (LF3$_R$). And his complaint about (H) is not that it fails to deliver a satisfactory account of the former fact, but that it fails to show that the latter fact is determined solely by the facts that constitute the former. In any case, notice that the fact that a particular norm is treated by the members of a community as their legal system's rule of recognition is a descriptive, and not a normative, fact. It follows that the Kelsenian worry about contravening the *is-ought* gap does not arise for any answer to (Q2) put in terms solely of social facts. These are indications that the Possibility question is not (Q2).

A different metaphysical question would concern (LF3$_R$), rather than (LF2$_R$). Perhaps this question can be formulated as:

(Q3)   What facts constitute or amount to a particular norm's being the rule of recognition of a community's legal system?

This question initially appears to be exactly what the Possibility question is getting at, but my suspicion is that it ends up collapsing into (Q4). Let me discuss that question first before returning to (Q3).

Perhaps what the Possibility question asks is not an empirical or metaphysical question of the preceding sorts, but is instead a first-order *legal* question. In that case, it could be formulated as:

(Q4)   What legally validates a particular norm as the rule of recognition of a community's legal system?

But notice that if we take seriously the functional role of rules of recognition as the ultimate norms of legal validity, (Q4) cannot be taken as a genuine, non-spurious question. A rule of recognition is supposed to be the ultimate standard of legal validity in a jurisdiction, and that means that there cannot be a set of facts or considerations that legally validates a particular norm as the rule of recognition of a jurisdiction. Raz, for one, has vacillated on this point. Sometimes, he seems to say that a rule of recognition is legally validated in virtue of its being accepted and followed as the ultimate legal norm (e.g. 1977, pp. 150–1); at others, he asserts that it is a mistake to talk about the legal validity of a rule of recognition (e.g. 1998, p. 381). The former would be the allegedly legal positivist answer to the Possibility question if that question were construed as (Q4); but the latter is premised on the correct understanding of the functional role of rules of recognition.

Returning to (Q3), let us say that a particular norm, say N, has been identified as the rule of recognition of a particular community's legal system. (Q3) entertains the possibility of asking what facts make it the case that N is the rule of recognition of that legal system. Let us say that we proceed to address this question by identifying some set of facts F as singling out N as enumerating the criteria of legal validity in the relevant legal system. But then, it seems to me, N would not have been a norm that sets out the *ultimate* criteria of legal validity in the legal system, but only a norm that (at best) sets out the *penultimate* criteria. For the real rule of recognition of the legal system would not be N, but instead a norm that incorporates references to F, the facts that we would invoke to answer (Q3)—or since (Q3) is in the end ill-posed, some question in the neighborhood of (Q3).[27] A legal theory that specifies the ultimate legal- and illegal-making features in a legal system would be analogous to a moral theory that specifies the ultimate right- and wrong-making features. The latter theory would articulate an ultimate principle of morality, such as the principle of utility or the categorical imperative. Analogously, the former theory would articulate an ultimate principle of legality of a legal system, and that is what Hart calls a "rule of recognition". And that in turn would mean that (Q3) is really not different

---

[27] Notice that legal philosophers who take something like (Q3) seriously acknowledge that the facts that we would invoke to answer that question are ones to which lawyers and other participants in the legal system would appeal to answer first-order legal questions. Shapiro, for example, says that "one must know which facts ultimately determine the existence and content of legal systems" to show that "the law is thus-and-so" (2011, p. 25). And Greenberg (2006b, p. 283) follows Dworkin in appealing to the ways that lawyers and others argue in actual first-order legal disputes to discredit purely social factualist answers to (Q3), or a question very much like it. What I am arguing in the text is that what are considered the ultimate determinants of legality in answering first-order legal questions are those that would have to be referred to in the rule of recognition given the functional role that Hart assigns to such a norm or rule. In the end, once (Q2) has been answered, and the first-order question of what the content of the rule of recognition of a legal system is has been answered, it is very far from clear that any question in the vicinity of (Q3) should be raised. Some of any lingering disquiet with this last position, I surmise, stems from a conflation of (Q2) with (Q3).

from (Q4). A question that asks for the facts in virtue of which a particular norm is the rule of recognition of a legal system would in effect be asking for the facts in virtue of which a rule of recognition is legally valid. If (Q4) is ill-posed, as I argued in the preceding paragraph, then so is (Q3).

It follows that none of (Q1)–(Q4) could be thought the right construal of the Possibility question. But once we exclude these, is there any genuine question that remains in the Possibility Puzzle?

6. ADDITIONAL POSITIVISMS

For significant stretches of *Legality*, Shapiro seems inclined to read the Possibility question as a question about the reasons or duties to act as rules of recognition, or more generally as laws, call for. Perhaps then we should consider the following additional versions of the Possibility question:

(Q5)   What makes it the case that the members or officials of a community have reasons to follow the rule of recognition of their legal system?

(Q6)   What makes it the case that the members or officials of a community have duties or obligations to follow the rule of recognition of their legal system?

Taking these questions seriously would entail presupposing that theories about the nature of law have the burden of providing accounts of the following facts, in addition to (LF1)–(LF3$_R$):

(LF4$_R$)   Necessarily, the members or officials of a community have reasons to follow the rule of recognition of their legal system.

(LF5$_R$)   Necessarily, the members or officials of a community have duties or obligations to follow the rule of recognition of their legal system.

"Necessarily" is inserted in these formulations because these presumably describe noncontingent characteristics of communities with laws. And the supposedly legal positivist positions would be that these normative facts are determined by social facts alone. In fact, contemporary legal philosophers have often spoken as if some more general versions of these theses—the unsubscripted versions asserting reasons or duties to follow laws, rather than rules of recognition more specifically—are things that need to be accounted for. I shall not write out such theses, but merely label them as "(LF4)" and "(LF5)"—that is, without the subscript "R".

With these new LF-facts, we come to the more squarely Dworkinian strain in the Possibility Puzzle. In "The Model of Rules II", having summarized Hart's legal theory as committed to a thesis—"belong[ing] to moral as well as to legal philosophy"—that "no rights or duties of any sort can exist except by virtue of a uniform social practice of recognizing those rights and duties", Dworkin goes on to complain that no mere existence of such social practices can generate duties and rights (1972, pp. 48–51). He introduces the problem as follows:

[E]very legal philosopher…has supposed that in at least some cases the judge has a duty to decide in a particular way, for the express reason that the law requires that decision.

But it is a formidable problem for legal theory to explain why judges have such a duty. Suppose, for example, that a statute provides that in the event of intestacy a man's property descends to his next of kin. Lawyers will say that a judge has a duty to order property distributed in accordance with that statute. *But what imposes that duty on the judge?* We may want to say that judges are 'bound' by a general rule to the effect that they must do what the legislature says, but *it is unclear where that rule comes from*.…Perhaps we can discover a basic legal document, like a constitution, that says either explicitly or implicitly that the judges must follow the legislature. *But what imposes a duty on judges to follow the constitution?* (p. 49; emphases added)

Dworkin's verdict is that Hart's theory based on the idea that the existence of a norm in a community consists of the community members' acceptance of that norm and the resulting social practice motivated by such acceptances fails to explain why those members are obligated to do as the norm demands. Citing Dworkin, Raz (1975/90, ch. 2, esp. pp. 56–8, 205 n.7) essentially repeats this criticism of Hart's theory. As discussed in Section 4 above, Raz calls Hart's theory a "practice theory of rules", and says that such a theory fails to explain how a practice necessarily is or generates reasons for action. Here, we see these philosophers reading Hart as construing the normative facts of $(LF5_R)$ and $(LF4_R)$, respectively, as determined solely by facts of social practices, and rejecting those allegedly Hartian proposals as satisfactory accounts of the relevant normative facts.

By the time of Gerald Postema's seminal 1982 article "Coordination and Convention at the Foundations of Law", the Dworkinian demand had hardened into a criterion of adequacy for theories about the nature of law. Postema sums up what he calls "the Normativity Thesis" as follows:

We understand law only if we understand how it is that laws give members of a community, officials and law-subjects alike, reasons for acting. Thus any adequate general theory of law must give a satisfactory account of the normative (reason-giving) character of law and must relate the framework of practical reasoning defined by law to the framework of morality and prudence.   (p. 165)

And after summarizing Hart's theory, Postema duly notes:

How is it that the fact of the behavior, beliefs, and attitudes of officials generate genuine duties for those officials? Consider the judge whose appeal to the alleged rule of recognition is challenged. Why should the fact that *other* officials follow the rule, and think *he* ought to follow it, give him any reason to do so? . . . Thus Hart . . . fails to give us an account of how the facts of judicial practice actually generate genuine official duties. His account is seriously incomplete.   (p. 171)

There has been a general consensus among contemporary legal philosophers that Hartian theories have the burden of showing how the social facts of the sort that they refer to amount to or generate reasons, or even obligations or duties, to act as the law says; and also that Hart's own theory falls short in this regard.[28] As will be sketched presently, Postema himself seeks to meet the demand by characterizing legal officials' commitments to rules of recognition, and their behavior motivated by those commitments, as amounting to coordination conventions that are meant to solve recurring coordination problems.

When Shapiro invokes the Possibility Puzzle in his critique of Hart in chapter 4 of *Legality*, the Puzzle largely assumes the shape of this Dworkin–Raz–Postema line of objection. Shapiro, presumably follow-ing Raz, calls Hart's theory a "practice theory" (2011, p. 95). He says that Hart's practice theory "depends essentially on the idea that the social practice of recognition among officials is sufficient to generate the

---

[28] In addition to the ones I have already quoted in the text, see e.g. Coleman & Leiter (1996); Gilbert (1999); Coleman (2001, lecture 7). See also Green (1983 & 1999); Smith (1994, p. 206 n.2).

fundamental rules of the legal system", and adds that this solution to the Possibility Puzzle fails because "it is false that social practices necessarily generate social rules" (p. 104). The fact that Shapiro here speaks specifically of generation of fundamental legal rules, or of rules of recognition, rather than of the reasons or duties to follow those rules, may be thought to indicate that he is here again demanding a legal positivism of (LF3$_R$), rather than of (LF4$_R$) or (LF5$_R$). But the surrounding discussion indicates that he is concerned about the latter facts, or at least that he does not recognize the distinction. Not only is he adopting Raz's talk of "practice theories", but immediately after dismissing Hart's theory for failing to solve the Possibility Puzzle, Shapiro discusses Postema's conception of official practices as coordination conventions as amounting to the best then-available solution to the Possibility Puzzle.

According to David Lewis (1969), on whom Postema heavily relies, whenever a group of people have a social practice—viz. a configuration of preferences and expectations, and behavior motivated by such preferences and expectations—that amounts to a solution to a recurring coordination problem, each of them has reasons to do his part to maintain the practice, the reasons that arise from his interests in solving the coordination problem and in satisfying thereby his preferences. If, as Postema suggests, legal officials' acceptances and following of a rule of recognition were conceived as amounting to a coordination convention in that sense, then each official would have reasons to maintain his adherence to that rule. This is Postema's proposal as to how it is that "the fact of the behavior, beliefs, and attitudes of [legal] officials generate genuine [reasons and] duties for those officials" (1982, p. 171), something that Hart allegedly failed to explain. Shapiro expresses "no doubt" that something like Postema's proposal would be a successful solution to the Possibility Puzzle (2011, p. 104). He also deems Postema's proposal a thoroughly legal positivist solution to the Puzzle: "Because coordination conventions are constituted purely by social facts and necessarily generate social rules, the thought is that they can serve as a positivist foundation for every legal system" (p. 105). Shapiro eventually rejects Postema's proposal, not because it fails to solve the Puzzle, but because it solves it in a way that implicates an inaccurate psychology. According to Lewis's conception, each member of a group who is committed to a pattern of conduct as a coordination convention is committed to that pattern because, and insofar as, other members are too. Shapiro (2011, pp. 108–10; see also

2002, pp. 392–3) observes that legal officials' and others' commitments to rules of recognition are not necessarily of such a narrow variety, and for this reason the relevant social practices should not be conceived as coordination conventions in Lewis's sense. In the characterization of laws as plans (and plan-like norms), and the thesis of plan positivism, Shapiro sees a conception of legal officials' and others' commitments to rules of recognition, and of their behavior motivated by such commitments, that is psychologically more accurate, and at the same time just as capable in solving the Possibility Puzzle as Postema's proposal based on coordination conventions. Here, the bootstrapping that plan positivism supposedly affords is the key to duplicating Postema's success in solving the Possibility Puzzle.

But here is the crucial question: Why think that theories of the nature of law should try to account for (LF4$_R$) and/or (LF5$_R$)? Why should we presume that officials or people more generally have reasons or even obligations or duties to do as their rules of recognition demand? Such claims, and the more general versions (LF4) and (LF5) are not obviously compelling. The laws or the rule of recognition of a community may call for actions that are morally, or more generally normatively, objectionable. And in such cases, the mere fact that a norm is a law, or that it is the rule of recognition, of the community would not, or at least would not obviously, imply that the members and officials of the community would have reasons to follow that norm. Now, to be sure, it is very much a live possibility that the most plausible theory about the nature of law implies that people have reasons (and even duties) to do what the laws of their community call for. But that would be a surprising substantive result. The point is that there is no obvious real ground for thinking that we should treat as a criterion of adequacy for a theory of the nature of law that it be able to explain how laws or rules of recognition as such necessarily generate reasons or duties to follow those norms.[29]

---

[29] Enoch (2011) has made the argument of this paragraph with thoroughness and persuasiveness. He does not, however, make the distinction between the norms that are the laws or rules of recognition on the one hand and those that are treated as such on the other, as I do. In other words, it is unclear that he would endorse my arguments of Section 4. In order to simplify and shorten my exposition in this section, I have stuck to the discussion of the norms that are rules of recognition. But a more thorough discussion of the relevant issues would also have covered the norms that are treated as rules of recognition, and the LF-theses about such rules.

Dworkin's discussion in Section 1 of "The Model of Rules II" (1972) that started contemporary legal philosophers down the path of trying to account for the normative facts under discussion suffers from multiple conflations. In the eleven pages of that section (as reproduced in *Taking Rights Seriously*), Dworkin's description of Hart's position is at times sufficiently accurate, and the criticisms are at times sufficiently perceptive of some genuine shortcomings of Hart's own exposition of his theory, as to appear quite compelling. And because Dworkin's conflations and elisions are often quite subtle, it would take a paper of at least the length of the current one to explain adequately where and how exactly the mistakes creep into Dworkin's discussion. I will have to be terse and dogmatic in my diagnosis here of what is going on in these crucial eleven pages.[30] Hart offered an account of the social facts in virtue of which some particular norm can be thought one of a community's laws or its rule of recognition. In other words, he offered social factual accounts of (LF2) and (LF2$_R$). What Dworkin ends up doing in Section 1 of "The Model of Rules II" is: (i) to take these accounts as Hart's accounts of (LF3) and (LF3$_R$) as well as of (LF2) and (LF2$_R$); and then (ii) to take these as having the ambition of affirming or vindicating (LF5) and (LF5$_R$). Both moves are unwarranted. But they have proved extremely influential, and even most critics of Dworkin have gone along with him on these moves. Shapiro appears no exception.

7. GREENBERG'S "RATIONAL-RELATION REQUIREMENT"

In sum, neither tributary to the line of thinking that generates the Possibility Puzzle seems well-motivated. Before closing this part of the paper and going on to examine Shapiro's particular bootstrapping proposal, however, I want to take a brief (and admittedly tentative) look at Mark Greenberg's intriguing line of reasoning to the effect that any theory about the nature of law must meet what he calls "the rational-relation requirement".[31] Very early in *Legality* (2011, pp. 25, 408 n.25),

---

[30] In my estimation, these eleven pages—or more particularly pp. 49–51 in which all of the important moves are made—are the most important pages of the post-1961 legal philosophy. To put it a bit melodramatically, this is where things went very badly wrong for legal philosophy, in my opinion, and we have not recovered since.

[31] My use of "tentative" is meant to register my current lack of comfort with Greenberg's line of reasoning. Greenberg kindly sent me detailed written comments on this section of the paper.

Shapiro registers Greenberg's influence on his approach, and Greenberg's reasoning could be considered an intriguing variation on the Dworkinian tributary to the Possibility Puzzle.[32] My goal in this section is to strengthen my case against Shapiro's approach to thinking about the nature of law by taking a critical look at Greenberg's line of reasoning.

Beginning with "How Facts Make Law" (2004), in a series of papers, Greenberg has laid out a particular conception of the metaphysical relation between what he calls "law practices" or "law-determining practices" on the one hand, and "legal facts" or "legal-content facts" on the other. The former are "descriptive facts—paradigmatically facts about the attitudes, sayings, and doings of members of constitutional assemblies, legislatures, courts…" (2006a, p. 114; cf. 2004, pp. 162–3). These are the psychological and behavioral facts that many legal philosophers call "social facts", and I shall stick to that terminology. And by "legal facts", Greenberg has in mind facts "about the content of the law" of any legal system (2006a, p. 114; cf. 2004, p. 162). It is reasonably clear that he has in mind what I have above identified as the facts of the (LF3) variety, or the facts about what the law of a jurisdiction is, rather than the other kinds of legal facts that I have distinguished.

Greenberg begins by observing that legal facts are partly determined by, or obtain partly in virtue of, certain social facts. He further claims that how certain social facts determine legal facts, or which specific social facts are determinative of legal facts, must be something that is rationally explicable or intelligible. As Greenberg sums up,

[A] full constitutive account of the legal facts must do more than specify constitutive determinants that modally determine the legal facts; the constitutive determinants must constitute *reasons* why the legal facts obtain. Reasons, in the relevant sense, are considerations that make the explanandum intelligible in rational terms…. (2006b, p. 268)

If this were right, then the nature of legal facts would not be explained adequately by characterizing them only as metaphysically determined

---

I have not been able to address all of his concerns, as reacting to some of them would have required a far longer section than would have been appropriate in this paper. And I am still feeling my way with respect to some others of his concerns.

[32] The influencing appears quite mutual. Greenberg's conception of legal positivism seems to owe much to Shapiro's works.

by certain social facts, where the relevant relation of metaphysical determination is cashed out in terms of legal facts' supervenience on nonredundant subvening facts. The relevant subvening social facts, while amounting to modally necessary and sufficient conditions for the obtaining of the supervening legal facts, would not furnish rational intelligibility. It follows that some additional facts in light of which the modal determination relation is made rationally intelligible, additional facts that are not a subset of the nonredundant supervenience base consisting of aforementioned social facts, must be invoked (Greenburg 2004, p. 159; cf. 2005). As Greenberg puts it at one point, "[s]omething must determine which aspects of law practices are relevant and how they together contribute to the content of the law" (2004, p. 174). This is "the rational-relation requirement" that adequate theories about the nature of law allegedly must meet.

One might have thought that in any jurisdiction, the jurisdiction's ultimate criteria of legal validity, or what Hart calls "the rule of recognition", does the requisite job of specifying the legal relevance and implications of certain social facts. But Greenberg anticipates this answer and finds it wanting. Using the term "models" to refer to the norms that specify which legal practices contribute to the contents of laws and how, Greenberg counts Hartian rules of recognition as providing one conception of such models (2004, pp. 178–9; 2006b, p. 271). But he thinks that the intelligibility question applies to the models themselves, and the fact that a particular model is the correct model in a particular jurisdiction must be rationally explicable or intelligible (2004, p. 179; 2006b, pp. 277–9).

I am unsure that I have a firm enough handle on Greenberg's line of thinking and what is motivating it. But it seems that here Greenberg could be characterized as proffering rational-relation or intelligibility requirements of two different strengths. The weaker of the two versions says that which social facts determine the legal facts—once again, of the (LF3) variety—of any jurisdiction must be rationally explicable or intelligible. This version is satisfied by an invocation of the relevant rule of recognition. But there is a stronger version that is not thereby satisfied. According to this strong version, why a particular rule of recognition is the correct "model" that maps certain social facts to legal facts must itself be rationally explicable or intelligible. In other words, with this strong rational-relation or intelligibility requirement, Greenberg can be

seen as pressing a question that is a hitherto unarticulated variation
of (Q0). That variant could be formulated as:

(Q7)   What reasons are there for a particular norm to be the rule of
       recognition (or model) of a community's legal system?

The reasons demanded here are supposed to make sense of, make intelligible, the correctness of a certain rule of recognition as the model of a
legal system.

But can a good sense be made of (Q7)? It seems to me that in response
we can rerun the arguments that I outlined in Sections 5 and 6. It is
unclear what kind of intelligibility is being demanded by (Q7). First, it
is quite clear that the kind of intelligibility at stake is not one satisfied by
causal explanations as to why a particular rule is, or came to be, accepted
as the rule of recognition (or model) by a community of people. Second,
given the relevant sense of "legal facts"—namely, those of the (L3)
variety—it is also clear that what is demanded is not a metaphysical
explanation of what psychological and behavioral facts constitute the
facts that some rule is *treated as* the rule of recognition (or model) in a
community. Third, although he is not entirely clear on this in his original paper (2004, pp. 187, 190–2), later on Greenberg makes explicit
that the kind of correctness he is concerned about when he talks about
"correct models" is *legal* correctness (2006a, p. 126 & n.41; 2006b,
p. 267). But then, it is puzzling why appeals to any facts or considerations beyond rules of recognition (or models) would be needed. To
look beyond, it seems, is to ignore the functional role of rules of recognition as the ultimate criteria of legal validity or correctness. And fourth,
it is not clear that there is a metaphysical explanation of the sort that
steers successfully between the two—metaphysical and legal—that we
have just considered. Greenberg (2006b, p. 283) is quite clear that the
kinds of considerations that would answer his (Q7) would be those that
would be accessible to, and be appealed to, by lawyers and others who
take part in first-order legal deliberation and disputes. It would follow,
it seems, that such considerations would be those that would have to
appear in correct formulations of rules of recognition (or models).

A significant glitch seems to stem from Greenberg's subscription
to the "practice theory" interpretation of Hart's legal theory (2006a,
p. 126; 2006b, pp. 271–2; 2011, p. 69). Because he thinks that rules,
including rules of recognition, as Hart conceives them, are constituted

by practices, or by the psychological and behavioral facts that make up practices, Greenberg thinks that rules of recognition can render intelligible the determination relation between social facts and legal facts only if the relevant psychological and behavioral facts—in other words, certain social facts themselves—can render the relation intelligible. He therefore spends considerable time combatting the view that social facts by themselves could furnish the requisite intelligibility (2004, pp. 178–84; 2006b, pp. 271–84). I find these portions of his argument largely compelling. But as I argued in Section 4 above, the practice theory interpretation ignores the crucial distinction between the facts about what norms are treated as the law by the members of a community and the facts about what the community's law is—i.e. between the (LF2) and (LF3) facts. It is only the former facts, in Hart's thinking, that consist of or are constituted by social facts. Because of his subscription to the practice theory interpretation, a particular and significant possibility escapes Greenberg's notice—namely, the possibility of rules of recognition themselves, rather than the social facts that constitute a community's acceptance of those rules, making intelligible the determination relation between social facts and legal facts.[33]

Fifth, and finally, there seems little to be said for a presumption that rules of recognition (or models) are morally or normatively justifiable, or generative of moral or normative reasons or duties.[34] Greenberg ends up opining that the additional facts that need to be invoked to provide rational intelligibility of the correctness of models are evaluative or normative facts (2004, pp. 187, 190–7; 2006b, pp. 284–9). For example, a model that designates legislators' joint intentions as determinative of

---

[33] In private communication, Greenberg acknowledged that he and I have different conceptions of Hartian rules of recognition. Still, he argued, he addresses a Hartian answer to (Q7) that is premised on something like my own conception of that notion when he discusses what he calls "Hartian bridge principles" in the later pages of (2006b). I do believe that "Hartian bridge principles" are closer to rules of recognition as I conceive them than what Greenberg calls "models" are. But even Hartian bridge principles, as Greenberg formulates their template (2006b, p. 276), are restricted to those norms that specify social facts as the sole ultimate determinants of legality. It would be far better to conceive rules of recognition as enumerating whatever facts or considerations are the ultimate determinants of legality in legal systems. (See the discussion in Section 4, pp. 14–15 above.) With this last conception of rules of recognition, we would not be motivated to raise anything like (Q7).

[34] I should note that I am not here saying that Greenberg works with such a presumption. Greenberg denied doing so in private communication. I am merely covering all of the possibilities outlined in Sections 5 and 6.

what the law is could be made intelligible by the fact that deference to
legislators' joint intentions enhances the relevant community's realization
of the ideal of democratic governance. But while the possession of such
evaluative or normative properties may enhance the moral or normative
correctness of the relevant model, it is not at all clear that they enhance
its *legal* correctness, which presumably is what is at stake.

Given the centrality of the rational-relation requirement for his
purposes, Greenberg offers remarkably little to motivate it. He observes
at one point:

[L]aw is fundamentally not only a human creation, but one that is constructed
in such a way that the existence of particular legal facts must always be fundamentally intelligible to rational creatures who know all the facts except those
that are specifically legal.   (2006b, p. 279)

This and like statements (e.g. 2004, pp. 164–5, 170–3; 2006a, pp. 135–6)
are what Greenberg offers, and they strike me as hardly more than mere
assertions of the rational-relation requirement. The fact that we are able
to figure out legal facts by investigating certain social facts is accounted
for by appeals to rules of recognition. If some stronger kind of intelligibility or rational explicability is required, that is not really something
that we can infer from the kinds of observations that Greenberg offers.
Repeatedly, Greenberg has analogized his own position about the rational-
relation requirement to Donald Davidson's view that certain principles
of rationality are constitutive of psychological facts (e.g. 2004, pp. 160,
164 n.18; 2006b, p. 287). I do not find the analogy particularly helpful,
however. Davidson's view is that beliefs, intentions, and other propositional attitudes are constructs within an integrated theory that is structured by the principles of rationality, consistency, and coherence.[35] This
is why Davidson believes that psychological facts are infused with
rationality facts, and are autonomous from physical facts that are marked
by a different set of constitutive principles.[36] To accept the proffered
analogy, we would have to think that our interpretation and attributions
of laws are similarly moves within a holistic theory that is structured by

---

[35] As Davidson remarks at one point, "[e]ach interpretation and attribution of attitude is a
move within a holistic theory, a theory necessarily governed by concern for consistency and
general coherence with truth, and it is this that sets these theories forever apart from those that
describe mindless objects, or describe objects as mindless" (1974b, p. 154).

[36] See also Davidson (1970; 1973; 1974a; 1975). I have benefitted from helpful discussions
of the Davidsonian thinking in Child (1994, ch. 1) and Kim (2003).

certain evaluative or normative principles—e.g. certain principles of political justice—that are distinct from both (i) the principles of rationality that (according to Davidson) are constitutive of the subvening or constituting social facts, and (ii) any legality-determining principles that would be captured by rules of recognition. Such a line of thinking does not strike me as having the level of plausibility approaching that of the Davidsonian line on psychological facts.[37]

It is open to Greenberg to argue that legal facts are constituted by the same principles of rationality that, according to Davidson, are constitutive of psychological or social facts.[38] As Bratman (2011, pp. 74–5) has observed, Shapiro could be seen as pursuing the just-described line of reasoning. In effect, he could be seen as arguing that the normative principles that are constitutive of planning are constitutive of legal facts. I will be scrutinizing this line of reasoning and the inferences Shapiro draws from it in Sections 8 and 9. But this is a line of thinking the likes of which Greenberg explicitly avoids. As indicated above, he thinks of social facts as descriptive facts, and his claim is that there are

---

[37] I am also not wholly won over by a disanalogy that Greenberg alleges. Greenberg contrasts legal facts' dependence on social facts with aesthetic facts' dependence on non-aesthetic facts, and argues that the rational-relation requirement does not apply to the latter relation as it does to the former (2004, p. 160; 2006a, pp. 116–17). I myself am not so sure that the two cases are as different as Greenberg makes them out. In the aesthetic case, artists and critics are people who are especially skilled in figuring out which non-aesthetic facts are determinative of aesthetic facts. Artists are additionally skilled in realizing the latter facts by manipulating the former; and critics in articulating the dependence relations and conveying them to the rest of us. For some illuminating discussions of these and related themes, see e.g. Sibley (1965); Zangwill (2007, ch. 2). As Greenberg points out, in the aesthetic case, there is no need to further make intelligible why certain dependence relations obtain. We are unbothered by the idea that it may just be a brute fact that certain aesthetic facts are determined by certain non-aesthetic facts. Of course, we might be able to offer certain causal explanations—e.g. sociobiological explanations—as to why we accept or are sensitive to certain dependence relations rather than some alternatives. We could also make normative assessments of certain dependence relations. And we could even consider metaphysical accounts regarding which psychological and behavioral facts amount to our judgments or practices of cognizing and being motivated by certain dependence relations between aesthetic and non-aesthetic facts. But as far as *aesthetic* explanations are concerned, our curiosity and investigations bottom out with the dependence relations themselves. Now, the question is whether the case is any different with the dependence of legal facts on certain social facts. Is there a need or demand for any explanations beyond the three types that we have just enumerated? I rather doubt it, and do not see any reason that Greenberg has provided to think otherwise.

[38] Dworkin (1986, ch. 2) can be seen as pursuing this line of reasoning by inflating or thickening the principles of rationality that allegedly are constitutive of social facts. And so can Shapiro, as I will be noticing presently. See footnote 2 above for a related discussion.

evaluative or normative principles constitutive of legal facts that are extrinsic to social facts.

In sum, I am skeptical that Greenberg's arguments for the rational-relation requirement in theorizing about the nature of law furnishes a more viable gloss on the Possibility Puzzle than the other ones we considered in Sections 5 and 6. We are entitled to think, I believe, that the Puzzle is a pseudo-problem. And this conclusion in turn discredits the felt need to bootstrap from the mere holding of some conative attitudes to the contents of those attitudes being the case. The widespread belief among contemporary legal philosophers that such a bootstrapping is necessary to affirm or vindicate legal positivism (or any other conception of the nature of law, for that matter) is unwarranted. What the contents of the law are is one issue, and what the nature of psychological attitudes that takes such contents as objects is a different, orthogonal issue. In other words, there is no good reason to think that a single set of facts should be construed as the facts in virtue of which both (LF2) and (LF3) obtain.[39] Whether we have reasons or obligations to do as the law says is yet a third issue. Consequently, the facts that constitute (LF2) should not be thought the same facts in virtue of which (LF4) or (LF5) obtains. Neither legal positivism nor any other view of the nature of law should be saddled with such conflations.

8. INSTRUMENTAL RATIONALITY

I hope I have done enough in the preceding four sections to discredit the felt need to bootstrap from the mere holding of the psychological attitudes, which partly make up a community's treating some norms as their laws, to the contents of those attitudes being the case. Now, even if the desire to bootstrap is ill-motivated, the conception of the relevant psychological attitudes—i.e. the ones that partly constitute the legal practice—as plan-attitudes may be justified on other explanatory grounds. And it may further be the case that plan-attitudes do in fact enable a bootstrapping of the sort that Shapiro seeks. As it turns out, Shapiro's arguments for the planning theory is substantially based on its

---

[39] Elsewhere, I have argued that contemporary legal positivists' commitments to delineate a single set of facts in virtue of which (LF2) and (LF3) obtain are borne out of a fallacy, which I called "the fallacy of double duty". See Toh (2012 & forthcoming).

perceived advantage in solving the Possibility Puzzle, and what he says about its other advantages, it seems to me, does not quite give the planning theory an upper hand over alternative conceptions of the relevant psychological attitudes.[40] But in this section and the next, I want to scrutinize his claim or assumption that some principle(s) of instrumental rationality enables bootstrapping from the mere having of plan-attitudes to the contents of those attitudes being the case. That issue is of interest even if the desire to bootstrap is discredited.

I should warn the reader that the way that Shapiro ultimately addresses the issue of bootstrapping is quite complex and involved, and I will not be able to lay out all of his moves in one go. By the middle of the next section, I believe, I will have accurately characterized what amounts to Shapiro's official proposal, but in this section I will be dealing with what is only a provisional version of his proposal. I have found this somewhat unsatisfactory approach unavoidable in my attempt to scrutinize all of the components of Shapiro's proposal and the motivations behind them in a methodical way. I also suspect that Shapiro is considerably attracted to the provisional version that I will be discussing, and that it could be considered an alternative proposal. But in any case, I urge the reader to bear in mind that, until we reach the next section, what I present as Shapiro's proposal is merely a provisional version of his proposal.

Once again, Shapiro seems to think that unlike in the cases of other conative psychological attitudes and their contents, the mere existence of plan-attitudes renders the relevant plan-contents apt or correct. In effect, Shapiro seems to accept something along the lines of the following about plans:

(IR1)   If a person has a plan-attitude to φ, then he is to φ.

Assuming that a person has reasons to do what he is to do, we can have the following variation as well:

(IR1')   If a person has a plan-attitude to φ, then he has reasons to φ.

I am here assuming that a plan-content specifies the agent who is to carry out the action that the content refers to; and I am also assuming for the sake of simplicity that the agent referred to by the plan-content

---

[40] This is something that even some very sympathetic readers of *Legality* have observed. See e.g. Yaffe (2012).

is the holder of the relevant plan-attitudes.[41] The key point for our purposes here is that if (IR1) were really the case, then it would serve as a bridging principle between the "existence conditions" of plan-attitudes and the "existence conditions" of plan-contents, and Shapiro would then be able to deflect the charge of equivocation.

But is (IR1) correct? Shapiro (2011, pp. 123, 142–3, 183) seems to think that (IR1)—or, since (IR1) is my own formulation, something very much like it—is one of, or is implied by, the principles of instrumental rationality. But as he also notes (p. 416 n.4), the exact contents and justifications of the principles of instrumental rationality are controversial. What Shapiro seems to be invoking here are the norms of consistency and of means–end coherence that, according to Bratman (1987, pp. 30–2), planning agents must observe for their plan-attitudes to serve their characteristic roles of guiding and coordinating behavior.[42] But in arguing that planning is characterized by such constitutive norms, Bratman does not appear to be endorsing something like (IR1). Instead, what Bratman actually endorses as "the heart of the requirement of means–end coherence" (2009, p. 13 & n.2; cf. 2011, p. 79), is a principle governing combinations of attitudes that can be formulated as:

(IR2w) If a person has a plan-attitude to ε, and believes that μ-ing is a necessary means to his ε-ing, then he has reasons to have a plan-attitude to μ, or to give up his plan-attitude to ε.

There is a principle that bears a superficial resemblance to (IR2w), which is closer to Shapiro's (IR1) than (IR2w) itself. It is:

(IR2n) If a person has a plan-attitude to ε, and believes that μ-ing is a necessary means to his ε-ing, then he has reasons to have a plan-attitude to μ.

Notice that the difference between these two principles has to do with the last clause of (IR2w). This last clause makes quite a bit of difference, and its inclusion indicates that (IR2w) is a principle that should be

---

[41] See (3C*), which I discussed in Section 2, p. 5.

[42] Aside from referring to these pages from Bratman (1987), Shapiro does not say much about how the requirements of instrumental rationality bear on the issue at hand. He merely says that to adopt a plan and not to take steps to carry it out would be irrational, and would amount to behavior that defeats the whole purpose of having plans.

given a "wide-scope" reading, to use John Broome's (1999) terminology. In other words, (IR2w) can be translated as:

(IR2w′)   A person has reasons to see to it that: (If he has a plan-attitude to ε, and believes that μ-ing is a necessary means to ε, then he has a plan-attitude to μ).

Notice that "reasons to" has a wide scope that covers the entire conditional in (IR2w′), whereas it has a narrow scope that covers only the consequent in (IR2n).

Now, although (IR1) and (IR2n) are not quite the same, they are quite close. And they seem to suffer from the same problem. Both (IR1) and (IR2n) allow or enable detachments of normative consequents through modus ponens, and that allows for normatively unpalatable results. Judy could have a plan, not for something as anodyne as going to the zoo on Saturday, but for something horrible, like poisoning her children. It would be odd, to say the least, to think that it follows merely from the fact that Judy plans to poison her children that she thereby gains reasons to poison her children, or reasons to plan to poison her children (or that Judy has reasons to buy rat poison at her local hardware store, or to plan to do so, if she were to think that doing so is the only available means to carry out her plan to poison her children). The wide-scope reading like (IR2w) is designed to prevent such objectionable detachment. Now, unfortunately for Shapiro's purposes, "detachment" is another word for "bootstrapping" in this context. What Shapiro needs is a principle that would license or enable bootstrapping, but any version of a principle of instrumental rationality that would be suitable for that purpose would yield normatively objectionable consequences. There is an alternative to the objectionable version—namely, the wide-scope version. But that version would be preferable exactly because it would not enable detachment or bootstrapping.

There has recently been an explosion of discussion about instrumental rationality in the philosophical literature, and some philosophers (e.g. Schroeder 2004; Kolodny 2005) have argued forcefully for the viability of some narrow-scope requirements. My own sympathies lie with the wide-scopers (e.g. Broome 1999; Brunero 2010) in this debate, but Shapiro may be able to rely on the available arguments for narrow-scope readings. But the point is that he needs to argue for narrow-scoping in order to ensure detachability/bootstrapping, and thereby affirm a plan positivism of the sort that he is after. And that would necessitate a type of detachability or bootstrapping that does not have normatively objectionable consequences. Given how much is covered by *Legality*, the lack of a discussion of this vital issue for Shapiro's project appears to me a serious and curious lacuna. For all I know, there also may be a way to settle for a wide-scope reading like (IR2w) and still generate a plancontent positivism of the sort that Shapiro is after. But again, that would need to be argued for. It may also be worth pointing out that wide-scope requirements of instrumental rationality may be constitutive not only of plan-attitudes, but also of some other kinds of psychological attitudes as well. Perhaps mere desires and valuings are not constrained by such a requirement, but there is a good case to be made for thinking that preferences are.[43] Hart is not voluble in his characterizations of "acceptances" of norms, the psychological attitudes that he sees as constituting legal practices. But if we conceive such psychological attitudes as characterized by the norms of coherence and consistency the way that plan-attitudes and preferences are, then they too could be seen as constrained by a wide-scope requirement of instrumental rationality like (IR2w). If (IR2w) or something like it were really good enough for plan positivism, then it would follow that any advantage that the planning theory of law is supposed to have over Hart's theory based on ruleacceptances is illusory.

There is a version of the instrumental rationality requirement that is, in my opinion, at least as compelling as (IR2w). R.M. Hare (1968) long ago observed that, in order to be credible, what a practical conditional would have to have as its antecedent is not the fact that the person has a conative attitude, but instead the content of that conative attitude. We can incorporate an analogous point about a belief about the necessary means. What we get is then something like:

(IR3)   If a person is to ε, and μ-ing is a necessary means to his ε-ing, then he has reasons to μ.[44]

What Hare himself argues about are not plan-attitudes, but desires. He points out that if we were to think of the fact that a person holds a desire

---

[43] See Davidson (1985), pp. 195–201, which is a reply to Bratman (1985).
[44] In addition to Hare (1968), see Darwall (1983, pp. 14–17); Dreier (2009, §§6–8); Blackburn (2010, §8).

as implying that he is to act according to the content of the desire, we would get all kinds of normatively incorrect and unpalatable results. That is analogous to what we above observed about Judy's case. And we can generalize Hare's argument and conclusion, and that is what I have done with (IR3). Notice that (IR3) is generic and neutral among the different kinds of conative psychological attitudes and their contents. It is in fact a generic version of what Stephen Darwall (1983, pp. 54–5) calls "existence internalism".[45] Whichever kind of conative psychological attitude is involved, what could make it the case that a person has reasons to act as the content of that attitude calls for is not the fact that a person has that attitude, but instead what the content says. If the content is the case—i.e. if it is normatively correct or apt—then people have reasons to carry out it or its necessary means. Otherwise, not.

In sum, contrary to what Shapiro argues, it seems quite unlikely that we can bootstrap our way from a mere holding of any psychological attitudes to their contents being the case. If (IR1) were right, then it would have enabled Shapiro to blur the distinction between plan-attitudes and plan-contents, and thereby deflect the charge of equivocation. But (IR1) is not credible, and whatever appearance of credibility it has seems to be mere reflections of either (IR2w) or (IR3). Notice that according to (IR3) in particular, what can make it the case that a person has reasons to act according to a plan-content (or the content of any conative attitude) is not the fact that he holds a plan-attitude (or any conative attitude) with that content, but instead the normative correctness or aptness of the content. In other words, the distinction between plan-attitudes and plan-contents seems to resurface at this late stage to vitiate Shapiro's plan positivism, and along with it Shapiro's case for legal positivism.

9. PERSPECTIVAL REASONS

Perhaps Shapiro is mindful of the worries about (IR1) that I have outlined in the preceding section. In any case, halfway through his book, he opts for a proposal that is quite different from the one that we have been considering. Shapiro wants to be able to say that laws, or more precisely the social facts that constitute legal practices, generate reasons to act as the laws say.

---

[45] More specifically, it could be called "the 'is to'-reason existence internalism". Cf. Darwall (1997).

At the same time, he wants to avoid having to say that all laws of a community, no matter how horrible, actually furnish genuine reasons for the members of that community to do as the laws say. Finally, he also wants to avoid having to say, with natural law theorists, that laws that fail to meet certain minimal normative standards are not laws, not genuine laws, not laws in some full-blooded sense, or something of the sort.[46] Negotiating through these demands, Shapiro (2011, pp. 184–92) opts for the position according to which laws furnish reasons only in a "perspectival" sense.[47] To talk about what the law calls for—i.e. what it requires, prohibits, or permits—is to talk about what reasons we have "from the legal point of view" (p. 185), which is not necessarily the normatively correct point of view.[48]

Shapiro further explains that the legal point of view is the point of view of a person—a hypothetical person, to be sure—who is wholly committed to the laws of his community as the normatively correct norms. If we take the laws of a community as forming a normative theory (which may differ from the correct normative theory in varying degrees), then claims about what the laws of a community call for are attempts at specifying what such a possibly imperfect normative theory calls for. Shapiro explains that such claims could be characterized as conditional claims (p. 187). In effect, he seems to be saying that (C) could be analyzed as (C′) below:

(C)   From the point of view of the legal system of a community that requires its members to φ, a member has reasons to φ.

---

[46] See e.g. Dworkin (1986); Finnis (1980); Murphy (2004).

[47] Shapiro's "perspectival" account is heavily indebted to Raz's account of "detached" legal statements, or statements "from the legal point of view", and Raz himself attributes the insight behind his account to Kelsen. See e.g. Raz (1974; 1977; 1981); see also Baker (1977); Finnis (1980, pp. 234–6). I have scrutinized Raz's account at length in Toh (2007). As I will explain presently, however, there is a twist in Shapiro's perspectival account that I believe (though I am far from sure) distinguishes his account from Raz's. In effect, both Raz and Shapiro can be seen as presenting variants on the Kelsenian "maneuver", described briefly in Section 5 above, of construing laws or the basic norm as "presupposed" rather than fully endorsed.

[48] By talking about reasons that obtain "from the legal point of view", we may be talking about a set of pro tanto reasons—i.e. genuine or real reasons which a deliberating person would have to weigh in his determination of what he ought to do all things considered. But Shapiro explicitly disavows such an *adjectival* reading of the "point of view" talk. According to the *perspectival* conception, which is an alternative to the adjectival conception, the reasons that are generated by laws do not have the status of being genuine reasons. In other words, they cannot or should not enter into anyone's practical reasoning unless they happen to coincide with what genuine reasons call for.

(C′)   If the norms of the legal system of a community are normatively correct, and if those norms require the community's members to φ, then a member has reasons to φ.

(C′) is not a genuine normative claim about what anyone is to do, but is instead a mere analytic claim.[49]

With Shapiro's perspectival account and its conditional analysis, we could revise (IR1) or (IR1′) as follows:

(IR4)   If some plan-content is normatively correct, then (if a person has a plan-attitude with that plan-content, then he has reasons to carry out that plan-content—i.e. to act according to that plan-content).

Collapsing the two antecedents, we get:

(IR4′)   If a person has a plan-attitude with a normatively correct plan-content, then he has reasons to carry out that plan-content—i.e. to act according to that plan-content.

(IR4′), like (C′), is analytic, and therefore is not a substantive principle as (IR1′) is. Shapiro can then claim that what is really a part of the ultimate determinants or grounds of the law is not a substantive principle like (IR1′), but instead an analytic "principle" like (IR4′). And it is (IR4′) that generates the reasons for action, and the reasons it generates are only perspectival "reasons" and not genuine reasons. Since (IR4′) is not a substantive principle, despite its membership among the ultimate determinants of the law, Shapiro can hold fast to legal positivism as he conceives that view about the nature of law—that is, stick to his view that the ultimate grounds of law are all social facts or non-normative considerations, and that investigations to determine what the law calls for are all empirical or non-normative investigations (2011, e.g. pp. 27, 42–3, 57).[50]

---

[49]   I believe (though I am far from sure) that this conditional analysis distinguishes Shapiro's perspectival account from Raz's. Raz construes statements from the legal point of view as normative statements, not analytic statements, albeit simulated or pretended normative statements. For this reason, it seems to me, Raz would not accept Shapiro's conditional analysis. See Raz (1975/90, pp. 172–7). I propose on Raz's behalf a non-conditional analysis in Toh (2007, esp. p. 414). For a conditional analysis like Shapiro's, which also is influenced by Raz, see Marmor (2009, ch. 7). I assess Marmor's views in Toh (2010).

[50]   Alternatively, as Bratman (2011, pp. 74–5) has helpfully suggested, even if substantive norms of instrumental rationality were constitutive of planning, Shapiro could argue that only

What should be observed, however, is that the perspectival account and the conditional analysis it includes are problematic for Shapiro's planning theory. For one thing, why should we now think that plans are all that special? We could generalize (IR4'), and get:

(IR5)   If a person has a conative psychological attitude with a normatively correct content, then he has reasons to carry out that content—i.e. to act according to that content.

In fact, there is no real need to mention, or any benefits to be derived from mentioning, any psychological attitudes in formulating such conditional principles. If we dispense with such mentions altogether, then we end up with:

(IR6)   If a person is to φ, then he has reasons to φ.

(IR5) and (IR6) are no less plausible, and no less analytic, than (IR4'). And if (IR5) or (IR6) were all it would take to solve the bootstrapping problem, then other theorists about the nature of law who characterize the existence of legal systems as consisting of other kinds of conative psychological attitudes and behavior motivated by such attitudes could help themselves to the perspectival account and its conditional analysis, and thereby address satisfactorily the bootstrapping problem. For example, Hart, who characterizes the relevant psychological attitudes as acceptances of norms, could invoke a version of (IR5)—just as easily as a planning theorist like Shapiro invokes (IR4')—to solve the bootstrapping problem. Nothing that a planning theorist has makes him a more capable bootstrapper than Hart and many other possible theorists, it seems.

We can sum up the situation as follows. What do we gain by going with the planning theory of law? Shapiro's answer, or at least the central part of that answer, is that we do a better job than legal positivists of before in solving the bootstrapping problem. Now, how does the planning theory help us in solving the bootstrapping problem? One possible answer Shapiro can give is that the characterization of laws as plans and

such norms are "essential to law", and that distinctively moral norms are not, or at least not in the same way. Bratman suspects that this last denial is what makes the planning theory a part of the legal positivist tradition. This charitable reading is in some tension with Shapiro's own explicit language, but I believe that it catches the spirit of what Shapiro is up to. It also meshes with my own treatment, in footnote 3 above, of the possibility that psychological facts are suffused with the norms or principles of rationality.

plan-like norms implies that (IR1), which is a norm of instrumental rationality that is constitutive of the activity of planning, is among the ultimate determinants or grounds of law. And insofar as (IR1) generates reasons for action, the planning theory solves the bootstrapping problem. But, as I have argued, this answer is problematic. (IR1) is implausible, and attempts to repair it—in the form of (IR2w) or (IR3)—would show that what really could generate reasons for action is not any norm that is constitutive of planning, but instead any normatively correct contents of the relevant plans. According to the second possible answer that Shapiro could resort to, and the one that he actually does seem to resort to eventually, (IR4), which is an analytic implication of the concept "plan" or some cognate concept, generates perspectival "reasons" to do as the plans say. But if the capacity to generate such perspectival "reasons" is all it takes to solve the bootstrapping problem, then many other kinds of conative psychological attitudes appear just as serviceable as plan-attitudes. And as far as genuine reasons for action are concerned, (IR5) and (IR6) would indicate once again that what really could generate reasons for action are normatively correct contents, regardless of the psychological attitudes that those contents are objects of. In the end, the characterization of laws as plans seems theoretically idle and unmotivatedly restrictive.

10. CONCLUSION

Shapiro's *Legality* has a strong claim to be considered the most significant book-length contribution to legal philosophy in the last thirty years. And the theory of law that the book presents, the planning theory of law, digs deep in gathering its resources and fans wide in its explanatory ambitions. And unlike some other major works in recent legal philosophy, *Legality* attempts to expose all of its key moves to the reader's scrutiny, and succeeds in doing so to a great and admirable extent. I believe, however, that some of what it presupposes or takes for granted in conceiving the task of investigating the nature of law, and in conceiving the main available theoretical options, warrant re-evaluation. I myself am skeptical of some of those presuppositions, and I believe that legal philosophy could be set on a more secure and productive path by abandoning those presuppositions. My primary goal in this paper was to identify perhaps the most central of those questionable presuppositions—namely, the thought that we need some way to bootstrap from the mere existence of some conative psychological attitudes, which partly make up the legal practice, to the contents of those attitudes being the case. Secondarily, I have sought to highlight some of the particular features of the planning theory that obscure from our view the difficulties and the questionable legitimacy of such bootstrapping. Chief among these features is the absence of a clear distinction between plan-attitudes and plan-contents in Shapiro's exposition. Given its author's resourcefulness, the planning theory may very well be defensible in ways that I am not suspecting. But I hope that my arguments will at least prompt Shapiro to address the worries of the sort that I have here raised about his theory.[51]

REFERENCES

Baker, G.P. (1977). "Defeasibility and Meaning", in P.M.S. Hacker & J. Raz (eds.), *Law, Morality, and Society* (Oxford: Clarendon Press).
Blackburn, Simon (2010). "The Majesty of Reason", in S. Blackburn, *Practical Tortoise Raising* (Oxford: Oxford University Press).
Brandt, R.B. (1979). *A Theory of the Good and the Right* (Oxford: Clarendon Press).
Bratman, Michael (1985). "Davidson's Theory of Intention", in B. Vermazen & M. Hintikka (eds.), *Essays on Davidson: Actions and Events* (Oxford: Clarendon Press).
Bratman, Michael (1987). *Intention, Plans, and Practical Reason* (Cambridge, MA: Harvard University Press).
Bratman, Michael (2009). "Intention, Belief, and Instrumental Rationality", in D. Sobel & S. Wall (eds.), *Reasons for Action* (Cambridge: Cambridge University Press).
Bratman, Michael (2011). "Reflections on Law, Normativity, and Plans", in S. Bertea & G. Pavlakos (eds.), *New Essays on the Normativity of Law* (Oxford: Hart Publishing).
Broome, John (1999). "Normative Requirements", *Ratio* 12: 398–419.

[51] I benefitted from generous and instructive comments and questions from audiences at an Ethics Discussion Group (EDGe) meeting at the University of Michigan in March 2012, a legal philosophy seminar at the University of Girona in July 2012, and a legal philosophy seminar at Bocconi University in Milan in May 2013. I also thank Bill Edmundson, Mark Greenberg, George Letsas, Stanley Paulson, David Plunkett, Scott Shapiro, and Wil Waluchow for helpful and encouraging comments on earlier drafts. I am most indebted to Brian Leiter for an e-mail correspondence that instigated the writing of this paper, and to Peter Railton for illuminating discussions over the three-day stretch surrounding the EDGe event which saved me from a number of significant mistakes.

Brunero, John (2010). "The Scope of Rational Requirements", *The Philosophical Quarterly* 60: 28–49.

Bulygin, Eugenio (1982). "Norms, Normative Propositions, and Legal Statements", in G. Fløistad (ed.), *Contemporary Philosophy: A New Survey*, vol. 3 (The Hague & Boston, MA: M. Nijhoff).

Cherniak, Christopher (1986). *Minimal Rationality* (Cambridge, MA: MIT Press).

Child, William (1994). *Causality, Interpretation, and the Mind* (Oxford: Clarendon Press).

Coleman, Jules (2001). *The Practice of Principle* (Oxford: Oxford University Press).

Coleman, Jules & Brian Leiter (1996). "Legal Positivism", in D. Patterson (ed.), *A Companion to Philosophy of Law and Legal Theory* (Oxford: Blackwell Publishers).

Darwall, Stephen (1983). *Impartial Reason* (Ithaca, NY: Cornell University Press).

Darwall, Stephen (1997). "Reasons, Motives, and the Demands of Morality: An Introduction", in S. Darwall, A. Gibbard, & P. Railton (eds.), *Moral Discourse and Practice* (Oxford: Oxford University Press).

Davidson, Donald (1970). "Mental Events", repr. in D. Davidson, *Essays on Actions and Events* (Oxford: Clarendon Press, 1980).

Davidson, Donald (1973). "Radical Interpretation", repr. in D. Davidson, *Inquiries into Truth and Interpretation* (Oxford: Clarendon Press, 1984).

Davidson, Donald (1974a). "Psychology as Philosophy", repr. in D. Davidson, *Essays on Actions and Events* (Oxford: Clarendon Press, 1980).

Davidson, Donald (1974b). "Belief and the Basis of Meaning", repr. in D. Davidson, *Inquiries into Truth and Interpretation* (Oxford: Clarendon Press, 1984).

Davidson, Donald (1975). "Thought and Talk", repr. in D. Davidson, *Inquiries into Truth and Interpretation* (Oxford: Clarendon Press, 1984).

Davidson, Donald (1985). "Replies to Essays I–IX", in B. Vermazen & M. Hintikka (eds.), *Essays on Davidson: Actions and Events* (Oxford: Clarendon Press).

Dreier, James (2009). "Practical Conditionals", in D. Sobel & S. Wall (eds.), *Reasons for Action* (Cambridge: Cambridge University Press).

Dworkin, Ronald (1972). "The Model of Rules II", repr. in R. Dworkin, *Taking Rights Seriously* (Cambridge, MA: Harvard University Press, 1977).

Dworkin, Ronald (1986). *Law's Empire* (Cambridge, MA: Harvard University Press).

Enoch, David (2011). "Reason-Giving and the Law", in L. Green & B. Leiter (eds.), *Oxford Studies in Philosophy of Law*, vol. 1 (Oxford: Oxford University Press).

Finnis, John (1980). *Natural Law and Natural Rights* (Oxford: Clarendon Press).

Gardner, John (2000). "Law as a Leap of Faith", repr. in J. Gardner, *Law as a Leap of Faith* (Oxford: Oxford University Press, 2012).

Gardner, John (2001). "Legal Positivism: 5½ Myths", repr. in J. Gardner, *Law as a Leap of Faith* (Oxford: Oxford University Press, 2012).

Gardner, John (2008). "Some Types of Law", repr. in J. Gardner, *Law as a Leap of Faith* (Oxford: Oxford University Press, 2012).

Gardner, John (2012). "Law in General", in J. Gardner, *Law as a Leap of Faith* (Oxford: Oxford University Press).

Gardner, John & Timothy Macklem (2011). Review of Scott Shapiro, *Legality* (2011), *Notre Dame Philosophical Reviews* (http://ndpr.nd.edu/news/27609-legality/).

Gibbard, Allan (1990). *Wise Choices, Apt Feelings* (Cambridge, MA: Harvard University Press).

Gilbert, Margaret (1999). "Social Rules: Some Problems for Hart's Account, and an Alternative Proposal", *Law and Philosophy* 18: 141–71.

Green, Leslie (1983). "Law, Co-ordination and the Common Good", *Oxford Journal of Legal Studies* 3: 299–324.

Green, Leslie (1999). "Positivism and Conventionalism", *Canadian Journal of Law and Jurisprudence* 12: 35–52.

Green, Leslie (2012). "Introduction" to H.L.A. Hart, *The Concept of Law*, 3rd edn. (Oxford: Clarendon Press).

Greenberg, Mark (2004). "How Facts Make Law", *Legal Theory* 10: 157–98.

Greenberg, Mark (2005). "A New Map of Theories of Mental Content: Constitutive Accounts and Normative Theories", *Philosophical Issues* 15: 299–320.

Greenberg, Mark (2006a). "On Practices and the Law", *Legal Theory* 12: 113–36.

Greenberg, Mark (2006b). "Hartian Positivism and Normative Facts: How Facts Make Law II", in S. Hershovitz (ed.), *Explaining Law's Empire* (Oxford: Oxford University Press).

Greenberg, Mark (2011). "The Standard Picture and Its Discontents", in L. Green & B. Leiter (eds.), *Oxford Studies in Philosophy of Law*, vol. 1 (Oxford: Oxford University Press).

Hare, R.M. (1968). "Wanting: Some Pitfalls", repr. in R.M. Hare, *Practical Inferences* (Berkeley & Los Angeles, CA: University of California Press, 1972).

Hart, H.L.A. (1958). "Legal and Moral Obligation", in A.I. Melden (ed.), *Essays in Moral Philosophy* (Seattle, WA: University of Washington Press).

Hart, H.L.A. (1961/94). *The Concept of Law*, 2nd edn., ed. P.A. Bulloch & J. Raz (Oxford: Clarendon Press, 1994).

Kelsen, Hans (1960). *The Pure Theory of Law*, 2nd edn., trans. M. Knight (Berkeley & Los Angeles, CA: University of California Press, 1967).

Kim, Jaegwon (2003). "Philosophy of Mind and Psychology", in K. Ludwig (ed.), *Donald Davidson* (Cambridge: Cambridge University Press).

Kolodny, Niko (2005). "Why be Rational?", *Mind* 114: 509–63.

Leiter, Brian (2009). "Explaining Theoretical Disagreement", *The University of Chicago Law Review* 76: 1215–50.

Lewis, David (1969). *Convention: A Philosophical Study* (Cambridge, MA: Harvard University Press).

Mackie, J.L. (1977). *Ethics: Inventing Right and Wrong* (Harmondsworth: Penguin Books).

Marmor, Andrei (2009). *Social Conventions: From Language to Law* (Princeton, NJ: Princeton University Press).

Murphy, Mark (2004). "Natural Law Theory", in M. Golding & W. Edmundson (eds.), *The Blackwell Guide to the Philosophy of Law and Legal Theory* (Oxford: Wiley-Blackwell).

Postema, Gerald (1982). "Coordination and Convention at the Foundations of Law", *Journal of Legal Studies* 11: 165–203.

Raz, Joseph (1974). "Kelsen's Theory of the Basic Norm", repr. in J. Raz, *The Authority of Law* (Oxford: Clarendon Press, 1979).

Raz, Joseph (1975/90). *Practical Reason and Norms*, 2nd edn. (Princeton, NJ: Princeton University Press, 1990).

Raz, Joseph (1977). "Legal Validity", repr. in J. Raz, *The Authority of Law* (Oxford: Clarendon Press, 1979).

Raz, Joseph (1981). "The Purity of the Pure Theory", *Revue Internationale de Philosophie* 35: 441–59.

Raz, Joseph (1998). "Postema on Law's Autonomy and Public Practical Reasons: A Critical Comment", repr. in J. Raz, *Between Authority and Interpretation* (Oxford: Oxford University Press, 2009).

Schroeder, Mark (2004). "The Scope of Instrumental Reason", *Philosophical Perspectives* 18: 337–64.

Shapiro, Scott (2002). "Law, Plans, and Practical Reason", *Legal Theory* 8: 387–441.

Shapiro, Scott (2011). *Legality* (Cambridge, MA: Harvard University Press).

Sibley, Frank (1965). "Aesthetic and Non-aesthetic", repr. in F. Sibley, *Approach to Aesthetics*, ed. J. Benson, B. Redfern, & J. Roxbee Cox (Oxford: Clarendon Press, 2001).

Skorupski, John (1993). "The Definition of Morality", repr. in J. Skorupski, *Moral Explorations* (Oxford: Oxford University Press, 1999).

Smith, Michael (1994). *The Moral Problem* (Oxford: Blackwell Publishers).

Toh, Kevin (2005). "Hart's Expressivism and His Benthamite Project", *Legal Theory* 11: 75–123.

Toh, Kevin (2007). "Raz on Detachment, Acceptance and Describability", *Oxford Journal of Legal Studies* 27: 403–27.

Toh, Kevin (2010). Review of Andrei Marmor, *Social Conventions: From Language to Law* (2009), *Ethics* 120: 617–22.

Toh, Kevin (2012). "La Falacia del Doble Deber y los 'Desacuerdos Teóricos' en el Derecho", in P.L. Sánchez & G. Ratti (eds.), *Acordes y Desacuerdos* (Madrid: Marcial Pons).

Toh, Kevin (2014/15). "Four Neglected Prescriptions of Hartian Legal Philosophy", *Law and Philosophy* 33 (2014): 689–724, republished with many corrections as "Erratum to: Four Neglected Prescriptions of Hartian Legal Philosophy", *Law and Philosophy* 34 (2015): 333–68.

Toh, Kevin (forthcoming). "Legal Philosophy à la carte", in D. Plunkett, S. Shapiro, & K. Toh (eds.), *Dimensions of Normativity: New Essays in Jurisprudence and Metaethics* (Oxford: Oxford University Press).

Williams, Bernard (1986). *Ethics and the Limits of Philosophy* (Cambridge, MA: Harvard University Press).

Wittgenstein, Ludwig (1921). *Tractatus Logico-Philosophicus*, trans. D.F. Pears & B.F. McGuinness (London: Routledge & Kegan Paul, 1961).

Yaffe, Gideon (2012). Review of Scott Shapiro, *Legality* (2011), *Philosophical Review* 121: 457–60.

Zangwill, Nick (2007). *Aesthetic Creation* (Oxford: Oxford University Press).

2

Quasi-Expressivism about Statements of Law: A Hartian Theory

STEPHEN FINLAY AND DAVID PLUNKETT

INTRODUCTION

Speech and thought about what the law is commonly function in *practical* ways to guide or assess conduct. Agents often make judgments about what the law is (henceforth 'legal judgments') in order to structure their deliberations about what to do, or to evaluate their own behavior. We make statements about the law ('legal statements') as a way to guide or evaluate the behavior of others. Judging that the law requires citizens to pay taxes to the government may motivate someone to pay her taxes, for example, and her statements of such a law may constitute criticism of others who fail to pay their taxes, or exhortations to them to pay. If some citizens end up before a court because of their failure to pay, the judge's legal judgments will commonly help direct her reasoning about what verdict to reach, and her legal statements may provide the vehicle by which the court's condemnation of their actions is expressed.

A complete metalegal theory (explaining how the law, and our thought and talk about it, fits into reality) should account for the full range of these practical features.[1] In this paper, we advance a broad approach to this task. To ease exposition, we focus on a central subset of claims about the law; those expressed by the use of sentences of the form 'It is the law that...', which we call *statements of law* or *legal statements*.

---

[1] Our understanding of 'metalegal theory' draws from Plunkett and Shapiro (2017); see also Toh (2013) for a similar treatment. Our topic could also be labeled 'general jurisprudence', which Plunkett and Shapiro understand as a subset of metalegal theory dealing with what is common to law, and thought and talk about it, across all jurisdictions.

Oxford Studies in Philosophy of Law Volume 3. John Gardner, Leslie Green, and Brian Leiter (eds)
This chapter © Stephen Finlay and David Plunkett 2018. First published in 2018 by Oxford University Press

Whether our theory can be expanded to other parts of legal thought and talk is an issue for future work.

Our theory has close affinities with the approach of metalegal *expressivism*, as recently championed by Kevin Toh.[2] Metalegal expressivism identifies the meaning of legal words and sentences not with any properties or facts that they represent, but with a conventional function of expressing the speaker's noncognitive (desire-like) attitudes or prescriptive (command-like) speech acts. This approach is tailor-made for explaining the practical uses of legal statements. But it has a hard time explaining why legal statements seem to *describe* something—and, moreover, something that strikes many as an objective matter of fact and a legitimate object of purely descriptive inquiry in the social sciences. This makes many uncomfortable with metalegal expressivism, and we think rightly so.

Whereas metalegal expressivism is modeled after the popular expressivist strategy in metaethics, our theory is modeled after a rival, "quasi-expressivist" strategy in metaethics, which one of us (Finlay) has championed in previous work. This strategy is quasi-*expressivist* because it agrees with expressivism that a central class of (legal or moral) statements is expressive of noncognitive attitudes or prescriptions. But it is *quasi*-expressivist because it diagnoses this as a feature of the *pragmatics* of these statements, rather than of their (purely descriptive) semantics.[3] This approach offers a straightforward vindication of the descriptive appearance of legal statements, while sharing the virtues of the expressivist's account of their practical functions.

While a quasi-expressivist theory of legal statements could be developed in various ways, we develop ours in a way friendly to *legal positivism*, understood as a view about what explains legal facts (about what the content of the law is in a given jurisdiction at a given time). Specifically, we understand legal positivism as holding that legal facts are *ultimately grounded* entirely in contingent social facts, of the kind studied by the

---

[2] See Toh (2005; 2011). For an alternative way of developing metalegal expressivism, see Etchemendy (2016).

[3] Cf. Enoch and Toh (2013) for exploration of the pragmatics of legal statements on the model of 'thick' ethical terms, and Silk (forthcoming) for a descriptivist view with close affinities to ours. Shortly before publication, Jeff Goldsworthy alerted us to Holton (1998), which also supplements a Hartian form of positivism with a pragmatic explanation of certain practical features of legal statements. Unlike ours, Holton's analysis appeals to specifically *moral* attitudes, and isn't quasi-expressivist.

social sciences (e.g. descriptive facts about the activity of legislators and judges), and *not* in moral facts (e.g. normative facts about what distributive justice requires or the moral merit of the actions of judges).[4] Our focus on "grounds" is addressed to the issue of constitutive explanation, of what legal facts consist in, rather than to causal or epistemic issues. And our focus on "ultimate" grounds in particular is meant to make room for *inclusive* legal positivists, who allow that moral facts can play a derivative role in grounding legal facts on the basis of certain contingent social facts, such as a constitution explicitly referencing *justice* as a constraint or basis for law.[5] This is in contrast with *exclusive* legal positivists, who hold that moral facts are never even part of the grounds of legal facts.[6] By this definition, what unites legal positivists is the view that only social facts (and not moral facts) are the *necessary* grounds of law; insofar as any moral facts are grounds of law at all, they are so contingently because of the obtaining of social facts. Legal *anti*positivists, such as Ronald Dworkin and Mark Greenberg, hold by contrast that, necessarily, moral facts (in addition to social facts) are amongst the grounds of law.[7]

Our theory is developed in a positivist-friendly form for two main reasons. First, positivism has important virtues, such as easily accommodating the existence of morally bad laws and legal systems, and we believe it to be correct. Second, a quasi-expressivist approach has greater significance when paired with positivism. Positivists might seem prima facie to have a harder time accounting for various practical features of legal speech and thought than antipositivists. But if a quasi-expressivist approach can explain these features without endorsing legal

---

[4] This understanding draws on Greenberg (2006), Plunkett (2013), Rosen (2010), and Shapiro (2011). Our theory is also compatible with 'legal positivism' on many other definitions.

[5] See Coleman (1982), Waluchow (1994), and the postscript to Hart (1961/2012) for defenses of inclusive legal positivism.

[6] See Green (1990), Raz (1980), and Shapiro (2011) for defenses of exclusive legal positivism. Note that exclusive legal positivists can grant that some laws reference moral facts, such as facts about what justice requires. For example, they can hold that the law directs us to *consult* moral or extra-legal norms, just as morality might direct us to follow the rules of grammar without incorporating them into morality itself. See Raz (1979/2002).

[7] See Dworkin (1986; 2011) and Greenberg (2006; 2014). Given the potential connotations of the "ultimately" talk here, it is worth noting that all of these views (inclusive legal positivism, exclusive legal positivism, and antipositivism) are compatible with social facts or moral facts being grounded in further facts.

antipositivism, this neutralizes some (though not all) of the motivations for antipositivism.

Our theory is additionally formulated in an explicitly *Hartian* framework, drawing on the jurisprudential views of H.L.A. Hart.[8] This enables us to introduce it in terminology familiar to philosophers of law, and also facilitates a secondary, interpretative goal of the paper. The final part of the paper argues that Hart's views in *The Concept of Law* are best reconstructed as a (positivist) form of quasi-expressivism. We argue against rival interpretations of Hart's theory of legal statements, including pure expressivist readings (Kevin Toh, Scott Shapiro) and hybrid expressivist readings (as suggested by some passages from Joseph Raz).[9] This secondary goal is separable from our primary thesis. One could embrace a quasi-expressivist theory of legal statements while rejecting our reconstruction of Hart. Or one could accept our reconstruction of Hart, while rejecting quasi-expressivism about legal statements. We pursue these goals together in part to give credit where it is (arguably) due. But more importantly, we do so because if this is the best reconstruction of Hart's view then engaging with quasi-expressivism is all the more important for the many legal philosophers who identify as broadly Hartian or who draw on Hartian resources—and for Hart's critics, since quasi-expressivism provides resources for defending a Hartian theory against influential objections.

§1. QUASI-EXPRESSIVISM: FROM MORALITY TO LAW

Section 1 introduces the key features of a quasi-expressivist approach to statements of law, develops it in a concretely Hartian form, and argues for its superiority over its rivals. First, we introduce a standard Hartian view of the content of legal thought and talk, or the semantics of legal language and the nature of legal facts, as *rule-relational*. This theory is both descriptivist and positivist-compatible. We then explain how it can capture the practical character of certain statements of law, by showing how a directly analogous *end*-relational view of the content of moral thought and talk provides quasi-expressivist solutions to parallel problems in metaethics (as argued by Finlay). We extend these solutions from the

---

[8] Especially Hart (1961/2012).
[9] See Raz (1993), Shapiro (2011), and Toh (2005).

metaethical to the metalegal case, and observe their advantages over rival proposals. In adopting this approach we do not assume that a relational, quasi-expressivist theory is the correct view in metaethics. Rather, we aim to demonstrate why such an approach might be appealing, and how it can be applied, in relation to parallel puzzles in metalegal theory. A quasi-expressivist view may be correct in the metalegal case even if incorrect in metaethics, and indeed we'll suggest that some central objections in the metaethical domain don't have plausible metalegal counterparts.

§1.1. Semantic Foundations: The Rule-Relational Theory

While a quasi-expressivist view of legal statements can in principle be combined with any descriptivist theory of their semantics, we will develop it from a particular view, for the following reasons. First, we think this semantics is broadly on the right track. Second, it is structurally parallel to the metaethical theory from which our quasi-expressivist account is derived by analogy. Third, it supports a particular kind of quasi-expressivist account, the details of which are especially attractive. Fourth, it is friendly to legal positivism, which enables us to demonstrate quasi-expressivism's potential as a response to antipositivist arguments. Finally, it lays the groundwork for our critical reconstruction of Hart's views in §2.

A semantic theory is "descriptivist" in case it identifies the literal and conventional content of the target sentences with an ordinary proposition, which represents the world as being a particular way and is true if and only if the world is so.[10] Such propositions are the contents of ordinary *beliefs*, understood as attitudes with a mind-to-world direction of fit. Hence, sincere assertion of a descriptive sentence '*p*' is a speech act of expressing the speaker's belief that *p*. To develop a descriptivist theory of statements of law, one must therefore identify which propositions are the semantic contents of sentences of the form 'It is the law that L'. What properties, relations, states of affairs, etc. are statements of law *about*?

An obvious but trivial answer is that these statements are about *law*. But what is law? Is it even something that exists "in the world", as a

---

[10] For ease of exposition we here overlook semantically incomplete sentences, which require supplementation from context to determine a proposition.

descriptivist semantics requires? A key insight—emphasized by Kelsen, Hart, and many other legal philosophers—is that laws don't exist in isolation, but only as parts of particular *legal systems*, such as New Zealand Law and American Law.[11] This relativity-to-a-system is plausibly also built into the conceptual and semantic competence of ordinary users of legal language. Claims or judgments about what the law is are made (explicitly or implicitly) relative to particular legal systems, and statements of law are commonly qualified in ways that plausibly function to identify particular legal systems or subsystems; e.g. '*In New Zealand*, it is the law that...', '*According to the Californian road code*, it is the law that...'. This suggests a *relational* theory of the semantics and metaphysics of law: legal statements describe some kind of relation in which things stand to a legal system.

Defining law in terms of a relation to a "legal system" is unsatisfyingly circular, of course. This circularity can be eliminated by developing our relational theory in an explicitly Hartian direction. In *The Concept of Law*, Hart argues that law can be analyzed as a union of first-order rules (e.g. governing behavior) and second-order rules (rules governing rules). Among the second-order rules of a legal system is what Hart calls a *rule of recognition*. This can be defined abstractly as specifying the criteria for a rule to be a part of a given system of rules, or, in Hartian terminology, the conditions of *legal validity* within the system.[12] This yields a relational account of the nature of law itself. Facts about what the law is, relative to a particular legal system, are facts about what rules are valid according to the relevant rule of recognition. Plausibly there are objective facts about many such relations (allowing for some indeterminacy).

On the corresponding, *rule-relational* semantic theory we adopt here, a statement of the form 'It is the law that L (in X)' semantically expresses the proposition that L is a rule (requiring, permitting, or empowering

---

[11] In Kelsen's words, "Law is not, as it is sometimes said, a rule. It is a set of rules having the kind of unity we understand by a system" (Kelsen 1945, 3). See also Gardner (2012b), Hart (1961/2012), Marmor (2011), Raz (1980), and Shapiro (2011).

[12] Hart normally writes as if there is *one* rule of recognition per legal system (also a common practice in the secondary literature), though occasionally hints at the possibility of multiple rules of recognition; see, for example, Hart (1961/2012, 95). For arguments in favor of this reading, and for the idea itself, see Marmor (2011) and Raz (1975/2002). We assume one rule of recognition per system to simplify discussion and without prejudice on this issue, following common practice; e.g. Gardner (2012c, 283).

some kind of behavior) satisfying the criteria of the rule of recognition R of legal system X. A legal statement that doesn't explicitly refer to a rule of recognition in this way implicitly relies on the salience of such a rule in the context. Not all relational or even rule-relational metalegal theories need be committed to giving rules of recognition this role in the semantics, which might be resisted for various reasons.[13] One might prefer, for example, to posit relativity to more specific rules or sets of rules (e.g. *US Tort Law*) in different contexts. As we adopt this Hartian view here largely for purposes of illustration, we will not address various objections against the details of Hart's appeal to rules of recognition.

Significant questions can be raised about the metaphysics of *rules*. But while such questions matter for many debates in the philosophy of law we can here remain neutral. All we need is that appeal to rules of the relevant kind is compatible with legal positivism as we have defined it, as we believe. Consider board games like Monopoly, and sports like football, which have rules prohibiting certain actions, permitting others, etc. It is very plausible that social facts (of some kind) are alone the ultimate grounds of those rules. It is also plausible that there are objective facts about how things stand in relation to those rules; e.g. whether a given move is permitted in Monopoly. These relational facts might arguably not themselves be "social facts" in a narrow sense, but so long as they are not grounded in any moral facts and the rules themselves are grounded entirely in social facts as we suggest, they are consistent with positivism about games. Our theory of legal statements requires nothing beyond rules and relations of this kind, and so we take this appeal to legal rules to be compatible with legal positivism.[14]

---

[13] One might share the worry that Scott Hershovitz expressed to us, that ordinary legal speech couldn't plausibly be *about* something as abstract as a rule of recognition—an instance of a general concern about semantic theories attributing complex thoughts to ordinary speakers. One might therefore look for different relata, but our theory can allow that speech and thought about the law requires merely a recognition that some criterion of law in the relevant system exists, and the ability to represent it in such *de dicto* terms, without knowing what it is. Hartians can insist that in the absence of this recognition, one lacks the concept of law.

[14] Some recent arguments suggest a radical form of antipositivism that extends even to board games; see Dworkin (2011), Greenberg (2006), and Hershovitz (2015). If such a view is correct then our proposals will fail to help the positivist, although our other aims in this paper would be unharmed. However, antipositivism seems far less plausible for board games than for law.

§1.2. *The Practical Uses of Legal Statements*

In this section we identify several different practical functions of legal talk and thought, and show how a (positivist-friendly) rule-relational theory of the content of legal statements can explain them. The challenge is to explain how mere assertions about the relations in which conduct or rules stand to other, socially grounded rules could function in these practical ways. To meet this challenge we draw on recent developments in metaethics. A parallel challenge confronts relational semantic theories about the content of moral statements concerning (e.g.) what is "good", or what "ought" to be done. According to the *end*-relational theory one of us (Finlay) has championed, these statements assert propositions about the statistical relations in which actions (for example) stand to "ends", or potential future states of affairs.[15] So to say that S *ought* to do A (in order that *e*), for example, is to assert approximately that *e* is more likely if S does A than if S does anything else. But how could the mere assertion of such ordinary propositions possess the practical features of moral claims? In metaethics, a set of pragmatic resources we call *quasi-expressivist* has been developed to answer this kind of challenge.[16] These resources can also be applied directly in the metalegal case, to explain how rule-relational statements can possess parallel features. We will explain how these solutions work in the metaethical case, and show how to draw the analogy to statements of law.

§1.2.1. Motivation and Expression

Consider, first, practical features of moral judgment that are *speaker-centric*. A central metaethical challenge is to explain the special connection between moral judgment and motivational attitudes in the speaker. Why is it, for example, that judging that you ought to do A reliably (and perhaps rationally) leads to your being motivated to do A, and telling somebody that they ought to do A expresses your approval of doing A? According to the (popular though controversial) thesis of *motivational internalism*, this connection between moral judgment and motivation holds by necessity. A primary argument for expressivism and against

---

[15] e.g. Finlay (2004; 2014). For other relational theories in metaethics, see Copp (2007), Harman (1975; 1996), Railton (1986), and Wong (1984).

[16] For the most developed version of this strategy, see Finlay (2014). It is introduced in Harman (1996) under the label 'quasi-absolutism'; for other versions, see, for example, Copp (2001), Phillips (1998), Railton (2008), and Strandberg (2012).

descriptivism in metaethics is that no purely descriptive judgment, or mere belief in any kind of properties or facts, could explain this "internal" connection. It is easily seen how this objection applies to a relational metaethical theory like Finlay's: a mere statement or belief that A raises the probability of some state of affairs has no necessary connection with speaker motivation.

A rule-relational theory of law faces a parallel objection. There is at least a special class of statements about law that seem essentially practical, in that the speaker tends to be reliably motivated to comply with what she asserts to be the law, and thereby to express pro or con attitudes towards the relevant conduct. We will call these *internal* statements of law, in contrast to *external* statements of law, which we discuss subsequently. (We take ourselves to be following Hart's famous and influential distinction between "internal" and "external" statements of law.[17] But it is controversial what distinction Hart intended, and different legal philosophers use this terminology in different ways. We employ these terms stipulatively, without commitment to whether this use aligns perfectly with Hart's, let alone other philosophers' use.[18]) This characteristic of legal statements is among the primary motivations for metalegal expressivism. It may seem incompatible with the rule-relational theory, since merely describing a relationship between positivistic rules does not have any essential connection with motivational attitudes in the speaker. But relational theories can answer this objection. We start by sketching the metaethical case, then draw the analogy to the metalegal case.

We concede that the end-relational theory, which interprets moral statements as asserting ordinary propositions about relations to ends, does not support any necessary connection between the beliefs expressed and motivational attitudes in the speaker. Notice, however, that motivational internalism is only plausible, at best, in relation to uses of 'ought' that are not explicitly relativized. For example, compare 'In order to poison your enemy without detection, you ought to feed them arsenic' with 'You ought to feed your enemy arsenic'. Only utterance of the latter is naturally taken to express positive motivational attitude toward feeding anyone arsenic. But distinctly *moral* uses of 'ought' are characteristically

---

[17] See Hart (1961/2012, esp. 89 and 102–10).
[18] Some philosophers, including Toh (2005), use 'statements of law' narrowly as a term of art for what by our definitions are strictly internal statements.

nonrelativized. One might therefore conclude that terms like 'ought' are *ambiguous* between a relational, non-moral meaning and a non-relational, moral meaning—rejecting a relational theory of peculiarly *moral* statements. However, there is an alternative explanation of this same observation, which is semantically more parsimonious.

If the semantics of 'ought' are indeed end-relational, then asserting an unrelativized sentence such as 'You ought to feed your enemy arsenic' can only communicate a complete proposition if some end is salient in the context. In that case the end can be left unstated, since the audience is able to identify it without help. So to explain the intimate connection between moral statements and motivation, the end-relational theory simply needs to explain why the use of terms like 'ought' has an especially close connection to motivational attitudes whenever an end is left implicit rather than explicitly stated. Finlay argues that this challenge is easily met.[19] The normal (though by no means only) circumstances in which the end can be assumed are where it is salient in virtue of being of *shared concern to both speaker and audience* (perhaps only under this description). In these circumstances there is a tight, obvious connection to motivation: any agent who has a desire or concern for an end *e* will (rationally) be motivationally disposed towards whatever they believe to stand in such an instrumental relation to *e*.

The end-relational theory is then able to explain how, by using (unrelativized) normative words like 'ought', speakers *express* their motivational attitudes. In normal contexts, a person uttering an unrelativized 'ought' sentence speaks *as if* the unstated end is salient as the object of her concern. This is an instance of "pragmatic presupposition": uttering a sentence that would normally make a helpful contribution to a communicative exchange only on the condition that some unasserted proposition *p* is true.[20] If the audience does not already recognize that *p* is true, they will engage in "presupposition accommodation", and understand the speaker to be communicating the additional information *p* that her utterance presupposes. By uttering an unrelativized 'ought' sentence, a speaker therefore communicates (or *expresses*) the additional information that she has favorable attitude toward the unstated end. Since she can therefore be

---

[19] Finlay (2004; 2014, ch. 5); see also Harman (1996, 15–16).

[20] Dowell (2016) observes that these cases lack some canonical features of pragmatic presupposition identified in Stalnaker (1974). We think the classification is apt nonetheless, as the practice involves presupposing something and is pragmatic rather than semantic.

expected also to have derivative favorable attitude toward the action she is asserting to be most promotive of that end, she will also pragmatically express favorable attitude toward the action itself.

This account accommodates the expressive elements of moral discourse that motivate metaethical expressivism, but remains descriptivist because it explains these as pragmatic features, arising from the way in which words like 'ought' are used in particular contexts, rather than as semantic features located in the conventional meaning of the words themselves. Like expressivism, it holds that (unrelativized) 'ought' statements characteristically express noncognitive attitudes, but unlike expressivism it holds this to be an entirely pragmatic feature of these statements, generated from a purely descriptivist semantics that is uniform between different kinds of use of 'ought'; hence the *quasi-expressivist* label.[21]

A parallel quasi-expressivist story can be told in the metalegal case. Clearly, not all statements of law are essentially normative or practical. The existence of external statements of law (unlike the existence of external moral statements), as pure descriptions of fact, is uncontroversial. This is particularly obvious for talk about laws of other times and places; e.g. when a contemporary American citizen says 'By the Hammurabi Code, it is the law that L' or 'In China, it is the law that L'. As Hart observes, the paradigms of internal statements of law rather involve utterances of simpler, unrelativized sentences, of the form 'It is the law that L'.[22] If all thought and talk about law is rule-relational, then these utterances must be implicitly relativized to some rule of recognition sufficiently salient in the context, which the audience is expected to identify without explicit cues. In general (but not invariably) these will be contexts where the rule of recognition is the object of a particular kind of motivational attitude for both the speaker and audience, an attitude we'll call *acceptance*.

An agent "accepts" a particular rule of recognition R, in our sense, if she is disposed to use the rules she believes to meet its criteria for law directly as a guide for her own and others' conduct when in the relevant jurisdiction. This notion of acceptance, modeled broadly on Hart's

[21] Following Björnsson and Finlay (2010) and Finlay (2014). Harman (1996) labels his similar account 'quasi-absolutist', focusing instead on the relativist's mimicry of moral absolutism. The term is inspired by the label 'quasi-realism' for the project of explaining the realist appearances of moral discourse with purely antirealist resources (Blackburn 1993).

[22] See Hart (1961/2012, 102).

discussion of rule-acceptance in *The Concept of Law*, is capacious. One might accept a rule of recognition (or particular law) because of its perceived moral merits or authority, for example, or for purely prudential or self-interested reasons. Alternatively, one might accept it merely instinctively, and not in response to any perceived reasons.[23] For any agent who accepts a particular rule of recognition R, for any reason or cause, there will obviously be a contingent but intimate connection between believing some first-order rule L to meet the criteria for legal validity provided by R, and being motivated to act in accordance with L. This provides a quasi-expressivist explanation why internal statements of law would characteristically both imply and express motivational attitudes.

The generality and explanation of this connection between unrelativized and internal use of legal statements can be expected to diverge in some ways from the case of moral statements. On the one hand, the fact of *jurisdictional uniqueness*—that often only a single rule of recognition (or legal system) has social efficacy in any one jurisdiction at any one time—is a strong source of salience competing with the speaker's and audience's attitudes of acceptance, which isn't present to the same degree in the case of moral statements.[24] Certainly, agents who don't accept the law of the land can easily make unambiguous external statements of law by uttering unrelativized sentences—as when professional thieves debate property law to determine which of their activities to conceal from police. On the other hand, the statistical normality of acceptance of the legal system with efficacy in one's own jurisdiction (whether socially conditioned, or for moral, prudential, or other reasons) restores some of the connection's strength.[25] In any case, the presence or absence of explicit relativization to a rule of recognition will be only loosely correlated

---

[23] We take no stand on whether certain agents (e.g. high-ranking judges) must accept certain rules for particular kinds of reasons in order for there to be a legal system. Hart denied, for example, that there could be a legal system in which all the officials accepted the rule of recognition only for prudential reasons (Hart 1961/2012, ch. 6), a claim rejected by other philosophers, including Gardner (2012a) and Shapiro (2011). The pragmatic account of Holton (1998) utilizes this Hartian claim to explain why internal legal statements would implicate claims about moral justification.

[24] A moral analog: moral ends may have the status of social norms, enabling "amoralists" to make unrelativized statements about moral value without corresponding motivational attitudes (Finlay 2014, 190–2); cf. Phillips (1998).

[25] Copp (2001) and Strandberg (2012) suggest analogous bases for metaethical quasi-expressivism in terms of *generalized conversational implicature*; see also Holton (1998) for a similar view of legal implicatures.

with a legal statement's status as internal or external. Any signal that a legal statement is internal, whatever the mechanism, will support a quasi-expressivist explanation why it expresses the speaker's motivational attitudes.

§1.2.2. Making Demands: The Prescriptivity of Legal Statements

We turn now to consider *audience*-centric practical features of moral and legal statements, in particular their illocutionary force of *prescription*. Addressing moral or legal claims to agents ('You ought to do A'/'It is the law that you do A') often has a central function of commanding that the addressee do A. In the metaethical case, we suggested above that in paradigmatic circumstances, ends will be salient on account of being of shared concern both to speaker *and* audience in the context. The audience's attitudes will be especially salient in second-personal assertions, of the form 'You ought to do A'. To be told that a particular action is the option that most promotes an end *e*, which you happen to desire, is to be given reliably and rationally motivating information, and is naturally classified as a speech act of *recommendation*. This extension of the quasi-expressivist solution can also be applied directly to the rule-relational theory of law. To be told that rule L meets the criteria for legal validity provided by the rule of recognition R you yourself accept is to be given reliably and rationally motivating information. It thereby constitutes a legal recommendation to comply with L.

This still omits the *categoricity* characteristic of moral and legal prescriptions, however. Consider the metaethical case: sometimes unrelativized 'ought' claims are addressed to audiences who transparently do not share the speakers' own concerns or preferences. This is especially characteristic of the *moral* 'ought' statements that address "categorical imperatives" to agents, demanding compliance regardless of the agent's desires (contrasting with mere "hypothetical imperatives"). Many legal statements have a similarly categorical quality, such that telling an agent "It is the law that you do A" functions prescriptively despite his declarations of indifference towards (or nonacceptance of) the rules of the relevant legal system.

Perhaps it is enough to explain the categoricity of moral talk that the speaker expresses her own motivational attitudes (as outlined in §1.2.1), thereby pressing her own second-personal authority on her audience—as some expressivists have thought. The end-relational theory supports a further explanation of this prescriptive feature, however.[26] When a speaker utters an unrelativized 'ought' sentence, by speaking as if one end were uncontroversially salient she behaves as if her attitudes were shared by her audience, even though (in prototypically moral contexts) this presupposition is transparently false. Taking a wider view of our linguistic practices, this can be recognized as a familiar kind of rhetorical device we'll label *moralism*.[27] Communicating something—especially about your audience—that you are clearly in no epistemic position to assume true is a familiar way of expressing a demand or "expectation" that it be made true. Consider the typically moralistic force of saying "We don't do that around here", for example, or "You will take out the trash".[28] An unrelativized use of 'ought' when the audience transparently does not share the speaker's attitude towards the end can therefore be predicted to function, pragmatically and rhetorically, to express a demand that they share (or at least respect) the speaker's attitude towards the end, and derivatively towards the action being claimed to promote it. A semantics of "hypothetical imperatives" can in this way aim to accommodate our practice of addressing "categorical imperatives" to others.[29]

A parallel quasi-expressivist story can be told about the categorically prescriptive character of certain (especially second-personal) legal statements, on behalf of the rule-relational theory. When the audience transparently doesn't accept the rule of recognition accepted by the speaker (e.g. in legal addresses to scofflaws), to talk as if one rule of recognition were uniquely salient in the context will sometimes be to talk *as if* that rule of recognition was accepted by the audience. This will rhetorically express a demand that it be accepted, and derivatively, that the law being claimed to follow from it also be accepted and obeyed.

We concede that this story may not be as compelling in the metalegal case as it (arguably) is in metaethics. This is because, again, jurisdictional uniqueness will often be sufficient by itself to make a particular rule of recognition salient. (An exception involves cases of "bedrock legal disputes", discussed below). But a quasi-expressivist account of categorical legal prescriptions can be supported by other mechanisms. If the speaker is evidently aiming to advise or influence the agent, for example, then

---

[26] See especially Finlay (2004; 2014, 180–8).
[27] See Finlay (2014, 186–7).
[28] Cf. Barker (2000) and Stevenson (1937, 24–5), on a "rhetorical objectivity effect".
[29] See Finlay (2004, 220; 2014, ch. 7). Cf. Foot (1972).

she is talking as if the agent accepts the relevant system of law; in contexts where this presupposition is transparently unjustified, a rhetorically expressed demand can be predicted as described above. The rule-relational theory therefore supports a quasi-expressivist explanation of the categorical prescriptivity of internal legal statements.

§1.3. Bedrock Legal Disputes

Thus far we have focused on how a quasi-expressivist, rule-relational theory can explain key practical features of legal talk and thought, in a way consistent with legal positivism. To bolster this case, we now consider an influential objection against legal positivism and show how a quasi-expressivist account can help positivists to respond.

In *Law's Empire*, Ronald Dworkin points to cases where speakers persist in a dispute about what to count as "the law" in a particular jurisdiction, despite complete, mutually recognized agreement on all relevant empirical facts.[30] Following terminology introduced by Plunkett and Sundell, we'll call such disputes *bedrock legal disputes*.[31] Dworkin argues that there are many bedrock legal disputes in actual legal practice, and, moreover, that many of them express genuine disagreements. Antipositivists can easily explain such disputes as involving disagreement over the moral facts they allege to be among the ultimate grounds of law, such as (on Dworkin's theory in *Law's Empire*) facts about which principles provide the strongest moral justification for the relevant social practices.[32] In contrast, it is less clear what positivists should say if they grant the existence of such disputes. Consider that on a straightforward positivist view, these disputes will often involve speakers employing different criteria for determining legal validity-in-the-system.[33] At least

---

[30] Dworkin (1986). Cf. Dworkin (2006; 2011).

[31] We use 'dispute' to refer to exchanges that *appear* (but may fail) to express genuine disagreement, following Plunkett and Sundell (2013a; 2013b). Dworkin's label *theoretical disagreements* has become general currency among legal philosophers; we avoid it partly because his definition builds in parts of his own analysis we don't endorse (e.g. that these disputes concern what he calls the *grounds of law*). For discussion, see Plunkett and Sundell (2013b).

[32] For a similar reading of *Law's Empire*, see Greenberg (2006).

[33] Part of Dworkin's objection to Hart's particular form of legal positivism is that such disagreements can (allegedly) arise between the very legal officials whose convergence in practice is what, for Hart, grounds a rule of recognition. On Hart's theory, such divergence seemingly entails that no rule of recognition exists in that jurisdiction, and hence no law does either. For discussion, see Shapiro (2011, ch. 10). Because of this, one might think that a Hartian theory, such as our own, should *not* endorse the claim that bedrock legal disputes involve speakers

prima facie, this seems to commit the positivist to denying that such disputes involve genuine disagreements. According to our rule-relational theory, for example, such intuitively and superficially conflicting statements of law are assertions that L is the-law-according-to-R1/not the-law-according-to-R2; assertions that are logically, conceptually, and metaphysically consistent with each other. So relational theories may seem committed to saying that participants in such disputes are merely talking past each other, expressing no genuine disagreement. Dworkin argues that the best versions of legal positivism do indeed have such commitments, and that this is a powerful reason to reject positivism.[34]

This objection to positivism parallels a well-known objection in metaethics based on the observation that moral disagreement can persist despite complete, mutually recognized agreement on all scientifically describable facts.[35] This presents a challenge particularly for relativistic theories, as easily illustrated with Finlay's end-relational theory. Settling all the relational facts about which actions best promote which ends does not settle the issue of what one morally ought to do, because the question remains of what end to pursue. Consider an assertion by a Benthamite utilitarian of the sentence 'Sometimes one ought to tell a lie'. An obvious end-relational analysis of this is as meaning that *sometimes one promotes utility most by telling a lie.* A Kantian deontologist might believe this proposition, but wouldn't thereby agree with the utilitarian's moral claim. So the end-relational theory confronts the objection that it cannot account for the existence of moral disagreements in such cases.[36] By contrast, the existence of fundamental disagreements of this kind is claimed to count in favor of expressivism, which explains them as disagreements "in attitude" (e.g. preferences or plans) rather than disagreements in belief. Metalegal expressivists claim the corresponding

---

employing different criteria for determining legal validity-in-the-system, but must instead explain bedrock legal disputes in some other way. However, this is not a problem for our view in this context. Our rule-relational theory isn't committed to Hart's views about which social facts ground rules of recognition, and we are concerned with a more general objection that is just one element of Dworkin's challenge to positivism in *Law's Empire* but receives greater emphasis in his later work; see Dworkin (2006; 2011). For discussion, see Plunkett and Sundell (2013b) and Shapiro (2011, ch. 10).

[34] Dworkin (1986). Cf. Dworkin (2006; 2011).

[35] Moore (1922/70).

[36] See, for example, Olson (2011).

advantage over descriptivist and positivist theories, explaining bedrock legal disputes as expressions of conflicting attitudes of acceptance.[37]

Many positivists respond by simply denying that there are bedrock legal disputes, or that bedrock legal disputes express genuine disagreements. This stance is more plausible than any parallel claim in defense of *metaethical* relativism, and if correct, then our view faces no real problem here. But the rule-relational theory also provides quasi-expressivist resources that positivists can deploy to allow that these exchanges involve an important kind of disagreement.[38] This strategy can again be adapted from metaethics.

Disagreement challenges to relational theories crucially assume that to vindicate intuitions of disagreement a conflict must be found in the utterances' asserted or semantic content. This assumption is challenged on the grounds that some disagreements are *pragmatic*, involving conflicts in what is expressed without being asserted—via such mechanisms as implicature. For example, one kind of such dispute involves *metalinguistic negotiation*, in which speakers use (rather than mention) a word differently in order to pragmatically communicate conflicting views about how it should be used.[39] A central kind of metalinguistic negotiation occurs when one speaker uses a term 'X' to express one concept (what she means by 'X') and another uses the same term to express a rival concept (what he means by 'X').[40] Potential examples are open to competing interpretations, but consider disagreement over whether Pluto is a *planet* between two scientists who agree on all Pluto's physical properties. If each speaker means something different by 'planet' then the literal contents of their assertions may both be true, but they nonetheless disagree in virtue of their incompatible views about how the word should be used—a disagreement they express by their competing metalinguistic uses of it.[41] Similarly, in bedrock legal disputes, speakers

[37] See Toh (2005; 2011). Toh's full account of bedrock legal disputes incorporates additional features not under discussion here. See also Toh (2008).

[38] These can supplement other positivist responses, including appeal to inclusive legal positivism or denial of the philosophical importance of such disputes. For other positivist resources, see Leiter (2009), Shapiro (2011), and the postscript in Hart (1961/2012). For a similar pragmatic contextualist treatment of bedrock legal disputes, see Silk (forthcoming).

[39] See Plunkett and Sundell (2013a; 2013b; 2014).

[40] Cf. Robinson (2009), who offers related thoughts in analyzing what he calls "bedrock moral disputes".

[41] As demonstrated in Plunkett and Sundell (2013a), standard linguistic markers for disagreement, such as 'That's false', 'You're mistaken', etc., are also typically licensed in metalinguistic negotiations. For connected discussion, see Khoo and Knobe (2018).

use a common word ('law') divergently despite apparent awareness that they agree on all relevant empirical facts. One option for legal positivists and/or rule-relational theorists is therefore to analyze such disputes as metalinguistic negotiations, as Plunkett and Sundell have argued.[42]

A related, quasi-expressivist solution can be directly derived from the pragmatic resources we introduced in response to the previous challenges (§1.2.1, §1.2.2), modeled after quasi-expressivist responses to parallel challenges for metaethical views like the end-relational theory.[43] This solution grants that many bedrock legal disputes involve speakers employing different criteria for determining legal validity-in-the-system. In §1.2.1 we argued that by making statements about the law that are implicitly relativized to a rule of recognition she accepts, a speaker pragmatically expresses acceptance of the first-order rule she thereby asserts to satisfy those criteria. So when A asserts that L is "the law" (relative to a rule of recognition R1 which she accepts as uniquely determining authoritative law in the jurisdiction), and B asserts that L is *not* "the law" (relative to a rule of recognition R2 which he accepts as uniquely determining authoritative law in the same jurisdiction), they pragmatically express conflicting attitudes of acceptance/nonacceptance towards L. A and B thereby have a disagreement in attitude over the law, as expressivists like Toh maintain, but communicated through the pragmatics rather than the semantics of their utterances. Additionally, by speaking as if one rule of recognition were uniquely salient in the context, A pragmatically presupposes that B accepts the same rule of recognition R1 she does (and vice versa), although this may be transparently false or unjustified. As argued in §1.2.2, this can be expected to function rhetorically as expression of a demand or prescription that B come to accept R1, and derivatively, L. By the same reasoning, B expresses the prescription that A come to accept R2, and derivatively, not L. The rule-relational theory thereby predicts that bedrock legal disputes would involve a quasi-expressivist disagreement in prescription.[44]

Some philosophers may here object, with Dworkin, that bedrock legal disputes intuitively involve disagreement over an objective matter

---

[42] See Plunkett and Sundell (2013b). This schematic strategy leaves open whether the expressed stances consist in beliefs or in desire-like attitudes.

[43] See Björnsson and Finlay (2010), Finlay (2014, ch. 8), and Harman (1996). For an opinionated comparison with the metalinguistic strategy, see Finlay (2016).

[44] See Ridge (2014) for the idea of disagreement in prescription.

of fact—over what the law really is, or what its grounds are—rather than being "mere" clashes of attitude. If so, then quasi-expressivist and meta-linguistic analyses may be committed to attributing an implausible degree of error to the self-understanding of ordinary speakers. We reply, first, that attributing such error to folk metalegal theory may not be a great cost, because ordinary speakers plausibly needn't possess sophisticated theories of their own practice. Second, one may challenge whether pretheoretical intuitions speak unambiguously and univocally against our proposal about the division of labor between semantics and pragmatics in disputes over what "the law is".[45] One can reasonably be skeptical of Dworkin's claims both about the need to preserve the "face-value" of bedrock legal disputes, and about what that "face-value" actually is.[46]

§1.4. The Normativity of Law

A common objection to positivist metalegal theories is that they omit the allegedly essential *normativity* of (at least internal) legal talk and thought. To evaluate the force of this against our proposals we first need to investigate what is meant by "normative" here, as this term is used in different ways by different philosophers, including in the philosophy of law.[47] A distinction is often drawn between normativity in a purely *formal* sense and in a *robust* sense.[48] Something is formally normative if it provides a standard or norm against which conduct (for example) can be compared, and found either to conform or not to conform. Formal normativity is mundane, found everywhere from the rules of games to standards of etiquette to shopping lists. By contrast, something is robustly normative if it possesses some kind of *authority* over agents, which in metaethics is often glossed in terms of providing *reasons for action*, or *rational requirements*.

We agree that law must have formal normativity, which positivism easily accommodates. Formal normativity poses no challenge to a rule-relational theory, because rules are paradigmatically things with which one might or might not conform. But like other positivists, we simply

---

[45] See Plunkett and Sundell (2014). For similar points in metaethics or more generally, see Finlay (2008; 2014, 241–4, 256–8), Plunkett (2015), and Plunkett and Sundell (2013a).

[46] See also Leiter (2009).

[47] See Enoch (2011a) on different ways legal philosophy uses the word "normative", and the confusion it causes. See also Finlay (forthcoming).

[48] Our terminology follows McPherson (2011).

deny that law as such necessarily has robust normativity. This is compatible with allowing that law as such necessarily *purports* to have robust normativity—perhaps by claiming moral correctness (as Robert Alexy maintains) or practical authority (as Joseph Raz maintains).[49] Laying claim to normativity doesn't entail actually having it, but may give law a claim to being "normative" in an attenuated sense that distinguishes it from most things with mere formal normativity, like rules of games.[50] However, we do not ourselves endorse this idea.

Law may be argued to have more than merely formal normativity on the basis of the practical features of its use in guiding and evaluating behavior, such as its connection to motivation and the categorical nature of legal prescriptions. These practical features are, of course, precisely what we have attempted to explain by appeal to quasi-expressivism, which can be viewed as a rival, positivist-friendly explanation of some of the alleged evidence that law essentially has (or claims) robust normativity. This explanation aligns with the expressivist's in appealing to the motivating role, expression, and conflict of noncognitive attitudes (of acceptance). But because of this, quasi-expressivism may be accused of sharing expressivism's perceived failure to accommodate the *objective* character of the prescriptivity of internal legal statements; i.e. that they purport to communicate authoritative facts rather than mere subjective wishes, and that we accept rules for our behavior *because* we believe them to be the law, not vice versa.

We reply, first, that unlike expressivism proper, quasi-expressivism at least accommodates the appearance that legal statements aim to describe objective, attitude-independent facts about law, which guide our actions and influence our attitudes toward first-order rules. In our treatment, acceptance of first-order rules is not explanatorily basic, but derivative from the combination of (i) beliefs in rule-relational propositions and (ii) (more fundamental) noncognitive attitudes towards a rule of recognition.

Second, we deny that legal prescriptions have any further, more robust kind of objectivity. In metaethics, many philosophers remain

---

[49] See Alexy (2002), and Raz (1979/2002; 1994). Having practical authority over an agent in Raz's sense involves an ability to change what it is rational for that agent to do; for discussion, see Hershovitz (2011). Raz famously argues from this to (exclusive) legal positivism, whereas Alexy advances his version in arguing against positivism; see Gardner (2012a) for a positivist response.

[50] See Enoch (2011a) and Plunkett and Shapiro (2017).

skeptical of quasi-expressivist attempts to explain the intuitive objectivity of moral prescriptions, insisting that they have a metaphysically objective kind of authority; for example that a genuinely *moral* end must have "to-be-pursuedness somehow built into it",[51] or be commanded by the world itself rather than merely by other agents.[52] In the metalegal case, however, parallel claims have nothing like the same plausibility. Legal requirements as such do not seem to entail rational or moral requirements, so there is no pressure to construe legal prescriptions as demands the world itself makes on us.[53] There is nothing obviously odd in the idea of a morally bad or heinous law, or entire legal system, which an agent has no genuine, rationally demanding (versus merely "institutional") reason to obey. We can naturally say that it really was a law of the United States in the early nineteenth century that fugitive slaves were to be returned to their owners, but that agents in that jurisdiction didn't have any genuine reason (prudence aside) for obeying that law. Antipositivists may dissent.[54] But to prosecute this case they must reject ubiquitous intuitions about such cases, and adopt what many will find highly revisionary views about what is and isn't law.

§1.5. *Quasi-Expressivism versus Expressivism*

Quasi-expressivism is a strategy that enables descriptivists to say many of the same things about internal legal statements as the expressivist. So it may be wondered why we should opt for quasi-expressivism over expressivism, especially since the expressivist's story is much simpler.[55] In this section we argue that quasi-expressivism enjoys significant advantages over expressivism proper.

One advantage concerns legal disagreement. The rule-relational theory has a straightforward explanation of disagreements about law between one speaker making an internal legal statement, and another speaker making an external legal statement concerning the same legal system. Intuitively, outsiders can make claims about the law in some

---

[51] Mackie (1977, 40).

[52] See, for example, Enoch (2011b), Parfit (2011), Scanlon (2014), and the response to Finlay in Joyce (2011).

[53] See Enoch (2011a) for further argument.

[54] See, for example, Dworkin (2011), Greenberg (2014), and Hershovitz (2015), according to whom (roughly) legal requirements are a subset of moral requirements.

[55] A parallel metaethical challenge is raised in Thomson (1996, 198).

legal system that disagree with the legal claims of a speaker who lives under and accepts that same law as a guide to her conduct (e.g. when we describe laws of first-century Rome). According to the rule-relational semantics, these are descriptive claims about the same subject: whether a particular first-order rule satisfies the criteria of a particular rule of recognition. By contrast, since these statements apparently don't express the speaker's pro-attitudes, metalegal expressivists like Toh seem committed to a separate account of the semantics of external statements of law, and therefore are hard-pressed to explain how such disagreements are possible.[56]

A second advantage is that quasi-expressivism avoids all expressivism's problems arising from rejecting traditional propositional contents for legal statements. Consider particularly the knot of difficulties known as the *Frege–Geach Problem*. An adequate semantics needs to account for the meaning of a word or expression not only in the assertion of simple, atomic sentences ('S ought to do A'/'It is the law that L'), but also when those sentences are used in nonassertoric ways, such as embedded in interrogatives ('Ought S to do A?'/'Is it the law that L?'), in attitude reports ('J believes that S ought to do A'/'J believes it is the law that L'), and in negations, disjunctions, and conditionals. This is a challenge for expressivism, since a speaker who uses 'ought' or 'law' in these other ways is typically *not* expressing the attitude that expressivist semantics associate with the word.

This problem has drawn enormous attention in metaethics over recent decades, and it remains highly controversial whether it can be solved.[57] By contrast, our rule-relational metalegal theory, like relational theories in metaethics, faces no such challenge. Because it identifies the semantic content of a simple declarative sentence about the law as an ordinary descriptive proposition with an ordinary kind of truth value,

---

[56] To avoid *radical* semantic disunity, expressivists could offer "inverted commas" analyses (popular in metaethics) of external legal statements as an indirect way of describing others' (internal) legal statements. However, this strategy famously fails to account for internal/external disagreements. They might, perhaps, appeal to pragmatic disagreement, but (i) it is unclear what the mechanisms of this might be, and (ii) this would undermine the simplicity argument for expressivism over quasi-expressivism.

For a similar objection offered in support of a pragmatic treatment of the speaker-endorsement expressed by internal legal statements, see Enoch (2011a, 23–4). For related discussion, see Enoch and Toh (2013).

[57] For discussion, see Schroeder (2008) and Woods (2017).

there are no puzzles about how it can be used nonassertorically. The expressive and prescriptive character of assertoric uses is explained pragmatically, as following partly from the fact that in sincere assertions the speaker *believes* the asserted proposition; an explanation that doesn't extend to nonassertoric uses, which don't indicate such belief.

A quasi-expressivist account of internal statements of law thus has the advantage of explaining the prevalence of both descriptivist and expressivist intuitions among philosophers of law. We conclude that in combination with a rule-relational semantics, it provides an account that compares favorably with rival approaches. While our case on its behalf is far from the final word, we hope to have made its virtues clear, inviting further critical exploration by other philosophers. We hope also to have demonstrated, more generally, that positivists have powerful but underappreciated resources for developing and defending descriptivist accounts of legal statements.

§2. A QUASI-EXPRESSIVIST READING OF HART

We believe it is no coincidence that our rule-relational and quasi-expressivist account of legal statements is so easily articulated by appeal to Hart's work in *The Concept of Law*. Hart's views on legal statements are the object of considerable controversy in the philosophy of law, and have been interpreted in a wide variety of ways, ranging from a flat-footed descriptivism about the practices of legal officials, to a form of pure expressivism, as well as a semantic hybrid of these. But in our opinion, Hart's overall position in *The Concept of Law* is best reconstructed by attributing him a view of just the kind we have proposed above.[58] We conclude this paper by advancing a reading of Hart as offering (i) a descriptivist and positivist rule-relational semantics, and (ii) a quasi-expressivist account of internal legal statements. We argue that this reconstruction makes the best sense of core claims Hart makes about legal statements, given the text and the overall jurisprudential views of *The Concept of Law*.

What is uncontroversial is that Hart aimed to give a thoroughly *naturalistic* analysis of law, making no appeal to what he described as the

---

[58] Note that we don't claim that Hart accepted everything we argued for above (e.g. our account of bedrock legal disputes).

"obscure metaphysics" of non-natural properties and relations.[59] In the philosophy of law this impulse has often led toward positivism, as it did for Hart. However, Hart was also concerned to refute certain (unproblematically naturalistic) views that legal statements either *describe* or *predict* the behavior of judges and other legal officials.[60] A central emphasis of *The Concept of Law* was that legal statements (and law itself) function to *guide* behavior, and not simply describe or predict it. Such views are inadequate, Hart claimed, because they leave out the internal point of view, "the view of those who do not merely record and predict behaviour conforming to rules, but use the rules as standards for the appraisal of their own and others' behavior".[61] A primary goal of *The Concept of Law* was therefore to provide a third option, one that neither posited obscure non-natural properties nor omitted the action-guiding character of law.

Kevin Toh has argued that "an expressivist analysis...is the third alternative Hart has in mind".[62] Toh's proposal that we give an expressivist reading of Hart's account of internal legal statements has since been taken up by others, including Scott Shapiro.[63] A primary reason Toh gives for this reading is that expressivism is tailor-made to accommodate both the action-guiding role of a statement (as expressing motivational attitudes) while remaining consistent with a naturalistic metaphysics. A similar line of reasoning can be used to support reading Hart's legal semantics as a form of *hybrid* expressivism, according to which the semantics of (internal) legal statements are both expressive of the speaker's acceptance of a rule (or other motivational attitudes) and descriptive of social (or relational) facts.[64] A hybrid reading of Hart is suggested by some key passages from Joseph Raz.[65]

---

[59]   Hart (1961/2012, 84).

[60]   Hart (1961/2012) treats such views (put forward by Scandinavian and American Realists) as forms of rule-skepticism rather than positivism, but they could be developed in positivist-friendly ways. For criticism of Hart's treatment, see Leiter (2013).

[61]   Hart (1961/2012, 98).

[62]   Toh (2005, 85).

[63]   See Shapiro (2011, ch. 4). Shapiro and Toh differ on the details of their expressivist readings of Hart.

[64]   For recent discussion of hybrid expressivism in metaethics, see the articles in Fletcher and Ridge (2014).

[65]   See Raz (1993; 1999). Raz's treatment is schematic, and doesn't identify the mechanisms by which Hart thinks speakers' acceptance is expressed. While Raz is often interpreted as offering a hybrid expressivist reading (as in Toh (2005)), his text doesn't conclusively rule out a quasi-expressivist reading (which Toh (2005) in effect acknowledges). This would make Raz's

However, these same desiderata are also satisfied by a quasi-expressivist account, attributing the attitudinally expressive features of internal legal statements to the pragmatics of legal discourse rather than to its semantics. So it is worth considering whether the alternative Hart had in mind was *quasi*-expressivism rather than expressivism proper (pure or hybrid). We hold that a quasi-expressivist interpretation fits Hart's writings better in multiple ways, and is the more charitable reading. We first argue (§2.1) that Hart embraced a rule-relational, descriptivist semantics. Subsequently (§2.2), we argue that he offered a version of quasi-expressivism rather than hybrid expressivism.

§2.1. Hart as Rule-Relational Theorist

Hart's theory of law uncontroversially posits the existence of a realm of objective relational facts relevant to law. As discussed above, he understands a legal system as a particular kind of union of primary rules (i.e. first-order rules) and secondary rules (i.e. rules about rules). These secondary rules most importantly include the rule of recognition, which provides the criteria for identifying particular rules (both first-order and second-order) as part of a given legal system, or legally valid within the system. (In turn, Hart holds that facts about the existence and content of the rule of recognition are explained by social facts, such as facts about the convergence of behavior among legal officials. This is crucial for the development of his view as explicitly a form of *legal positivism*, and for the defense of his theory as purely naturalistic.[66]) He clearly thinks that it is a matter of objective, naturalistic fact whether or not a particular rule meets the criteria of legal validity laid out by the rule of recognition, or whether this is indeterminate. These are facts about the logical relations in which first-order rules stand to the rule of recognition. Therefore, he would presumably think that we sometimes talk about these facts, and that statements of the form 'It is the law that L' are an integral part of such talk. Passages in *The Concept of Law* strongly suggest

---

interpretation much closer to ours, although differences may remain over semantic content, attitudes expressed, and pragmatic mechanisms involved.

[66] There is a vast literature on what Hartians should identify as the relevant social practices underwriting the rule of recognition, and whether they are conventions (see e.g. Marmor (2009) and Postema (1982)). As our focus is on the language and not the metaphysics of law, we will not wade into these issues here.

such a view of legal semantics. For example, he writes of specifically internal statements of law,

> To say that a given rule is valid is to recognize it as passing all the tests provided by the rule of recognition... We can indeed simply say that the statement that a particular rule is valid means that it satisfies all the criteria provided by the rule of recognition.[67]

Here the text clearly supports a descriptivist, rule-relational reading, and is an uncomfortable fit with an expressivist interpretation.

Further evidence is provided by the pains Hart takes to insist it is a mistake to talk about the "validity" of the rule of recognition. He writes,

> We only need the word 'validity', and commonly only use it, to answer questions which arise within a system of rules where the status of a rule as a member of the system depends on its satisfying certain criteria provided by the rule of recognition. No such question can arise as to the validity of the very rule of recognition which provides the criteria; it can neither be valid nor invalid but is simply accepted as appropriate for use in this way.[68]

This is in tension with Toh's interpretation that claims of legal validity are mere expressions of acceptance, because Hart is clear (as in this passage) that rules of recognition are indeed objects of acceptance. If Toh's reading is correct, this is the wrong thing for Hart to say. By contrast, a rule-relational interpretation vindicates Hart's insistence as appropriate. If to be "valid" is to meet the criteria of a rule of recognition for being a first-order rule of the system, then rules of recognition are not themselves legally valid.[69]

One potential obstacle to reading Hart as a descriptivist, cited by Toh, is his claim—in work published eight years before *The Concept of Law*—that "the primary function of these [legal] words is not to stand for or describe but a distinct function", roughly, the function of guiding behavior.[70] However, the evidential weight of this passage in favor of an

---

[67] Hart (1961/2012, 103).

[68] Hart (1961/2012, 109).

[69] For further discussion, see Green (1996).

[70] Hart (1953, 31). Technically this claim is compatible both with Hart's accepting that legal statements have a (non-primary) descriptive function, and with his not assuming that this distinction between primary/secondary function aligns with the distinction between semantics/pragmatics. However, Hart's retraction (discussed below) indicates he wasn't hedging in either way.

expressivist reconstruction of Hart's views in *The Concept of Law* is seriously undercut by the fact that Hart later disowned it. We quote at length:

Had I commanded...in 1953 the seminal distinction between the 'meaning' and the 'force' of utterances, and the theory of 'speech acts'...I should not have claimed that statements of legal rights and duties were not 'descriptive'...[71]

...in [1953] I fail to allow for the important distinction between the relatively constant meaning or sense of a sentence fixed by the conventions of language and the varying 'force' or way in which it is put forward by the writer or speaker on different occasions...Neglect of this distinction...vitiates parts of my account in [1953] of the meaning of statements of legal rights...It was just wrong to say that such statements *are* the conclusions of inferences from legal rules, for such sentences have the same meaning on different occasions of use whether or not the speaker or writer puts them forward as inferences which he has drawn. If he does put such a statement forward as an inference, that is the force of the utterance on that occasion, not part of the meaning of the sentence. What compounds my error is that though I speak of such sentences as capable of being true or false I deny that they are 'descriptive' as if this were excluded by the status which I wrongly assign to them as conclusions of law, and my denial that such sentences are 'descriptive' obscured the truth that for a full understanding of them we must understand what it is for a rule of conduct to require, prohibit, or permit an act.[72]

As Toh holds that Hart remained committed to expressivism about legal statements throughout his career, he confesses that he finds these disavowals "particularly baffling".[73] A virtue of our proposed reconstruction is that what Hart says here is exactly what it predicts he should. Granting that Hart's metalegal views in 1953 may well have been expressivist, this evidence suggests that at least by 1967 he had come to accept descriptivism about legal language.[74] This leaves open whether a descriptivist semantics should be assigned also to *The Concept of Law*, published in 1961; we'll return to this issue below.

---

[71] Hart (1983, 2).
[72] Hart (1983, 4–5).
[73] Toh (2005, 99n).
[74] In Hart (1983), Hart references his (1967/83) as correcting the earlier error of rejecting descriptivism. Although Hart is here explicitly addressing statements about *legal duties*, rather than statements of *law* (as we define them), he can reasonably be expected to hold parallel views of the latter.

Further evidence for a descriptivist reconstruction of Hart's mature views is his treatment (or lack thereof) of the Frege–Geach Problem, sketched above in §1.4, concerning the meaning of sentences in embedded or nonassertoric uses. This is arguably the central problem facing expressivism—whether about moral, legal, or any other kind of apparently descriptive discourse—and despite decades of sustained attention in metaethics the jury is still out on whether it can be solved. Toh thus rightly presents this as a serious issue for the metalegal expressivist theory he attributes to Hart. One would therefore expect that *if* Hart were indeed advancing a nondescriptivist legal semantics, then he would have been highly motivated to address how this problem might be solved, at least in broad outline. Yet Hart is silent on the topic, even in his later writings discussing and defending his views on legal discourse.[75] By contrast, this silence presents no problems for our proposed reconstruction. For if the practical features of legal statements are accommodated within the framework of a *descriptivist* semantics, the Frege–Geach Problem doesn't arise.[76]

For all we've said, it might still be thought that Hart's views specifically in *The Concept of Law* are best reconstructed as expressivist, or perhaps indeterminate between expressivism and descriptivism. For example, it may seem plausible that when *The Concept of Law* was published Hart was simply not aware of the Frege–Geach Problem—which was first raised in P.T. Geach's paper "Ascriptivism", published in 1960, just a year prior. However, on closer examination this conjecture seems exceedingly unlikely. Not only was Geach a colleague of Hart's at Oxford, but Hart's own earlier expressivist views (in the philosophy of action rather than jurisprudence) provided one of the principal and explicit targets of Geach's seminal paper.[77] Indeed, 'ascriptivism' has, following Geach, become the

---

[75] Toh points to some potentially relevant passages (e.g. on a logic of imperatives) in Hart (1982/2011); see section X of Toh (2005). However, Hart could have perceived a need for such a logic even if he were (as on our interpretation) merely a *quasi*-expressivist about the imperatival force of internal legal statements.

[76] For problems facing *hybrid* expressivist attempts to avoid the Frege–Geach Problem, see Schroeder (2008).

[77] See Geach (1960), in relation to Hart (1951). While Geach does not mention Hart by name, it is uncontroversial in the literature that Hart is his target (see, for example, the entry on ascriptivism in *The Blackwell Dictionary of Western Philosophy* (Bunnin and Yu 2009)). Hart's 1983 disavowals of legal nondescriptivism, quoted above, are in effect an acknowledgment of Geach's basic point. In the Preface to Hart (1968), he cites Geach's 1960 objections in explaining why he chose not to reprint Hart (1951) in that collection. Toh acknowledges that

standard label for Hart's own expressivist theory of action-statements. So we can rather presume that Geach's point would have been particularly salient to Hart at the time that he published *The Concept of Law*.

One final consideration in favor of a descriptivist over an expressivist reconstruction of Hart is the status of Hart's legal positivism as a *metalegal* theory (explaining how the law, and our thought and talk about it, fits into reality). Consider first the metaethical case. Metaethical expressivists rightly emphasize their neutrality with respect to questions about what explains why certain moral "truths" obtain, or what grounds moral "facts" (on appropriately minimalist readings of "truth" and "fact"). They don't take a stand, for example, on whether what we morally ought to do is ultimately explained by our contingent attitudes, any more than on whether consequentialism is true. This is because expressivism is a theory about what we are doing when engaged in moral thought and talk that doesn't itself require taking any stand on object-level moral issues. For expressivists, these are substantive or first-order moral questions that are not the province of metaethical theory.

Correspondingly, metalegal expressivism implies that claims about what grounds facts of law are substantive, first-order legal claims, and therefore express the speaker's attitudes of acceptance rather than describe objective facts about the nature of law. So metalegal expressivism is hard to square with the idea that legal positivism is a descriptive claim about the nature of law, to be proven or refuted through metalegal theorizing.[78] The issue is that many of Hart's methodological remarks strongly suggest that he accepted that the truth of legal positivism is established as *part of* what we are here calling his "metalegal" theory.[79]

Hart's remarks in the Preface to Hart (1968) are a problem for his expressivist reading; see Toh (2005, 102). (Thanks to Luis Duarte d'Almeida for helpful discussion of the relationship between Hart and Geach.)

[78] See Plunkett and Shapiro (2017). Toh apparently agrees, arguing in Toh (2008) that his preferred form of legal positivism (as a thesis one can advance by making an internal legal statement, not just external ones) is *compatible* with but not established by expressivism about internal legal statements. See also Toh (2013).

[79] See, for example, the methodological remarks in the postscript to *The Concept of Law*. Hart writes that his account, which we take to *include* a commitment to legal positivism, "is descriptive in that it is morally neutral and has no justificatory aims: it does not seek to justify or commend on moral or other grounds the forms and structures which appear in my general account of law, though a clear understanding of these is, I think, an important preliminary to any useful moral criticism of law" (Hart 1961/2012, 240). It should be noted, however, that Hart's varied methodological remarks in *The Concept of Law* point in different directions on

The same is true of the views put forward by many contemporary positivists.[80]

By contrast, descriptivist analyses fit more smoothly with taking on substantial commitments about the nature and grounds of law as part of one's metalegal theory. Such commitments can be both a part and a consequence of developing a descriptive semantic theory, and may easily include a form of legal positivism. A commitment to positivism follows, for example, from the Austinian view that legal statements refer to facts grounded in the commands of a sovereign. It also follows from the rule-relational view that legal statements describe relations to a rule of recognition whose existence and content is fully grounded in social facts. So on our rule-relational reading of Hart's views, his legal positivism can clearly be an element of his metalegal theory rather than a separate, first-order legal view about the content of law. For this and the other reasons we've observed, we think Hart is best interpreted as a descriptivist about legal statements.

§2.2. Hart as Quasi-Expressivist

Hart is perfectly clear that he thinks that (internal) legal statements express the speaker's attitude of acceptance. But is he best interpreted as attributing this expressive function to their semantics (as on a hybrid expressivism, or a subjectivism on which legal statements are descriptions of such attitudes) or to their pragmatics (as on quasi-expressivism)?

The language of his 1983 disavowal of nondescriptivism points strongly in the direction of pragmatics. He contrasts the "meaning...of a sentence fixed by the conventions of language" with the "'force' or way in which it is put forward by the writer or speaker on different occasions". A pragmatic reading is also supported by his failure to observe a contrast between "expressing" and "implying" in a passage in his *Essays on Bentham*. Hart first observes, against subjectivism, that it is vital to distinguish between reporting and expressing a noncognitive attitude, because many statements need to be understood as expressing the speaker's

---

this point. In particular, see his remarks in chapter 9, which support a reading on which his commitment to legal positivism flows partly from substantive moral and political commitments. This arguably suggests a different reading of the status of his legal positivism. See also his earlier Hart (1958), in exchange with Fuller (1958).

[80] For example Gardner (2012b), Leiter (2007), Marmor (2006), and Shapiro (2011).

attitude without reporting that she has it.[81] While this contrast between "expressing" and "reporting" an attitude is traditionally emphasized by expressivists, Hart also makes clear that the expression of the attitude needn't be a part of the literal meaning of a statement. He writes,

> Bentham was not alone in failing to grasp the distinction between what is said or meant by the use of a sentence, whether imperative or indicative, and the state or attitude of mind or will which the utterance of a sentence may express and which accordingly may be implied though not stated by the use of the sentence. When I say 'Shut the door' I imply though I do not state that I wish it to be shut, just as when I say 'The cat is on the mat' I imply though I do not state that I believe this to be the case.[82]

Here Hart appears to suggest that the attitudes are expressed via *implication*, which is a pragmatic mechanism. If he rather intended an expressivist (i.e. semantic) claim, then he would be running together 'express' and 'imply' in a way that is at worst confused, and at best idiosyncratic. Since the context is a discussion of (Bentham's view of) internal legal statements, this passage also fits best with a quasi-expressivist account of those kinds of statements in particular.[83]

Even so, this leaves open the questions of whether these passages represent Hart's view in *The Concept of Law*, and whether his view of the pragmatic mechanisms involved resembles our quasi-expressivist account. We think there is compelling evidence for positive answers in each case. Consider Hart's remarks on the relationship between internal and external statements of law. He identifies as a distinguishing characteristic of internal statements that they are standardly expressed by sentences of the form 'The law is that...', contrasting with the typical expression of external statements by sentences like 'In the UK they accept as law that...'.[84] This is to highlight a key element of our quasi-expressivist

---

[81] Hart (1982/2011, 249–50).

[82] Hart (1982/2011, 248–9).

[83] Thanks to Kevin Toh for bringing these passages from Hart (1982/2011) to our attention, and for helpful discussion.

[84] A puzzle for our reconstruction is that Hart at one point characterizes external legal statements as describing what people accept as law, rather than relations of legal validity (Hart 1961/2012, 103). We speculate he may be thinking that speakers taking an external point of view with regard to a legal system typically aren't interested in judging validity-within-the-system. In any case, he proceeds to qualify this as merely "normal", acknowledging external statements of legal validity.

story: that internal statements standardly do not specify which legal system or rule of recognition they are made relative to. He writes,

> The use of unstated rules of recognition... in identifying particular rules of the system is characteristic of the internal point of view. Those who use them in this way thereby manifest their own acceptance of them....[85]

Observe that Hart says it is by the "use" of "unstated" rules of recognition that we "thereby manifest" our acceptance. In other words, we express our attitudes by using a rule to which we omit reference. It does not seem a leap to interpret Hart as here articulating the quasi-expressivist claim that it is often through presupposition of a rule of recognition (speaking *as if* exactly one such rule were salient) that a speaker expresses her acceptance of it.[86]

In our opinion, all this evidence adds up to a strong circumstantial case for reconstructing Hart's view as combining a rule-relational theory of the semantics of legal statements with a quasi-expressivist view of the special subset of those statements that are internal. However, while we believe our reconstruction offers the best and most charitable way of reading Hart, we hesitate to claim this is the precise view animating every line of *The Concept of Law* and subsequent texts. Hart's relevant texts are often ambiguous, and different passages lend credence to rival readings.[87] Given that Hart was not primarily concerned about issues in the philosophy of language, and that the distinctions we now possess are more nuanced than those at Hart's disposal when he produced his core work in legal philosophy, it wouldn't be surprising to find indeterminacy between a range of different but closely related theories, such as pure, hybrid, and quasi-expressivism. However, without having the quasi-expressivist option squarely in view, it is also easy to mistake a text advancing such a view as vacillating inconsistently between descriptivism

---

[85] Hart (1961/2012, 102).

[86] A further alignment between Hart's text and our view is his (sometimes faulted) vagueness about whether the object of expressed acceptance (in internal legal statements) is the rule of recognition, the first-order rule, or the behavior it describes. Recall that our quasi-expressivist story predicts expression of acceptance toward multiple objects.

[87] In his *Essays on Bentham*, for example, Hart writes (criticizing Raz's alternative approach): "I find little reason to accept such a cognitive interpretation of legal duty in terms of objective reasons or in the meaning of 'obligation' in legal and moral contexts which this would secure. Far better adapted to the legal case is a different, non-cognitive theory of duty" (Hart 1982/2011, 159–60). See also Hart (1982/2011, 144–5). As Toh observes, this provides support for a pure expressivist reading, though we think it also can be reconciled with quasi-expressivism.

and expressivism. Hart's views about legal statements may therefore turn out to be more determinate (also: consistent and defensible) than interpreters have often assumed. These exegetical questions are ripe for further investigation.

CONCLUSION

This paper has advanced a rule-relational, descriptivist view of legal statements of a kind compatible with positivism. Views of this kind face a variety of challenges, concerning (inter alia) motivational and practical elements of internal legal statements, and the possibility and extent of legal disagreement. We demonstrated how some of these challenges can be met by appeal to a form of quasi-expressivism, and more generally, the rich pragmatics of legal statements. We formulated our proposal in an explicitly Hartian framework, and went on to argue that the best critical reconstruction of Hart's own position in *The Concept of Law* is a similarly rule-relational and quasi-expressivist theory. Since the philosophical promise and explanatory power of much of this package of relational semantics and quasi-expressivist pragmatics is independent of this particular Hartian articulation, however, we believe these linguistic resources can be put to gainful employment by Hartians and non-Hartians alike.[88]

REFERENCES

Alexy, Robert (2002). *The Argument from Injustice: A Reply to Legal Positivism*, trans. B.L. Paulson and S.L. Paulson (Oxford: Oxford University Press).
Barker, Stephen J. (2000). "Is Value Content a Component of Conventional Implicature?" *Analysis* 60(267): 268–79.
Björnsson, Gunnar and Stephen Finlay (2010). "Metaethical Contextualism Defended", *Ethics* 121(1): 7–36.

[88] Thanks to Luis Duarte d'Almeida, Scott Altman, Max Etchemendy, John Gardner, Jeff Goldsworthy, Scott Hershovitz, Robin Kar, Brian Leiter, Andrei Marmor, Eliot Michaelson, Tristram McPherson, Alex Sarch, Scott Shapiro, Tim Sundell, Kevin Toh, and Daniel Wodak for helpful feedback and discussion. An earlier version of this paper was presented at the Legal Philosophy Workshop at the University of Pennsylvania in May 2014. Thanks to everyone who provided feedback during that workshop. Our idea for this paper emerged from discussion at a workshop on metaethics and law at the University of Illinois College of Law in March 2011. Thanks to Robin Kar for organizing and inviting us to that workshop, and to the other participants for thought-provoking discussion.

Blackburn, Simon (1993). *Essays in Quasi-Realism* (Oxford: Oxford University Press).

Bunnin, Nicholas and Jiyuan Yu (2009). "Ascriptivism", in *The Blackwell Dictionary of Western Philosophy* (Malden, MA: Blackwell).

Coleman, Jules L. (1982). "Negative and Positive Positivism", *Journal of Legal Studies* 11(139): 139–64.

Copp, David (2001). "Realist-Expressivism: A Neglected Option for Moral Realism", *Social Philosophy and Policy* 18(2): 1–43.

Copp, David (2007). *Morality in a Natural World: Selected Essays in Metaethics* (Cambridge: Cambridge University Press).

Dowell, Janice (2016). "Review of Stephen Finlay's *Confusion of Tongues*", *Mind* 125(498): 585–93.

Dworkin, Ronald (1986). *Law's Empire* (Cambridge, MA: Harvard University Press).

Dworkin, Ronald (2006). *Justice in Robes* (Cambridge, MA: Harvard University Press).

Dworkin, Ronald (2011). *Justice for Hedgehogs* (Cambridge, MA: Harvard University Press).

Enoch, David (2011a). "Reason-Giving and the Law", in L. Green and B. Leiter (eds.), *Oxford Studies in Philosophy of Law*, vol. 1 (Oxford: Oxford University Press), 1–38.

Enoch, David (2011b). *Taking Morality Seriously: A Defense of Robust Realism* (Oxford: Oxford University Press).

Enoch, David and Kevin Toh (2013). "Legal as a Thick Concept", in W.J. Waluchow and S. Sciaraffa (eds.), *Philosophical Foundations of the Nature of Law* (Oxford: Oxford University Press).

Etchemendy, Matthew (2016). "New Directions in Legal Expressivism", *Legal Theory* 22(1): 1–21.

Finlay, Stephen (2004). "The Conversational Practicality of Value Judgement", *Journal of Ethics* 8(3): 205–23.

Finlay, Stephen (2008). "The Error in the Error Theory", *Australasian Journal of Philosophy* 86(3): 347–69.

Finlay, Stephen (2014). *Confusion of Tongues: A Theory of Normative Language* (Oxford: Oxford University Press).

Finlay, Stephen (2016). "Disagreement: Lost and Found", in R. Shafer-Landau (ed.), *Oxford Studies in Metaethics*, vol. 12 (Oxford: Oxford University Press).

Finlay, Stephen (forthcoming). "Defining Normativity", in D. Plunkett, S. Shapiro, and K. Toh (eds.), *Dimensions of Normativity: New Essays on Metaethics and Jurisprudence* (Oxford: Oxford University Press).

Fletcher, Guy and Michael Ridge (2014). *Having It Both Ways: Hybrid Theories and Modern Metaethics* (Oxford: Oxford University Press).

Foot, Philippa (1972). "Morality as a System of Hypothetical Imperatives", *Philosophical Review* 81(3): 305–16.

Fuller, Lon (1958). "Positivism and Fidelity to Law—A Reply to Professor Hart", *Harvard Law Review* 71(4): 630–72.

Gardner, John (2012a). "How Law Claims, What Law Claims", in M. Klatt (ed.), *Institutionalized Reason: The Jurisprudence of Robert Alexy* (Oxford: Oxford University Press).

Gardner, John (2012b). *Law as a Leap of Faith* (Oxford: Oxford University Press).

Gardner, John (2012c). "Law in General", in J. Gardner, *Law as a Leap of Faith* (Oxford: Oxford University Press), 270–302.

Geach, P.T. (1960). "Ascriptivism", *Philosophical Review* 69(2): 221–5.

Green, Leslie (1990). *The Authority of the State* (Oxford: Oxford University Press).

Green, Leslie (1996). "The Concept of Law Revisited", *Michigan Law Review* 94(6): 1687–717.

Greenberg, Mark (2006). "How Facts Make Law", in S. Hershovitz (ed.), *Exploring Law's Empire: The Jurisprudence of Ronald Dworkin* (New York: Oxford University Press).

Greenberg, Mark (2014). "The Moral Impact Theory of Law", *The Yale Law Journal* 123: 1288–342.

Harman, Gilbert (1975). "Moral Relativism Defended", *Philosophical Review* 84(1): 3–22.

Harman, Gilbert (1996). "Moral Relativism", in G. Harman and J.J. Thomson, *Moral Relativism and Moral Objectivity* (Malden, MA: Blackwell), 1–64.

Hart, H.L.A. (1951). "The Ascription of Responsibility and Rights", in G. Ryle and A. Flew (eds.), *Logic and Language (First Series): Essays* (Oxford: Basil Blackwell).

Hart, H.L.A. (1953). "Definition and Theory in Jurisprudence", *Law Quarterly Review* 70.

Hart, H.L.A. (1958). "Positivism and the Separation of Law and Morals", *Harvard Law Review* 71(4): 593–629.

Hart, H.L.A. (1967/83). "Problems of the Philosophy of Law", in H.L.A. Hart, *Essays in Jurisprudence and Philosophy* (Oxford: Oxford University Press).

Hart, H.L.A. (1968). *Punishment and Responsibility* (Oxford: Oxford University Press).

Hart, H.L.A. (1983). *Essays in Jurisprudence and Philosophy* (Oxford: Oxford University Press).

Hart, H.L.A. (1982/2011). *Essays on Bentham: Jurisprudence and Political Theory* (Oxford: Oxford University Press).

Hart, H.L.A. (1961/2012). *The Concept of Law*, 3rd edn. (Oxford: Oxford University Press).

Hershovitz, Scott (2011). "The Role of Authority", *Philosophers' Imprint* 11(7): 1–19.

Hershovitz, Scott (2015). "The End of Jurisprudence", *The Yale Law Journal* 124(4): 1160–204.

Holton, Richard (1998). "Positivism and the Internal Point of View", *Law and Philosophy* 17(5–6): 597–625.

Joyce, Richard (2011). "The Error In 'The Error In The Error Theory'", *Australasian Journal of Philosophy* 89(3): 519–34.

Kelsen, Hans (1945). *General Theory of Law and State*, trans. A. Wedberg (New York: Russell and Russell).

Khoo, Justin and Joshua Knobe (2018). "Moral Disagreement and Moral Semantics", *Noûs* 52(1): 109–43.

Leiter, Brian (2007). *Naturalizing Jurisprudence: Essays on American Legal Realism and Naturalism in Legal Philosophy* (Oxford: Oxford University Press).

Leiter, Brian (2009). "Explaining Theoretical Disagreement", *The University of Chicago Law Review* 76(3): 1215–50.

Leiter, Brian (2013). "Legal Realisms, Old and New", *Valparaiso Law Review* 47(4): 949–63.

Mackie, J.L. (1977). *Ethics: Inventing Right and Wrong* (New York: Penguin).

McPherson, Tristram (2011). "Against Quietist Normative Realism", *Philosophical Studies* 154(2): 223–40.

Marmor, Andrei (2006). "Legal Positivism: Still Descriptive and Morally Neutral", *Oxford Journal of Legal Studies* 26(4): 683–704.

Marmor, Andrei (2009). *Social Conventions: From Language to Law* (Princeton, NJ: Princeton University Press).

Marmor, Andrei (2011). *Philosophy of Law* (Princeton, NJ: Princeton University Press).

Moore, G.E. (1922/70). "The Nature of Moral Philosophy", in G.E. Moore, *Philosophical Studies* (London: Routledge & Kegan Paul).

Olson, Jonas (2011). "In Defense of Moral Error Theory", in M. Brady (ed.), *New Waves in Metaethics* (Basingstoke: Palgrave Macmillan), 62–84.

Parfit, Derek (2011). *On What Matters*, vol. 2 (Oxford: Oxford University Press).

Phillips, David (1998). "The Middle Ground in Moral Semantics", *American Philosophical Quarterly* 35(2): 141–55.

Plunkett, David (2013). "Legal Positivism and the Moral Aim Thesis", *Oxford Journal of Legal Studies* 33(3): 563–605.

Plunkett, David (2015). "Which Concepts Should We Use?: Metalinguistic Negotiations and The Methodology of Philosophy", *Inquiry* 58(7–8): 828–74.

Plunkett, David and Scott Shapiro (2017). "Law, Morality, and Everything Else: General Jurisprudence as a Branch of Metanormative Inquiry", *Ethics* 128(1): 37–68.

Plunkett, David and Timothy Sundell (2013a). "Disagreement and the Semantics of Normative and Evaluative Terms", *Philosophers' Imprint* 13(23): 1–37.

Plunkett, David and Timothy Sundell (2013b). "Dworkin's Interpretivism and the Pragmatics of Legal Disputes", *Legal Theory* 19(3): 242–81.

Plunkett, David and Timothy Sundell (2014). "Antipositivist Arguments from Legal Thought and Talk: The Metalinguistic Response", in G. Hubb and D. Lind (eds.), *Pragmatism, Law, and Language* (New York: Routledge), 56–75.

Postema, Gerald J. (1982). "Coordination and Convention at the Foundations of Law", *Journal of Legal Studies* 11(1): 165–203.

Railton, Peter (1986). "Facts and Values", *Philosophical Topics* 14: 5–31.

Railton, Peter (2008). "Naturalism Relativized?", in W. Sinnott-Armstrong (ed.), *Moral Psychology*, vol. 1 (Cambridge, MA: MIT Press), 37–44.

Raz, Joseph (1975/2002). *Practical Reason and Norms* (Oxford: Oxford University Press).

Raz, Joseph (1979/2002). *The Authority of Law: Essays on Law and Morality* (Oxford: Oxford University Press).

Raz, Joseph (1980). *The Concept of a Legal System: An Introduction to the Theory of Legal System*, 2nd edn. (Oxford: Oxford University Press).

Raz, Joseph (1993). "H.L.A. Hart (1907–1992)", *Utilitas* 5(2): 145–56.

Raz, Joseph (1994). *Ethics in the Public Domain: Essays in the Morality of Law and Politics* (New York: Oxford University Press).

Raz, Joseph (1999). "The Purity of the Pure Theory", in S.L. Paulson (ed.), *Normativity and Norms: Critical Perspectives on Kelsenian Themes* (Oxford: Oxford University Press).

Ridge, Michael (2014). *Impassioned Belief* (Oxford: Oxford University Press).

Robinson, Denis (2009). "Moral Functionalism, Ethical Quasi-Relativism, and the Canberra Plan", in D. Braddon-Mitchell and R. Nola (eds.), *Conceptual Analysis and Philosophical Naturalism* (Cambridge, MA: MIT Press/ Bradford), 315–48.

Rosen, Gideon (2010). "Metaphysical Dependence: Grounding and Reduction", in B. Hale and A. Hoffmann (eds.), *Modality: Metaphysics, Logic, and Epistemology* (Oxford: Oxford University Press).

Scanlon, T.M. (2014). *Being Realistic About Reasons* (Oxford: Oxford University Press).

Schroeder, Mark (2008). "What Is the Frege–Geach Problem?" *Philosophy Compass* 3(4): 703–20.

Shapiro, Scott (2011). *Legality* (Cambridge, MA: Harvard University Press).

Silk, Alex (forthcoming). "Normativity in Language and Law", in D. Plunkett, S. Shapiro, and K. Toh (eds.), *Dimensions of Normativity: New Essays on Metaethics and Jurisprudence* (Oxford: Oxford University Press).

Stalnaker, Robert (1974). "Pragmatic Presupposition", in M. Munitz and P. Unger (eds.), *Semantics and Philosophy* (New York: NYU Press).

Stevenson, Charles L. (1937). "The Emotive Meaning of Ethical Terms", *Mind* 46(181): 14–31.

Strandberg, Caj (2012). "A Dual Aspect Account of Moral Language", *Philosophy and Phenomenological Research* 84(1): 87–122.

Thomson, Judith Jarvis (1996). "Moral Objectivity", in G. Harman and J.J. Thomson, *Moral Relativism and Moral Objectivity* (Malden, MA: Blackwell), 65–154.

Toh, Kevin (2005). "Hart's Expressivism and His Benthamite Project", *Legal Theory* 11(2): 75–123.

Toh, Kevin (2008). "An Argument Against the Social Fact Thesis (and Some Additional Preliminary Steps Towards a New Conception of Legal Positivism)", *Law and Philosophy* 27(5): 445–504.

Toh, Kevin (2011). "Legal Judgments as Plural Acceptances of Norms", in L. Green and B. Leiter (eds.), *Oxford Studies in Philosophy of Law*, vol. 1 (Oxford: Oxford University Press), 107–37.

Toh, Kevin (2013). "Jurisprudential Theories and First-Order Legal Judgments", *Philosophy Compass* 8(5): 457–71.

Waluchow, Wilfrid (1994). *Inclusive Legal Positivism* (Oxford: Oxford University Press).

Wong, David B. (1984). *Moral Relativity* (Berkeley CA: University of California Press).

Woods, Jack (2017). "The Frege–Geach Problem", in T. McPherson and D. Plunkett (eds.), *The Routledge Handbook of Metaethics* (New York: Routledge), 226–42.

3

The Normative Force of Law: Individuals and States

LIAM MURPHY

The normative force of law that matters is its moral force. The central issue of this essay is accordingly what moral reason legal subjects have to comply with law. But first it is useful to identify and set aside other issues that might be associated with the "normativity" of law.[1]

I. LAW AND MOTIVATING REASONS

In his argument against the traditional English command theory of law, H.L.A. Hart focused on two distinct issues.[2] The command theory was, he thought, fairly obviously inadequate for being unable to explain constitutional continuity or nonimperative legal rules. But more important and interesting for Hart was the observation that the equation of legal norms with threats made by those in power distorted the deliberative role law actually plays in the typical person's practical life. His claim here is descriptive. It is that for many or most people, legal norms do not simply set prices on possible actions, where the price varies from context to context. We do not typically deliberate about the costs and benefits of following the law "for this case only," but accept the reason-giving force of law in general. This is what Hart called the "internal aspect" of legal rules.

This descriptive observation is completely compatible with there being no objective or real (justifying) reason why anybody ought to accept legal norms, and compatible with a large variety of (motivating) reasons why

---

[1] For a full investigation of the ambiguities associated with ideas of the "normativity" or "reason-giving force" of law, see David Enoch, "Reason-Giving and the Law," in Leslie Green and Brian Leiter (eds.), *Oxford Studies in Legal Philosophy: Volume 1* (OUP 2011), 1–37.

[2] H.L.A. Hart, *The Concept of Law* (3rd edn, OUP 2012), chs. II–IV.

Oxford Studies in Philosophy of Law Volume 3. John Gardner, Leslie Green, and Brian Leiter (eds)
This chapter © Liam Murphy 2018. First published in 2018 by Oxford University Press

people in fact do accept them. Thus I might accept legal norms out of a sense of self-interest, moral obligation, or a mere preference to conform.[3] This is the sense in which law, for Hart, can well be compared to a game. The rules of the game are what they are, and once you decide you want to play the game, there are right and wrong moves you can make; most players will be motivated to make right moves and not make wrong moves. But there is nothing in this account of the way in which legal rules figure in some people's deliberations that provides any reason, moral or otherwise, why anyone should play this game.

Hans Kelsen's position here is superficially different from Hart's since for Kelsen a valid legal norm is one that really does provide an "ought" and so the foundation of a legal system is, accordingly, an ought—the basic norm. In fact, however, barring quibbles over whether "validity" implies ought, and without attempting an accurate characterization of the development of Kelsen's thought over more than half a century, we can say that the two positions are identical. For Kelsen as for Hart social facts determine the content of the law. This is what makes them both legal positivists. But for Kelsen a special norm is required to animate those inert facts with obligation. That special norm has no substantive content of its own. It merely says that the norms enacted in accordance with the effective constitution ought to be obeyed. Anyone writing as a "legal scientist" can discuss the criteria of legal validity without actually accepting or "presupposing" the basic norm. The point of view of the scientist is one from which one can describe the normative system that is law as if the basic norm that would ground validity (obligation) were presupposed. We can make full sense of law as a normative system, a system of rules and principles, and we can note that for many people that system is a source of motivating reasons, without having to take a stand on the further question of whether there is in fact any categorical reason why anyone should pay attention to the law at all.[4]

2. LEGAL OBLIGATION

But doesn't even the legal positivist assume that where there is law, obligation must be present? Hart did write that any legal theory must explain

---

[3] Ibid., 203.

[4] See Hans Kelsen, *The Pure Theory of Law* (University of California Press 1967), 201–5, 217–19; for discussion, see Joseph Raz, *The Authority of Law* (OUP 1979), 134–43.

the sense in which law makes conduct "in *some* sense obligatory."[5] But by this he clearly did not mean that legal theory must explain the moral force legal norms actually have.[6] The closest he came to saying anything of the kind was when he repeatedly insisted on the opposite. That legal validity did not settle the issue of moral obligation was for Hart among the fundamental motivations of the entire positivist outlook.

Some contemporary legal philosophers do write as if positivist theory must explain how law as such can provide us with real reasons for action.[7] This is puzzling, since if the content of law is grounded in social fact it seems obvious that it will not always generate genuine reasons to comply. We could not have a general reason to comply with legally valid rules, just because that is what they are, no matter what their content and what the mode of their creation. More important, it is hard to see how the thought that there is always genuine reason to comply with law could ever arise if we start from the fundamental belief that law's content is grounded in social fact. The motivation for this combined view is mysterious.

What Hart had in mind when he wrote that legal theory must explain the sense in which law is a source of obligation was quite different. He believed that there was a distinct beast, a legal obligation, and that legal theory should be able to explain its existence. According to Nicola Lacey, Hart puzzled about the conditions for the existence of legal obligation until the end of his life.[8] This seems to me unfortunate, since nothing of importance seems to be at stake with disagreement about what legal obligation is.

In his 1966 essay, "Legal Duty and Obligation,"[9] Hart insists that the concept of legal obligation is distinct from that of moral obligation; he thus rejects the position of many that moral obligations are the only real obligations around. Hart's position seems on the face of it plausible;

---

[5] Hart, *The Concept of Law*, 6.

[6] Scott Shapiro, *Legality* (HUP 2011), 97, writes that Hart, "in all of his many writings, never explicitly explains how his positivistic theory is compatible with Hume's Law" (that you can't get an ought from an is). But Hart never suggested that you could get a genuine objective reason for action from the mere fact of legal validity.

[7] See e.g. Jules Coleman, *The Practice of Principle* (OUP 2001), 74–102.

[8] Nicola Lacey, *A Life of H.L.A. Hart: The Nightmare and the Noble Dream* (OUP 2006), 354.

[9] H.L.A Hart, "Legal Duty and Obligation," in Hart, *Essays on Bentham* (OUP 1982), 127–61.

but what then is a legal obligation? There's one simple answer Hart could have given: a legal obligation is just what we have when we are subject to a valid duty-imposing legal rule. This would be to treat the idea of legal obligation as entirely internal to the system. It prompts the objection that on this account legal obligations, just as such, are no more real than the obligations imposed by duties of etiquette or by the rules of a game we are playing. My own view is that a Hartian positivist should be happy to accept this result, but Hart apparently never did find it appealing.

I believe that the reason is that he was always attracted to a reductive, nonrealist account of moral obligation. If this kind of explanation is appropriate for the moral case, it is natural to provide it for the legal case as well. From this point of view, there is no normative priority to the moral; in both cases, the task is to explain the conditions under which people are inclined to say that various kinds of obligations exist. If, by contrast, we are comfortable with the idea of real, objective moral obligation or reasons for action, the important question about legal obligation is whether it implies moral obligation or not.

In *The Concept of Law*, Hart explained the existence of both moral and legal obligation in terms of his general account of social rules. "Rules are conceived and spoken of as imposing obligations when the general demand for conformity is insistent and the social pressure brought to bear upon those who deviate or threaten it is great." We then distinguish between moral and legal obligation by pointing to the involvement of certain distinctive kinds of feelings, the role of coercion, the possibility of deliberate change, and so on.[10] Applied to morality, Hart's account of rules and the conditions under which they generate obligation was quickly attacked by Dworkin and others, and it is one of the parts of the book that he expressly repudiated in the *Postscript*, noting that he now believed that the social rules account was appropriate only for the legal case.[11] But this retreat was on technical grounds having to do with whether moral rules were in a certain sense conventional. Hart did not abandon his purely sociological, reductivist approach to both moral and legal obligation. His remarks make quite clear that, for both, he offers merely an account of the conditions under which it is proper to say that a certain special kind of rule exists in a society. The issue of what those

---

[10] Hart, *The Concept of Law*, 82–91, 167–80.
[11] Ibid., 254–9.

with realist or objectivist commitments would think of as actual obligation is simply not confronted.[12]

It is, however, possible to take for granted an objectivist position about moral obligation and still benefit from Hart's discussion of legal obligation. Leaving aside moral obligation as a separate issue, there remains an interesting question about the difference between a legal system that is merely effective, in that its subjects generally comply, and one that is (we might say) descriptively legitimate in that there is both a demand for conformity and general acceptance of the legitimacy of that demand.[13]

If this is the right way to understand Hart, what we are left with is a dispute about the nature or concept of legal obligation. There are three contending accounts: the purely nominal account according to which legal obligation attaches to any valid duty-imposing rule, the moralized account according to which there is no legal obligation without moral obligation, and Hart's sociological account.

This, it seems clear, is a purely verbal dispute. It is plausible to restrict the idea of legal obligation to cases where there is a moral obligation, but also plausible to deny this. It is plausible to restrict the idea of legal obligation to cases where the facts fit Hart's sociological account, but also plausible not to. Suppose someone says that they have a legal obligation to turn in their dissident neighbors to the secret police. A variety of responses seems acceptable, so far as the nature or concept of legal obligation is concerned. No, you have no obligation to do that, in fact it would be immoral. Yes, you have a legal obligation since the law is valid, but you have no moral reason to do it. No, you have no legal obligation because no one but the authorities would expect you to follow that legal rule. These are just different plausible ways of understanding what a legal obligation is, and I don't see any scope for so much as an argument that one of them is best.

---

[12] Hart did not offer a purely descriptive account of moral and legal rules. For him, the normativity of moral or legal rules lies in the attitudes of those who accept those rules. As discussed in Section 1, this still does not give us objective reasons for action, even for those who accept the rules. For an excellent account of Hart's metaethical views, see Joseph Raz, "H.L.A. Hart (1907–1992)," *Utilitas* 5 (1993): 145, 148–9. This section discusses the cognitivist aspects of Hart's view.

[13] Hart, *The Concept of Law*, 160.

But it doesn't matter, because we don't need the idea of legal obligation. We have the ideas of the content of the law in force and of moral obligation. That the former matters is part of the argument of this essay; the latter obviously does. Hart's discussion reminds us of a third criterion that is also worth remembering: in addition to the content of valid law and moral obligation, there is the issue of the legitimacy of the law in a descriptive sense. All three issues, validity, moral obligation, and descriptive legitimacy, are important. But it is also clear that we can discuss each of them without making use of the idea of legal obligation. When claims about the conditions of legal obligation are made, it is easy enough to disambiguate, and continue the discussion using other terms. Nothing gets lost in that translation, I believe.

3. AUTHORITY, LEGITIMACY, AND POLITICAL OBLIGATION: SOME DEFINITIONS

By way of stipulative definition that seems consistent with the practice of most legal and political philosophers, we can say that to have (real, *de jure*, legitimate) political *authority* is to be in a position to prescribe moral obligations for others; to have the right and the ability to do this.[14] It follows that there is no political authority without subjects having a general moral obligation to obey the law, and vice versa. I have always found this notion of authority to be somewhat unhelpful for political philosophy, since it seems foreign to the way actual governments and legal subjects understand their relationship—at least since the demise of the idea of the divine right of kings.[15] States do, I believe, typically claim the right to issue and enforce directives, but that leaves open whether they claim in addition that subjects have a moral obligation to obey.

In any event, our concern here is not with what states claim, but what is morally the case. There are two issues: whether the state's issuing and enforcing directives is justified, and whether subjects have a duty to obey. Some philosophers use the label "legitimacy" narrowly, to refer to the first of these issues alone; others insist that a legal system cannot

---

[14] See e.g. Joseph Raz, "Authority and Justification," *Philosophy & Public Affairs* 14 (1985): 3.
[15] See Allen Buchanan, *Justice, Legitimacy, and Self-Determination: Moral Foundations for International Law* (OUP 2007), 233–60.

count as legitimate unless both conditions are met, thus bringing the notion of legitimacy close to that of authority as defined earlier.[16] An important moral issue lies behind this terminological diversity—whether justification for a practice of directing people to act in various ways and backing that up with force can be found in the absence of a general duty to obey, and vice versa. Since my own answer to this moral question is yes, it is terminologically convenient to use "legitimacy" in the narrow sense of the moral justification of the issuing and enforcing of directives.[17]

A related moral issue is whether subjects have some kind of general duty to support the institutions that constitute the state. This issue is most naturally labeled one of "political obligation," and so that is the terminology I use. (Here again there is terminological diversity, however, as for many writers "political obligation" refers to the obligation to obey the law.) I do not in this essay pretend to address the issues of legitimacy or political obligation for their own sakes, but only as they are implicated in different views one might have about the duty to obey the law.

4. THE DUTY TO OBEY AND THE THEORY OF LAW

The issue of whether there is an obligation to obey the law interacts directly with the dispute between positivists and nonpositivists about the grounds of law. This poses an initial problem. The grounds of law are the considerations that determine the content of the law in force. We can define positivism as the view that social facts alone, and never moral considerations, determine the content of law.[18] Nonpositivism is the view that moral considerations are always among the grounds of law, either as a filter to catch grossly unjust directives, or in the form of a moralized interpretation of legal materials.

Dworkin's "moral reading," which aims to interpret legal materials in their morally best light, is the most important version of nonpositivism.[19] But Dworkin's legal theory contains several other strong commitments that are not essential to nonpositivism as just defined. The most important of these for current purposes is that he approaches the theory

---

[16] e.g. John A. Simmons, *Justification and Legitimacy* (CUP 2001), 137.

[17] For discussion, see William A. Edmundson, *Three Anarchial Fallacies: An Essay on Political Authority* (CUP 1998), 7–47.

[18] This ignores, for the sake of simplicity, the possibility of "inclusive" or "soft" positivism.

[19] See Ronald Dworkin, *Law's Empire* (HUP 1986).

of the grounds of law with the premise that legal rights and obligations are, generally speaking, real—that is, objective, moral—rights and obligations. On this approach, the question of whether a norm is plausibly regarded as having moral force is part of the inquiry into whether it is a legal norm in the first place. Positivism doesn't assume that law is not morally significant; but it does insist that a belief that it is morally significant cannot govern our investigation into its content.[20] This is true even for Raz, as although in his view law claims that it gives us genuine obligations to obey, he does not hold that we should interpret law so that this claim is more likely to come out true. In fact, he argues that the claim is usually false, though there is plenty of valid law around.[21]

Kelsen, as we have seen, did hold that insofar as the *Grundnorm* was presupposed, law was genuinely normative. There is an interesting scholarly debate to be had about just what he meant by presupposition of a norm, and about just what legal normativity implied for him. It is possible to read him as equating legal normativity, where it exists, with the normativity of morality and justice, but also possible to read him as insisting, in line with the purity of the pure theory, that they must be distinct. For current purposes, however, there is no need to enter into the debate about how best to read Kelsen on normativity. Suppose that he believed that law is a source of oughts distinct from morality (and self-interested rationality). We can leave such a view to one side. The idea of a distinct realm of categorical reasons for action, emerging from legal practices, is both mysterious and implausible. If law gives rise to real obligations, they are going to be moral obligations. If we suppose, on the other hand, that Kelsen believed that legal oughts were not some different species than moral oughts, we have different grounds for not pursuing his position. For whatever else may be said about Kelsen's views and their development, it is crucial to take account of his lifelong rejection of moral objectivity. Like Hart, Kelsen simply did not offer a view on the relation between valid law and objective moral obligation.[22]

---

[20] Such a stance is also compatible with nonpositivist theories of the grounds of law, just not Dworkin's.

[21] Raz, *The Authority of Law*, 233–49; Joseph Raz, *Ethics in the Public Domain: Essays in the Morality of Law and Politics* (OUP 1994), 325–38.

[22] Kelsen's moral subjectivism no doubt considerably weakened his ability to defend the constitutional order of the Weimar Republic against critics. See David Dyzenhaus, *Legality and*

Most discussions of the obligation to obey the law in moral and political philosophy implicitly assume a positivist position. These discussions take for granted that law can have any content and be created by all kinds of regimes, democratic or despotic. So it is hardly a surprise (the nonpositivist might quietly observe) that the conclusion of these inquiries is usually that there is no general duty to obey the law.

It would seem, then, that we cannot discuss the question of the duty to obey without at the same time taking a stand on the grounds of law.[23] This would be unfortunate, since the normative force of law, if such there is, would be one main reason to inquire into its grounds in the first place. However, this problem can be avoided. Positivist and nonpositivist accounts agree in very many cases about the factors that will actually play a role determining the content of law.[24] For often the moral factors that nonpositivist accounts of law locate within the boundary of law are inert, even if they are always in principle relevant. No one thinks that ten years imprisonment for murder is unconstitutional in the United States, or that the law against murder violates the law of equal protection, or that only marriage between persons of the same sex is permissible under English law. Though some insist that these conclusions depend in part on moral reasoning and others deny it, agreement on the truth of these propositions doesn't depend on agreement about why they are true. And there is in any case considerable agreement about why they are true. Positivists and nonpositivists agree a great deal about the grounds of law; it is not just that they may end up with the same conclusions about particular legal issues. All sides agree that legal sources such as validly enacted statutes, judicial decisions, and constitutional provisions are among the sources of law. And when there is no live moral issue, a straight reading of such sources will determine law's content for positivist and nonpositivist alike. When discussing the duty to obey, therefore, we should have in mind not the death penalty, same-sex marriage, and the regulation of sexual conduct among consenting adults,

---

Legitimacy: Carl Schmitt, Hans Kelsen, and Hermann Heller in Weimar (OUP 1997), 158–60. But it does save his theory from absurdity. It is obviously not plausible, morally speaking, to claim that whatever the rules established in accordance with the effective constitution may be, they impose objective moral obligations. If legal validity implies real obligation, legally valid rules couldn't have any old content and be posited in any old way.

[23] Philip Soper, *The Ethics of Deference: Learning from Law's Morals* (CUP 2002).
[24] See Liam Murphy, *What Makes Law* (CUP 2014), 103–7.

but rather road rules, duties of care, the law of theft, and the like. We should discuss the law that falls into the overlap among plausible theories of the grounds of law.

Since the traditional question is whether there is a duty to obey law as such—just because it is the law and not because of its content or even, perhaps, the way it was made—it can be objected that this narrowing of focus to only some of what on some theories counts as law makes it impossible to provide an answer. But in fact it only makes it impossible to defend a positive answer. If there is no content-independent prima facie duty to obey the law that falls into the overlap, then there is no content-independent prima facie duty to obey the law. This will be my conclusion.

A more particular objection is that there cannot be *any* overlap in the implications of a theory of law like Dworkin's that assumes that there is a general duty to obey the law and those of theories that leave that issue open.[25] My observations just now that positivist and nonpositivist theories will in many cases agree about the factors that are relevant to answering some legal question ignored this issue. Nonpositivism is just the view that moral considerations always play a role in fixing the content of law. But once we add to nonpositivism the distinctive Dworkinian claim that legal duties are in their nature real moral duties,[26] do we still find an overlap with positivist theories? It might be thought that we could not, since for Dworkinian nonpositivism the status of answers to legal questions is categorically different than for positivist approaches. For Dworkinians, the question of whether there is a general duty to comply with law is empty. So mustn't I have left this particular version of nonpositivism aside when I inquire into the normative force of what falls into the overlap?

I do not think so. A theory of the grounds of law cannot simply announce that legal rights and obligations are real (moral) rights and obligations. That does not help us determine the content of the law. What we need is an account, such as Dworkin's interpretivist moral reading, that tells us how we figure out what the law is. That account may itself have been shaped in part by the interpretive assumption that

---

[25] I thank George Letsas, Stefan Sciaraffa, and Nicos Stavropoulos for pressing me on this.

[26] The claim is also made by others, of course, perhaps most prominently by Mark Greenberg; for a recent statement, see Greenberg, "The Moral Impact Theory of Law," *Yale Law Journal* 123 (2013/14): 1288.

legal rights and obligations are real rights and obligations, and so the content of the moral reading will turn in part on a certain theory about the duty to obey—in Dworkin's case the theory of associative obligations, discussed below. But this does not mean that we cannot say what the law is according to this account unless we accept the theory of the duty to obey. Once we have determined the area of overlap, we can ask whether the account of the duty to obey that partly shaped the interpretivist moral reading really does establish a general duty to obey.

5. THE DUTY TO OBEY: INDIVIDUALS

We can finally turn to our main question—whether there is a prima facie duty to obey the law. A prima facie duty is one that could be overridden in particular cases by other factors of sufficient moral weight.[27] I am not aware of any argument for an absolute or non-overridable duty to obey the law, whatever its content may be. And by a duty to obey the law, we mean a duty to obey the law *as such*, because it is the law, and not because of its content or the way it was made.[28]

I have nothing new to say about the most familiar deontological argument for a duty to obey the law, Locke's argument of actual contract, or consent. Both elements of Hume's argument against this account in the *Treatise of Human Nature* and "Of the Original Contract" are convincing. Suppose that I have promised to obey the law, perhaps when I became a naturalized citizen of my adopted country. Though I cannot argue the case here, I agree with Hume that the duty to keep promises is itself instrumentally grounded—I should keep promises made primarily because of the value of the practice of doing so (though more can be at stake where reliance is present). But if that is so, there is every reason to look directly to the instrumental case for obeying the law—the good that a practice of general obedience generally brings about. It is true that

---

[27] The term "prima facie duty" comes from W.D. Ross, *The Right and the Good* (OUP 1930) and was used by him just to mean a duty that might be overridden by other moral considerations or duties. Shelly Kagan points out that "prima facie" really means "at first glance" which is not what Ross meant since the duties Ross discusses are not shown to have been illusory when overridden, and that Ross really should have used "pro tanto" as Kagan and many others now do; see Kagan, *The Limits of Morality* (OUP 1989), 17. But since "pro tanto" is not in general use, and it is clear enough what we mean by "prima facie" in this context, I'll stick with the old terminology.

[28] Leslie Green, *The Authority of the State* (OUP 1988), 225–6.

if I have promised to obey, there are other instrumental benefits to add to the mix, but on the face of it they seem swamped by the direct benefits of obedience.

The second part of Hume's argument is that most individual legal subjects have not in any case promised to obey the law; they were born into a society where obedience is simply expected of them. Tacit consent, inferred from continuing presence in the jurisdiction, is implausible because most people have no realistic alternative.

The argument of "fair play" is subject to a similarly well-known and compelling objection. This argument is based on the plausible idea that if I have chosen to share in the benefits of a cooperative scheme, it would be morally objectionable to free ride on the burdensome compliance of others by not shouldering the burdens of compliance myself. But most individuals cannot be said to have chosen to participate in the cooperative scheme that is governance by law. And when benefits are forced on one, the fair play argument does not have any purchase.[29]

Quite apart from that familiar objection, however, it cannot simply be assumed that following the law amounts to assuming the burdens of cooperation in the sense relevant for the fair play argument.[30] There certainly can be valid legal requirements, such as some pointless bureaucratic requirement, the universal flouting of which would not reduce the benefits people receive from the overall legal scheme or otherwise undermine it. Even if every legal subject had asked for the benefits of the legal system, the argument from fair play would not support a fully general duty to obey the law. It would support a duty to shoulder one's share of the burdens of sustaining the beneficial scheme; but that is not the same thing.

I believe a similar point applies to Dworkin's argument[31] that a prima facie duty to obey the law can be grounded in associative obligations.[32] Dworkin's key idea is that law can transform a group of people living together by "geographical accident" into what he calls a political community. The members of a political community, in his special sense, bear

[29] Robert Nozick, *Anarchy, State, and Utopia* (Basic Books 1974), 90–5.

[30] Kent Greenawalt, *Conflicts of Law and Morality* (OUP 1989), 138–47; Raz, *The Authority of Law*, 237–9.

[31] Dworkin, *Law's Empire*, 195–215.

[32] This account will not ground an entirely content- and context-independent duty to obey unless we presuppose Dworkin's theory of law, according to which the various conditions for the existence of an associative obligation are guaranteed to be satisfied by valid law, since the content of law will be determined with those conditions in mind as constraints.

associative obligations to each other akin to those held among members of a family. Law creates this political fraternity by providing a moral bond in the form of moral principles that are shared, despite disagreement about ideals of justice and sound policy.

We may accept for the sake of argument that where members of a group share principles to govern their interaction despite their moral disagreements at the level of ideal theory, their relationship acquires a special moral quality such that they owe obligations to each other that they do not owe to outsiders. We may also accept that the content of that obligation is to be true to the shared principles that constitute the community in the first place. Even if we grant all this, however, it does not follow that there is a general obligation to obey the law, because there is no reason to think that all and only the principles we share will be expressed in the law.[33] We do not simply enact into law our shared moral values or commitments; we enact into law rules, principles, and standards that are appropriately enacted into law, given our shared values and commitments, and given the special considerations that have to be taken into account when we are making law, not expressing our values and commitments. To take a simple example, the Anglo-Saxon world surely shares a commitment to a moral principle of easy rescue. Yet, rightly or wrongly, Anglo-Saxon lawmakers have generally felt that it would be inappropriate to give that principle legal expression.[34] Similarly, there are good reasons why the reach of contract law should not extend to all promises that (as we agree) have moral force.

But even though not all principles we share have appropriate legal expression, wouldn't fidelity to a community of principle nonetheless *include* fidelity to those principles that do get expressed in the law? No, because legal principles may not merely fall short of shared moral principles, they may, on their surface, mislead in a more fundamental way. It would be wrong, for example, to conclude from the law of property and its related doctrines in torts and criminal law that underlying that whole scheme is some shared commitment to a Lockean theory of moral property rights. Whatever one thinks about this one example, it cannot be denied that much of the content of law does not wear its rationale on its face.

---

[33] Liam Murphy, "The Political Question of the Concept of Law," in Jules L. Coleman (ed.), *Hart's Postscript: Essays on the Postscript to The Concept of Law* (OUP 2001), 397–409.

[34] See Liam Murphy, "Beneficence, Law, and Liberty: The Case of Required Rescue," *Georgetown Law Journal* 89 (2001): 605.

Legal principles do not all simply announce moral principles with the same content; many of them are part of an artificial normative scheme whose justification must be found elsewhere. And from the fact that some shared value is served instrumentally by enacting some principle into law, it does not follow that that value is best promoted by each individual being faithful to that legal principle in every case.[35]

If we are to have general moral reason to follow legal rules, the most promising source may seem to be the process of their making. Many have thought that democratically enacted legislation does bring with it a standing duty of compliance because of the moral significance of the procedure. Any argument along these lines is limited, of course, both to the case of (good enough) democracies and to legislation. But in any case, it seems to me that the argument does not go through. Consider, for example, Thomas Christiano's suggestion that to fail to abide by democratic legislative directives is to treat one's fellow citizens unequally and thus unjustly. "Citizens who skirt democratically made law act contrary to the equal right of all citizens to have a say in making laws when there is substantial and informed disagreement."[36] There is serious ground for doubt whether actually existing democracies respect an equal right of all citizens to have a say in making laws. But we can leave that aside, and grant that an ideal democracy satisfies the equal right of citizens to have a say in making laws and is for that reason (if not for that reason alone) a superior mode of lawmaking. Other forms of lawmaking, we may say, violate this equal right. What is unclear is why an individual's failure to obey democratically made law also violates the right.

Assume an ideal electoral and legislative process that respects the equal right of all to have a say in making laws. When I disobey the law that results, I am not asserting that the democratic process was not the right way to make law, nor that I have the right to tell others what to do,

---

[35] The same general kinds of consideration lead me to reject Samuel Scheffler's recent argument for a duty to obey the law in "Membership and Political Obligation," *Journal of Political Philosophy* 26 (2018): 3–23. I agree with Scheffler that membership in a political community can be noninstrumentally valuable. It also seems plausible that where membership in a group is noninstrumentally valuable, members have reason to do their share, as defined by norms of the group that express what it is that "the group wants and needs of them," to help sustain it and contribute to its purposes. But I do not believe that all of even democratically made law can be seen as norms that express that, or as norms "of the group" in the necessary sense.

[36] T. Christiano, *The Constitution of Equality: Democratic Authority and Its Limits* (OUP 2008), 250.

or even to make a special exception for myself. The moral reasons for adopting a particular process of lawmaking are not automatically grounds for obedience, unless we simply assume that we have an obligation to obey law made in the right way.

We cannot assimilate democratic lawmaking to cases where groups of people agree to adopt a certain procedure, regarded as fair, for resolving their disagreement. Suppose two of us have to paint the house, but both prefer to use the roller to paint the walls and ceiling than the brush to paint the woodwork. We agree to draw straws. We should comply with the outcome of the chosen procedure; but this is because we agreed in advance to do just that. The case of democratic governance is different from this simple case in two ways. First, I might agree to or support a method for making law without this entailing an agreement or promise to obey. Second, as is obvious, democratic procedures are not based on universal agreement; they are imposed on the population, independent of actual consent. Even if some degree of actual support among the population—legitimacy in the descriptive sense—is treated as a condition of normative legitimacy, unanimous support is clearly unavailable.

In some cases, it seems that we ought to follow the decision made in a fair procedure, even if there was no advance agreement to do that. When the members of a group have agreed that some collective task will be performed by them, but disagree about the division of labor, it may seem unnecessary that each agree in advance to follow the results of a particular fair procedure. While each of us is grumbling that he does not want to go first, one of the group may draw my name out of a hat. Assuming we are all equally well suited to going first, there's no better procedure than that. So I should go first even though I didn't in any sense agree to the procedure in advance. But again, democratic government is not a bit like this, because we have not agreed in advance on a certain list of collective tasks that require a certain division of labor.

Christiano well expresses what seems to me to be a widely held view. I have so far been suggesting that its apparent appeal is due to a tacit association of democracy with some kind of universal consent. But perhaps what is at work is rather an idea that we are all morally required to do our part in the collective enterprise of promoting and maintaining valuable and just forms of social cooperation.[37] Democracy presents

---

[37] See John Finnis, *Natural Law and Natural Rights* (OUP 1980).

itself as the morally best means of resolving disagreements about how to go about that and should be supported for that reason, independent of any actual consent to anything. This seems an attractive view, but it still does not get us to a general duty to obey the law. We should obey the law, on this essentially instrumental line of thought, just in case that will further our duty to promote whatever social goals justify the existence of the (legitimate) coercive political apparatus in the first place. As discussed more fully later, we cannot simply stipulate that compliance with law will always have this effect.

Other defenses of democracy as a system of government, such as those that turn on the epistemic value of democratic procedures, or on the value of public deliberation, will, it seems evident, leave the same gap between justification of the system of government and the obligation to obey the law. (Jürgen Habermas's[38] account of the justification of any norm, legal or moral, closes the gap at the level of ideal theory, insofar as justification can only be found where certain ideal procedures have in fact been followed. But this does not imply a general duty to obey law under actual, nonideal conditions.)

All the arguments so far considered for a content- and context-independent duty to obey the law have a similar structure. They are all compatible with or explicitly invoke an instrumental understanding of the moral reasons in favor of governance by law as an institution; the attempt is then made to provide a deontological, or noninstrumental, account of the duty to obey.

Now by an instrumental understanding I mean that governance by law is valued in the first place because of its ability to secure certain good outcomes. Were it not for the value of those outcomes, we would not regard governance by law as morally desirable; law is not valuable just for its own sake. This position is of course compatible with legal governance being morally superior to other means of promoting security, overall welfare, justice, and so on, even if the other forms of governance could do a better job promoting such ends. Law as a means has noninstrumental virtues; there may, in fact, be no other fully morally acceptable means available for the promotion of these social goals. So the instrumental view of law is fully compatible with valuing law as one mode of governance among others because it can satisfy the values we

---

[38] J. Habermas, *Between Facts and Norms* (MIT Press 1996).

associate with the ideal of the rule of law.[39] It is also compatible with there being moral principles that apply only to the legal order, as part of what Rawls calls the basic structure of society,[40] and not directly to individuals. Thus some goals of legal governance, such as social justice, may make no sense independently of the existence of some institutional governance structures. What is ruled out by an instrumental view of law is that governance by law has some kind of intrinsic moral significance that it would have even if it contributed not at all to security, justice, higher levels of overall welfare, and the rest. On the instrumental view, though there are moral reasons to favor governance by law over other forms of governance, no form of governance, governance by law included, would have value for us if it did not bring about independent goods. The instrumental view of law is therefore compatible with the Utopian Marxist ideal of the withering away of the state.

A noninstrumental account of the value of governance by law could in principle provide a more direct route to the conclusion that there is a standing moral reason to obey the law. But I am not aware of any such account—at least not one that applies in the actual, nonideal world.

Kant's legal theory perhaps comes closest, since for Kant positive law plays a constitutive role, making real all "acquired" rights and specifying, for the situation where people are subject to a coercive power, the content of the one "innate" right to equal freedom.[41] Moreover, though there are grounds for criticism of the content of these rights as actually found in positive law, no individual is in a position to act on his view that the state has got it wrong. This suggests that positive law in some sense constitutes (some of what is) right and wrong. It also suggests that Kant's view that we have a duty to enter into the "rightful condition" that is life under a state should be understood in terms of the intrinsic moral value of being governed by law. It isn't that we need law because that is the best way to protect everyone's independently cognizable rights; it is that without law it is in some sense impossible for us to act rightly toward each other. Without law we are doomed to a life of sin; where there is law, we must always comply.

---

[39] See also Leslie Green, "Law as a Means," in Peter Cane (ed.), *The Hart-Fuller Debate in the Twenty-First Century* (Hart Publishing 2010).

[40] John Rawls, *Political Liberalism* (Columbia University Press 1996), 257–88.

[41] Immanuel Kant, *The Metaphysics of Morals*, ed. Mary Gregor (CUP 1996); for discussion, see Arthur Ripstein, *Force and Freedom: Kant's Legal and Political Philosophy* (HUP 2009).

In the first place, however, this is not an account of the intrinsic moral value of being governed by law. Governance by law may be necessary for the realization of the equal right to freedom, and not just a contingent causal condition.[42] But this does not make being subject to public authority an end in itself; the end remains the realization of the equal right to freedom. Second, while Kant does assert that we must all "obey the authority who has power over you" he immediately adds "in whatever does not conflict with inner morality."[43] The important point here is that Kant's doctrine of right is concerned with the grounds for the use of force. So while it does lead him (perhaps unnecessarily) to absurdly authoritarian views about resistance to the state, it doesn't address in any great detail the general moral significance of governance by law, nor in particular the question of when and whether passive noncompliance with law is morally permissible.[44]

So far as I can see, the instrumental view of law as I have laid it out is inescapable. There is of course nothing inconsistent in offering a deontological account of the duty to obey the directives of a system whose existence is at bottom justified in instrumental terms, and no way to prove that it could not work. Notably, the consent argument has the right form for this kind of approach. The consent argument is unlike the other arguments considered previously in that it doesn't leave a gap between the justification of the system and the conclusion of a general duty to obey. But this is because the consent argument applies entirely independently of the justification and indeed the quality of the system of governance by law—everything turns on the content of the contractual arrangement between subject and ruler with limits set only by considerations of contractual capacity and the absence of force and fraud. The argument applies directly to each subject but is entirely detached from the reasons anyone may have for valuing a situation of governance by law. In fact, once we leave aside the idea that governance by law has intrinsic moral significance for each subject, it is tempting to speculate that the only deontological argument that could in principle ground a general duty to obey is a voluntaristic one such as the argument

---

[42] Ripstein, *Force and Freedom*, 9.

[43] Kant, *Metaphysics of Morals*, 136.

[44] Thomas Hill, "Questions about Kant's Opposition to Revolution," *Journal of Value Inquiry* 36 (2002): 283.

from consent.[45] (The argument from consent is not the only possible voluntaristic argument. Thus Raz's idea that those who "identify" with or respect their legal system may acquire a duty to obey is voluntaristic, even though there is no relevant canonical moment akin to the making of a promise.[46])

Even if there are deontological reasons to favor certain forms of legal order over others—those that respect the autonomy of subjects, or the value of integrity, or are democratic, and so on—a further argument is required to link each legal directive to each subject's obligations. Take the morally best, humanly feasible legal and political system we can describe. Why should each subject always obey each law? Only, I suspect, if each of us has taken some voluntary step to bind us morally to all of the law.[47]

[45] I here echo much of what John Simmons writes about the duty to obey the law. See Simmons, *Moral Principles and Political Obligation* (PUP 1979); Simmons, *Justification and Legitimacy*; Simmons, "The Duty to Obey and Our Natural Moral Duties," in Christopher H. Wellman & John Simmons (eds.), *Is There a Duty to Obey the Law?* (CUP 2005). But with Greenawalt I disagree with Simmons that an account of the duty to obey the law must explain why we have special obligations to obey the law of one state (our own) in particular: Greenawalt, *Conflicts of Law and Morality*, 167. Simmons's motivation for this "particularity requirement" is not one that applies to my discussion: it is to challenge claims of legitimacy by the state, which he holds can only be made good if all citizens have a particularized moral obligation to obey. (It is worth noting that even the consent argument, which Simmons agrees is the only hope for a general duty to obey, could violate the particularity requirement, in that it is certainly possible to promise obedience to more than one state.) As I am here simply investigating what moral obligation we have to obey the law, there is no reason to insist in advance that our conclusion will have a certain content. In any event, an instrumental account of political obligation of the kind about to be discussed could certainly impose on individuals' stronger responsibility for maintaining the institutions of states to which they have closer ties. Furthermore, even if I have a fully impersonal responsibility to promote just and beneficial institutions wherever they may be, the relevance of my compliance with law to fulfilling that responsibility will generally be restricted to law that claims jurisdiction over me, which is for the most part the law of my current country of residence. For discussion of these issues, see Jeremy Waldron, "Special Ties and Natural Duties," in William A. Edmundson (ed.), *The Duty to Obey the Law: Selected Readings* (Rowman & Littlefield 1999). (The formal legal category of citizenship, naturalization oaths aside, is not especially relevant to the issue of the duty to obey. Think of the Palestinian citizen of Jordan who has lived all his life in Lebanon, or the Australian or Mexican citizen who has lived most of his life in the United States.)

[46] Raz, *The Authority of Law*, 250–61; Raz, *Ethics in the Public Domain*, 337–8.

[47] Stephen Perry has suggested the following account of political authority, which would, if its elements were substantively made out, ground a general duty: a lawmaker has the power to give others obligations just in case it would be good if it had that power. See Perry, "Political Authority and Political Obligation," in Leslie Green & Brian Leiter (eds.), *Oxford Studies in Philosophy of Law: Volume 2* (OUP 2013). This is related to Anscombe's idea that the state has authority because it is necessary that it does: Elizabeth Anscombe, "On the Source of the Authority of the State," in Joseph Raz (ed.), *Authority* (NYU Press 1990). Perry, unlike Anscombe, explicitly focuses in on what would explain the state's having the power to impose

Of course, if law as such has instrumental importance, we would expect there to be instrumental reasons for people at least sometimes to obey the law. Those who offer deontological arguments for a duty to obey need not and do not disagree about that. But the argument thus far suggests that the only moral reasons to obey the law are instrumental. And with that foundation, it is clear that we cannot build a content- and context-independent duty for individuals to obey.

The moral reason to obey the law is that it will do (if it will) more good than not obeying. For individuals, the good that it may do is that it will support the institutions of the state and promote what, through law, the state is trying to achieve. The instrumental duty to obey the law is thus subsidiary to an instrumental duty of political obligation. This is the position not just of the utilitarian tradition that follows Hume, but also of Rawls,[48] who characterizes political obligation in terms of a natural duty of justice—to support and promote just institutions. Rawls's account of political obligation is clearly consequentialist, or instrumental, though it is of course not utilitarian. (Rawls does, however, write: "There is quite clearly no difficulty in explaining why we are to comply with just laws enacted under a just constitution."[49] It is quite unclear to me how the instrumental natural duty of justice could do any such thing.)

There are clear benefits to the existence of institutions that can provide basic security, protect rights, preserve the environment, promote economic justice and overall welfare, and so on. And law as a mode of governance is clearly superior to alternatives, from the moral point of view, in view of its potential to achieve such goals while at the same time respecting the agency of persons. There may be law without the rule of law, but only legal systems can achieve the ideal of the rule of law, which is the best way to rule. All this is obvious enough as a matter of political

obligations on others as distinct from the good that the exercise of coercive force might do. Even leaving behind the puzzling form of this argument (it would be good, therefore it is), it is entirely unclear why there would *ever* be value in X having such a power with respect to Y. It might be good for subjects to believe that they have a duty to do what the government says; but why, independently of any effect on conduct, would the mere fact of the moral relationship—I get to tell you what you ought to do—have value? Even if the state is democratic, and so the duties are imposed after a fair process that treats us all equally, and so on, there still seems no plausible case that it would be good in itself for the state to have this "normative power." On these issues, see William A. Edmundson, "Political Authority, Moral Powers and the Intrinsic Value of Obedience," *Oxford Journal of Legal Studies* 30 (2010): 179.

[48] John Rawls, *A Theory of Justice* (HUP 1999), 99.
[49] Ibid., 308.

theory, even abstracting from debates about what exactly the conditions for a legitimate coercive political order are, and what account of justice we should be aspiring to.

Suppose a context where the political coercive order is legitimate and otherwise good enough so that revolution and overthrow is morally a worse option than supporting, while trying to improve, the content of the law, the context of its making, and the mode of its enforcement. On the instrumental account, it is clear that we subjects have, by way of political obligation, a duty not to undermine but rather to support the existing order. The issue then becomes whether this implies that we also have a duty to obey the law. And the answer, of course, is that it depends. It depends on whether we do more good—in terms of our twin aims of supporting the existing order and making things better—by complying or by not complying.

The basic structural point is this, and it applies even if the law is as good as it could be. We cannot reason directly from what it would be good and right to have enacted and enforced as law to what it would be good or right for individuals to do.[50] That we have the law in place that it is best to enforce (there is no better set of legal norms it would be better to enforce) does not imply that it is always obligatory for each person to follow the law. Of course, so long as the continued existence of the legal system is desirable, it pretty much follows that it would be bad if *everyone* disobeyed *all* the laws, since the consequence of everyone disobeying all the time, most likely, would be collapse of the system. But even disobedience by all might not undermine the overall structure, so long as it is restricted to certain parts of the legal order. Thus suppose we believe that the prohibition of recreational use of marijuana, or a requirement that undocumented persons be reported to the immigration authorities, would be bad policy. Suppose also pretty much everyone fails to comply. The state will not collapse. It might actually improve, in terms of the content of its law.

There is a puzzle about the case of general disobedience, of all law, that needs to be mentioned and then set aside. If no one complies, the (good enough) state falls, which, we presume, is a bad result. But it seems as if no one of us is to blame. Suppose general compliance; my becoming a noncomplier won't cause the state to fall. Suppose general

---

[50] See Edmundson, *Three Anarchial Fallacies*, 7–47.

noncompliance; my having stayed a complier wouldn't have saved the state. It is tempting to reason that no instrumental account can ever show why any individual ought to obey the law. But this temptation has its roots in a very general phenomenon—if we submit to it, we will conclude that no trivial act of pollution is bad because of its effects, no failure to vote is bad because of its effects, no failure to contribute money to famine relief is bad because of its effects, and so on. The general problem is how to explain individual responsibility in a context where, as Derek Parfit puts it, "we together" cause some harm.[51] It is a fascinating and important philosophical puzzle, but its generality allows me to leave it aside here.

Suppose I know that enough others are complying such that my non-complying act would not be part of a group of acts that together have a bad effect on the viability of the legal system.[52] If I reason that my non-compliance won't make any difference, could I be said to be free riding on the compliance of others?[53] This is not the argument from fair play. The thought is that if we together have an obligation to act so as to preserve the state, because of what it can achieve, it is unfair of any one person to count on sufficient compliance by others, taking any advantage that might result from his own noncompliance. "You only get not to comply because we are complying," say the compliers to the noncompliers, "and that's not fair." "If we could count on you to comply, it would be all right for us not to comply." This seems right, but the issue is rarely going to come up in a pure way. For most people most of the time, self-interest counsels compliance, in which case the compliance of the compliers is not a sacrifice or burden for them. Equally, the reason

---

[51] D. Parfit, *Reasons and Persons* (OUP 1984), 75–86.

[52] Exactly how to determine whether my act should count as part of such a group is an important part of the general puzzle about collective responsibility for bad outcomes. Obviously, the test cannot be whether, taken on its own, my act makes a difference. But neither should we say that all acts of the type that together make a difference are part of the group, since it may make no difference if there are many fewer complying acts. There is going to have to be some account of a vague boundary here. As I say, pursuing this important issue here would take us too far afield.

[53] Christopher H. Wellman, "Samaritanism and the Duty to Obey the Law," in Christopher H. Wellman & A. John Simmons (eds.), *Is there a Duty to Obey the Law?* (CUP 2005), 30–53 discusses this issue in the context of advancing an argument that the duty to obey the law arises out of a duty to rescue; for effective criticism of Wellman's "Samaritanism" argument, see A. John Simmons, "The Duty to Obey and Our Natural Moral Duties," in Wellman & Simmons, *Is there a Duty to Obey the Law?*; William A. Edmundson, "State of the Art," *Legal Theory* 10 (2004): 249.

for noncompliance might not be my own advantage as there may be none; in that case too there would be no free riding. In principle, then, a deontological requirement of fairness to complying others is fully compatible with the instrumental case for compliance. The circumstances of its engagement, however, are rather particular, and perhaps typically not present.

Suppose then that the level of compliance is sufficient to assure the stability of the state and the circumstances do not raise the fairness issue just discussed. If we now consider the case of an individual who is debating whether to comply with a legal rule, it is easy to see that the mere fact that it is a legal rule is likely to provide only very weak grounds for compliance. No one act of noncompliance will in itself bring the whole scheme down—not in virtue of its own effects, nor in virtue of the "bad example" it might provide. It may be that in this particular context, for this particular individual, following it may actually achieve little or nothing in the way of the benefits we associate with general compliance.

Now in the case of some very particular legal rules, individual acts of noncompliance can directly harm the overall institutional regime that is governance by law. I have in mind legal rules prohibiting the corrupting, through bribery or otherwise, of legal officials—judges, police officers, legislators, and so on.[54] In this case, the harm to the overall system is not dependent on the overall level of compliance.

Equally, there often will be moral reasons to act in accordance with a legal rule that are not related to the benefits of maintaining a legal order. Thus suppose some scheme of environmental regulation establishes a fair cooperative scheme that has effective results in cleaning up some river.[55] Even total noncompliance with this scheme would not endanger the legal order. But each potential polluter has instrumental moral reasons, supplemented by reasons of fairness, to participate in the scheme. These reasons, however, are content dependent; they are not guaranteed to be present just because the scheme is put in place by law. We typically have similar content-dependent moral reasons to pay our taxes.[56]

Furthermore, and needless to say, there are direct moral reasons to refrain from most of what is prohibited by the criminal law.

---

[54] I am grateful here to Leslie Green.
[55] See Raz, *The Authority of Law*, 247–9.
[56] I am grateful here to discussion with T.M. Scanlon.

All in all, we have to conclude that for individuals in a well-functioning state, the instrumental moral case to comply with the law just because it is the law is rather weak, and in any event hostage to all kinds of contingencies. What seems to matter much more than the obedience of individual subjects is their seeking reform of the state and the content of its laws to make it more legitimate, more just, and all around better. In a more or less effective state, where effective coercive measures in any event provide adequate reasons of self-interest for most people to obey most of the time, the moral case for compliance with law just doesn't seem to be very strong.

6. THE LAW-ABIDING CHARACTER

There is a further important aspect to the issue, however. We have considered the morality of compliance only as a question of what it is right or wrong to do. We have not evaluated the case for what Hume called the artificial virtue of political allegiance.[57]

Hume's moral theory focused solely on virtues of character, the motives and dispositions that receive moral approval or disapproval. He argued that some such motives and dispositions, such as parental love, are found in nature. Others, such as law abidingness and fidelity to promise, can only arise in the context of a conventional social practice and are therefore properly regarded as artificial. Hume believed that a standing disposition to comply with law would in the first instance be generated by self-interest; moral approval by others, on the other hand, is grounded in the recognition that this disposition has social utility. Now neither Hume's exclusive focus on virtue in his moral theory nor his claim that self-interest is the original ground of the virtue of compliance is essential to the structure of his argument. Instrumentalist moral theory generally should recognize value in dispositions and motives that themselves can be seen to make things go better.

That consequentialist moral theory should evaluate not just conduct but also character was most clearly argued by Sidgwick.[58] More recently, philosophers have appealed to this plurality of objects of evaluation

---

[57] Thanks to Thomas Nagel for discussion. For exploration of the idea that "law-abidance" might be a virtue in the classical, noninstrumental sense, see William A. Edmundson, "The Virtue of Law-Abidance," *Philosophers' Imprint* 6 (2006): 1.

[58] Henry Sidgwick, *The Methods of Ethics* (Hackett Publishing 1982).

to defend consequentialism against the charge that it requires strict impartiality at the level of disposition, motive, and desire.[59] These discussions show, in effect, that consequentialist ethical theory can explain the moral significance of the natural virtues.

The same general approach can be applied to Humean artificial virtues. An instrumental theory of the duty to comply should consider not just the reasons we may have to act in compliance with law; it should also consider the instrumental value of subjects having a general disposition toward compliance. If we have such a disposition, we typically don't reflect on the reasons for compliance, but simply act. But the disposition need not and should not be blind habit. When called on to reflect on such dispositions, we can justify them as tending to promote good outcomes. Since we are able to offer justificatory reasons for our standing policy of compliance, this complex of beliefs and motives is entirely compatible with Hart's account of what it is to accept the law, and the internal aspect of legal rules.

The question now becomes whether it is instrumentally for the best for legal subjects to have a standing disposition to comply. The importance of this possibility lies in the fact that the disposition might be for the best even if in some cases compliance is not for the best. Taking into account the possibility of error, especially a tendency to err in our own favor, we may do better, overall and in the long run of cases, not considering the merits of acting in a certain way on a case-by-case basis, but simply sticking to a firm policy. These points have been made by utilitarians attempting to answer deontological critics.[60] Yes, say the utilitarians, you should adopt a policy of never killing innocent people, even though on some occasions that will mean you do the wrong thing. You reconsider the grounds for your policy only when the circumstances are truly exceptional. If you fail to kill when the circumstances were not such as to justify reviewing the policy, but killing would have nonetheless been for the best, you will have done the wrong thing, though your motive not to kill was a good one. We might say that your failure to kill was blamelessly wrong,[61] since you acted on a motive it was right for you to have. This is not a compelling answer to the deontological critic, since

---

[59] Parfit, *Reasons and Persons*, 3–51; Peter Railton, "Alienation, Consequentialism, and the Demands of Morality," *Philosophy & Public Affairs* 13 (1984): 134.

[60] See R.M. Hare, *Moral Thinking: Its Levels, Method, and Point* (OUP 1982).

[61] Parfit, *Reasons and Persons*, 31–5.

the judgment that refraining from killing the innocent was wrong should be rejected. But in the context of the duty to obey, where deontological arguments for compliance are not plausible, the idea of it being right to adopt a standing policy to act in a way that will on occasion lead us to act less well than we otherwise might is clearly very important.

Nonetheless, it does not seem to be true that for individuals acting in their private capacity it is generally for the best to be disposed to comply with law without considering the pros and cons of the particular case. Law has varying content, and we are adept at sorting legal rules into relevant different categories without much thought. I can distinguish between legal rules prohibiting recreational use of marijuana, say, and rules of tax law. Most important, it is not difficult for us to identify cases where overall compliance with law can be counted on, so that my non-compliance won't harm the legal-political institutional order, from cases where that is not so. Thus though it may in some circumstances, and for some categories of legal rules, be for the best to develop a standing disposition to comply, there is no compelling reason to think that a disposition always to comply with law as such will be for the best.

7. THE DUTY OF STATES TO OBEY THE LAW

Everything changes when we turn to the law that applies to the state itself. Here we cannot restrict our focus primarily to the content of law and the mode of its making, assuming more or less effective (and legitimate) enforcement. There is no further set of institutions that will enforce the law that applies to states themselves. I will first discuss domestic law, before turning to international law in Section 8.

Though it is obvious, it is also often forgotten that there is no coercive apparatus that will enforce law against the government itself. In countries such as the United States or Germany, the institution of judicial review may blind us to this, since for justiciable constitutional and statutory questions the court is there to pronounce that some legislation is invalid or some executive act was contrary to law. But pronouncement, obviously, is not enforcement.[62] Enforcement of law happens when the executive branch of government uses coercive means to ensure compliance by

---

[62] See Jack Goldsmith & Daryl Levinson, "Law for States: International Law, Constitutional Law, Public Law," *Harvard Law Review* 122 (2009): 1791.

individual subjects of the state. When a highest court finds executive or legislative illegality, we rely on the relevant branches simply to comply. Of course, the executive branch may enforce the law against lower-level officials of that branch. But if the executive branch as a whole is not complying—in practice, if the highest-level officials are not complying—there is no further enforcement mechanism available. (I leave aside the possible case of high-level members of the executive branch being prosecuted by a later government for violation of the criminal law. Apart from the fact that such prosecution rarely if ever happens, in situations of stable democratic transition at any rate, the issue of government compliance is obviously not limited to the criminal law.)

A related issue here is the idea that coercive enforcement is a condition of the existence of law. Most legal philosophers now reject the thought that sanctions must be present before we can talk sensibly of legal order. But few emphasize that if we took that view, we would have to conclude not only that states are not subject to international law, but that they are not subject to law at all.[63] Though I believe it would be wrong to deny the importance of the possibility of coercion when distinguishing law from other normative systems, it is disastrous to insist that the presence of an actual coercive apparatus is a requirement for the existence of legal norms. That would lead us in exactly the wrong direction, away from the domain in which law has its greatest normative significance.

What moral reasons do legal officials in the executive, judicial, and legislative branches have to follow constitutional and ordinary domestic law? I should first mention and set aside the unlawful use of coercive force by the executive branch against its subjects.[64] Though I do not here attempt to offer a theory of legitimacy, it does seem plausible that any justification for the use of force that might attach to the state in virtue of its existence as the publically constituted coercive order (as opposed merely to being in a position to do something) will depend on the existence of law and the state's compliance with it. As I suggested previously, though law and legal institutions would have no moral significance if they could do no good, governance by and through law may be an essential condition of any legitimate coercive pursuit of those aims.

---

[63] For an exception, see Joseph Raz, *Practical Reason and Norms* (2nd edn, OUP 1999), 158.
[64] I am grateful here to Alexander Guerrero.

But the issue of official compliance is much broader than this specific case of unlawful coercion of subjects.

What general moral reasons do legal officials have to comply with law? They may have promised to do so, either by an explicit oath, or perhaps by an implicit promise that can be inferred from their action in accepting office or seeking it through the electoral process. This will not necessarily apply to all legal officials, in all kinds of legal orders. But even where there is an express promise, I do not believe, for the reasons given earlier, that this can provide a quick foundation for the duty to obey. Even if some deontological account of the morality of promise were available, it should still be clear that the really weighty reasons legal officials should obey lie elsewhere.

The main reason legal officials should obey the law is again instrumental. US constitutional electoral law has some glaring imperfections, such as the Electoral College, the overrepresentation of residents of low-population states in the Senate, and the very short electoral term for the House of Representatives. Wouldn't it be good if somehow the relevant officials could conspire simply to change the practice, without amending the law? It would be in one way good, but in another way extremely bad. When it comes to individuals, the "bad example" claim about non-compliance seems silly. When it comes to government officials setting examples for each other, and for the rest of us, it does not. Moreover, and more important, the very idea of the state being subject to law being taken seriously depends on states taking that idea seriously. Once the decision whether to comply starts to be treated as a matter of deciding whether there is a better way to do things, we quickly end up with the state not binding itself to law at all. The benefits of the constitutional state, in terms of continuity, stability, transparency, the avoidance of usurpation, and so on, depend on close to full compliance with law by the state itself.[65]

The importance of the various branches of government following the law is not limited to the structural parts of a constitution, or even to constitutional law itself. Suppose that the executive branch of some government deliberately flouts a statute requiring legislative authorization

---

[65] In their argument that the executive branch of the United States is not bound by law and it's a good thing too, Posner and Vermeule simply assume that the basic constitutional framework of the state will remain in place: Eric Posner & Adrian Vermeule, *The Executive Unbound: After the Madisonian Republic* (OUP 2011).

for the use of military force. There are obvious weighty moral reasons (quick action may save lives) that would support this in a particular case, as well as, on the other side, standing moral reasons in favor of broader public deliberation about the decision to risk lives in military action. It might seem that the additional moral reasons generated by a legal prohibition could not possibly have comparable weight. But the bad effects of official lawlessness are of a fundamentally different order of magnitude from those of individual noncompliance. And the effects are more severe, the higher up the political hierarchy you go. If the head of government flouts the law, or is found out subsequently to have done so, it is not so much a bad example we are dealing with, but a reasonable ground for wondering whether the very existence of the coercive political order is, after all, a good thing, or at least whether there is any long-run reason for having patience with the existing coercive political order, attempting to make it better, and so on, rather than expecting the worst and trying something new. Official lawlessness greatly increases the case for revolution and overthrow, which is not a good thing.

Modern political coercive orders are understood in good part in terms of their structural legal features (the separation of powers, the electoral system if there is one, and so on). We do not have to follow Kelsen[66] so far as to identify the state with law as a conceptual matter to see the central role law has in defining the substantive nature of our state. If the most fundamental structural law is not complied with, then while we may have a state, in the sense that we can point to those individuals and groups with a de facto near monopoly over the use of force, we will not have an institutional structure we can point to that might or might not deserve our allegiance over time; we will have only rulers. Noncompliance with ordinary law that applies to government has a similar effect, if extensive and flagrant enough. Any law that applies to a branch of government is an instance of the structure of the political order in operation. If the legislature legally can control the executive, within some areas, or there are constitutional limits on executive power, then those are defining features of the system. If we, the subjects of that system, cannot count on the executive to comply with law that applies to it, we cannot properly assess our reasons for supporting the overall political coercive order. The grounds for political obligation become opaque.

[66] Hans Kelsen, *General Theory of Law and State* (Transaction Publishers 2006).

These remarks concern legal duties that apply to officials in their official capacity, rather than as private individuals. The instrumental case for compliance with law that applies to a person in his private capacity is perhaps also stronger for those who happen to be high officials than it is for the rest of us, but this difference is not the one to which I am attaching so much importance.[67] It should also be noted that in arguing for a strong instrumental moral case for officials in the executive branch to follow the law that applies to them in their official capacity, there is no suggestion that these officials ought to *enforce* the law in all particulars as against individuals. There are familiar and plausible reasons the executive should, in accordance with law, due process, and so on, exercise discretion in the enforcement of law.[68]

Consider next the legislature, and constitutional restrictions on valid legislation. If judicial review is not available, and the executive branch regards itself as bound to enforce law that is not struck down by the judicial branch, then the law will not be complied with unless majorities in the legislature constrain themselves. Once again, law here determines the basic institutional structure of the state. There is only one subject of this part of the law, and if it ignores the law or gives it little weight, then the institutional structure is changed.

Last, that the judicial branch should resolve disputes according to law, in all but the most extreme circumstances—such as would warrant an attempt to undermine a grossly unjust or illegitimate system from within—is not something that needs much argument. What else should it be doing?

Prima facie duties can always be outweighed by unusual circumstances that provide a moral case for failing to comply. Perhaps during times of emergency the executive might justifiably flout settled law about the formal political process required in the conduct of war and about the means that may permissibly be used. The point is that the case in favor not only has to be strong on its own terms; it must also overcome the extremely powerful instrumental case in favor of governmental compliance with the law. We should not, I believe, become too exercised about these "exceptions." We should regard them for what they are, if they

---

[67] The greater instrumental case for compliance by officials considered in their private capacity is analogous to that for prominent nonofficial "leaders of society." See Raz, *The Authority of Law*, 237–8, on the Archbishop of Canterbury.

[68] I am grateful here to Barbara Fried.

are: morally justified violations of law. Similarly, though there is considerable theoretical interest in figuring out the proper way to understand the legal regulation of emergency executive power, where the law itself suspends part of the law, in particular the prospects of maintaining the rule of law in such a context, none of this should affect the main conclusion that, barring unusual circumstances, members of the three branches of government have very strong instrumental reason to comply with law.

So even without considering the issue of character, we find a strong case for states to comply with law. The argument does, however, carry over to the motives and dispositions that officials would best have. The temptation to violate law, especially within the executive branch, is surely often very strong, and on occasion grounded in the best of aims. There is much to be said in favor and little to be said against a very strong standing disposition to comply—since true emergencies in their nature provide effective notice that the standing grounds for compliance may in this case be outweighed by other factors.

Now a typical reaction of the wise skeptic at this point would be to point out that, yes, it's all very well, but official lawlessness is widespread and the mere conclusion that governments ought to obey the law doesn't mean that they will. Of course that is so. And so it is of course extremely valuable to investigate the purely prudential reasons that may explain official submission to unenforced law. Even without complex modeling and speculation about the motives of officials, it is clear enough as a matter of common sense that officials frequently have strong self-interested reasons to comply with the law. They turn on reputation, the ability to secure their "policy aims," and so on.[69] Moreover, wise constitutional designers from Madison on have been concerned to create institutional structures that will enhance the prudential reasons officials have for compliance. All of this might suggest that, although there is no institutional enforcement in the literal sense as against officials, in many or most legal systems, the incentives will be arranged such that officials will typically have very strong prudential reasons for compliance. It may be appropriate to regard this kind of deliberate adjusting of prices attached to choices as a kind of enforcement.

None of this undermines the central importance of determining whether, morally speaking, officials ought to comply.

[69] Daryl Levinson, "Parchment and Politics," *Harvard Law Review* 124 (2011): 657.

It is worth noting that much of the "positive" literature on compliance simply takes for granted that moral motivations will not be sufficient explanation for official compliance. The quest then is to produce more or less ingenious models that explain why nonetheless officials for the most part do comply. Properly understood, this literature asks a hypothetical question: Assuming that a desire or decision to do the right thing isn't the answer, why do officials comply? The truth is that we simply do not know why officials comply with the law when they do; common sense, however, would suggest that a sense of moral duty plays a considerable role, much of the time.[70] That this motive should be shored up by clever constitutional design that attempts to align interest with compliance goes without saying.

I have emphasized the importance of government compliance with law, even in the absence of judicial determinations of the law's content. Given that the content of law is not always immediately clear, in such cases government may cloak noncompliance with disingenuous legal interpretation. This has been the subject of some debate in the United States in the wake of the "Torture Memos" during the administration of President George W. Bush. Various proposals have been made for non-court but independent bodies whose role it would be to determine the content of law as it applies to government.[71] In the current US context, such a proposal may make a great deal of sense, but this is not the place to pursue these issues. We should remember that even if actual courts were always available to declare the content of the law as it applied to the other two branches, the issue of compliance would remain alive.

8. THE DUTY TO OBEY GLOBAL LAW

The duty of states to obey international law, or of any subject to obey any kind of global law, is instrumental; subjects should obey when it will do good, and because it will.

Among the deontological arguments for a duty to obey domestic law discussed in the previous sections, the argument from democratic process

---

[70] Though see Frederick Schauer for a more skeptical view: "When and How (If at All) Does Law Constrain Official Action?" *Georgia Law Review* 44 (2010): 769; Schauer, "The Political Risks (If Any) of Breaking the Law," *Journal of Legal Analysis* 4 (2012): 83.

[71] See, for example, Bruce Ackerman, *The Decline and Fall of the American Republic* (HUP 2010).

and associative obligations evidently would fare worse in the global than the national context.

However, the consent argument fares better, at least for international law. This is because, unlike in the domestic case, it can at least be argued with a straight face that states are not subject to international obligations that they have not expressly consented to. In the case of customary law, the argument relies on the doctrine of the persistent objector. Despite the fact that objecting is no doubt onerous, to infer implicit consent from the failure to object is hardly absurd in the context of the relations among states, not to be compared to Locke's idea that my presence on the king's highway counts as implicit consent.

The doctrine of the persistent objector may itself not be terribly secure.[72] But there are other elements of international legal doctrine that in the end clearly undermine the claim that international law imposes no obligation without consent. There is the idea of *jus cogens*, preemptory law that states cannot contract out of. More secure doctrinally speaking is the exception Hart focused on in his discussion of this issue: new states are taken to be subject to customary law as it exists at the time they come into existence. Last, international organizations such as the Security Council have taken on legislative roles that were arguably never anticipated in the original treaties.

In any event, the factual basis of the consent argument has never been its gravest weakness. The more important point is that there is more at stake with the global legal order than that the valuable practice of honoring international commitments should be supported. It is true that this is a valuable practice, both for each state and for people collectively. But just as the moral stakes of a president's compliance with law are hardly exhausted by the fact that he took an oath of office, there are much stronger reasons for a state to comply with international law than those that flow from any promise or expression of consent.

Another way to bring out the point is to consider the distinction between treaties and "soft-law" agreements that parties explicitly describe as not legally binding. If consent is the basis for the duty to obey, it applies equally in both cases. Since this is not the way participants in the system think of it, something has gone wrong. Of course soft-law agreements

---

[72] Hugh Thirlway, "The Sources of International Law," in Malcolm D. Evans (ed.), *International Law* (2nd edn, OUP 2006), 127.

impose obligations; the basis of that obligation is the importance of the practice of making and keeping international agreements. But something more is going on with the obligation to obey the law.

Though consent is not the ground of states' obligations to obey international law, the fact that most states have in fact consented to most of international law is, nonetheless, very important. The moral significance of the fact of consent lies not with its generation of a duty to obey, but in providing an element of accountability.[73] Of course, lawmaking by way of treaty is hardly to be thought of as a globally democratic legislative process, but the possibility of a state refusing to sign up adds considerably to the legitimacy of calling noncompliers to account and applying sanctions. The role of consent in international law is thus politically very significant, even though it is not the basis of states' duty to obey.

In the case of domestic law, the basis of the obligation to obey the law, where it exists, is the political obligation to support the institutions of the state. In the case of international law, the obligation is to support beneficial international institutions and beneficial coordinated state practices. That general compliance (supposing the content of the law isn't too bad) is generally speaking good seems hard to deny. International humanitarian law has arguably been enormously important in disciplining the conduct of war. To have a settled law of the sea that is usually complied with, even if it is less than fully just, is clearly preferable to having no law of the sea at all. Similarly the content of international environmental law is hardly what it needs to be, but to have international environmental law at all is a precondition of having good law. It wouldn't be a wise strategy to refuse to comply until law with the right content came about, since other states will have different views about what content is right.

In the case of individual subjects of domestic law, as we saw, the fact that general compliance is better than general noncompliance does not translate into an instrumental duty of obedience to all law all the time. But in the case of international law, it comes close to doing that. In part this is because of the weakness of the enforcement mechanisms available in international law. The more compliance is in effect voluntary, the more harm noncompliance may do. But it is also just a matter of numbers.

---

[73] Allen Buchanan & Robert O. Keohane, "The Legitimacy of Global Governance Institutions," *Ethics and International Affairs* 20 (2006): 405.

The situation is not as stark as the one I described for domestic law that applies to branches of government, where only one person or body may be the subject of the law. But there are very few states, relatively speaking, and individual acts of noncompliance by one or a handful of the two hundred odd states could and can make a very significant difference to the practice of compliance. It would seem to be especially important that states that can get away with illegality in self-interested terms should comply. The signal that noncompliance by powerful states sends—that only the weak or the foolish would follow the law if noncompliance were better in self-interested terms—is particularly destructive.

The moral case for compliance with international law, then, is simple. With so few legal subjects, each act of noncompliance has a reasonable chance of being part of a pattern of increasing noncompliance that snowballs into a situation where compliance is no longer the norm. The fact that self-interest may usually counsel compliance does not undermine this point. For the lower the overall level of compliance, the less considerations of reputation and so on will counsel compliance on self-interested grounds. Those who argue that there is never a moral duty for states to obey international law must believe that a world without international law would be as good as a world with it. They must believe that the world goes no worse if each state decides for itself what seems right and proper, rather than constraining itself to shared standards of conduct while trying to improve the content of those standards. It goes without saying that the current content of international law and the process of its making both fall way short of feasible alternatives. But to say that states should comply with international law as it now is because that will make the world better need involve no illusions about our nonideal world and is fully compatible with recognizing that the content of the law may be bad enough in a particular case that the benefits of noncompliance outweigh the harms.

9. THE FOCAL CASE: LAW FOR STATES

Though the reasons are quite different for domestic and international law, and though the case is stronger for domestic law, we can conclude that "law for states"[74] typically has stronger moral force than what is usually the case for domestic law applying to individual subjects.

---

[74] See Goldsmith & Levinson, "Law for States."

The upshot is that conventional thinking about what is the focal case of law, the municipal legal system effectively enforcing law as against individual subjects, is very misleading. It pushes to the margins law for states, both domestic and international. Since a central reason for being concerned about the content of law in the first place is that there are moral reasons to obey it, our focal case should to the contrary be that of the underenforced or unenforced law that applies to states.[75]

[75] This article draws on Liam Murphy, *What Makes Law* (CUP 2014), 109–43, 175–82 (copyright held by Cambridge University Press 2014, reproduced with permission). I am grateful to Sacha Baniel-Stark and Erick Rabin for excellent research assistance. The support of the Filomen D'Agostino and Max E. Greenberg Research Fund of New York University School of Law is gratefully acknowledged.

4

The Authority of Hate Speech

RAE LANGTON

I. HATE SPEECH AS DOING THINGS WITH WORDS

When we speak, we 'do things with words', and often we do things with words to people: advise them, marry them, warn them, and more, as J.L. Austin observed. Our topic here is hate speech, a category absent from Austin's otherwise generous catalogues.[1] But his insight that *saying is doing* applies to hate speech, as much as to anything else. When hate speech is minimized, or psychologized, shrunk down to expression of unpopular ideas, or injury of sensitive feelings, it is worth recalling that 'the harm in hate speech' involves its force as a speech act: it is in large part 'performative', as Jeremy Waldron, among others, has recently agreed.[2]

What is done with words can depend on patterns of authority. An Alabama slave law said, in 1861, that slaves are people and things: as 'rational human beings, they are capable of committing crimes; and in reference to acts which are crimes, are regarded as persons', but 'because they are slaves, they are incapable of performing civil acts, and, in reference

---

[1] Austin 1962. I am grateful to the organizers and participants of the Analytic Legal Philosophy Conference 2014 in Oxford, where I was 'Special Guest', and benefited enormously from the lively and forceful discussion of an early draft. I am also grateful to audiences in Graz in 2016, and Paris 2017 at the 'République des Savoirs', École Normale Supérieure. The essay's companion piece is 'Blocking as Counter-speech' (2018); versions of both are in my John Locke Lectures, given in 2015, publication forthcoming. For earlier work on authoritative speech acts and accommodation, see Langton 1993; Langton 2012; Langton 2017; and Langton and West (1999).

[2] Waldron 2012, 166, agreeing explicitly with MacKinnon 1993, and implicitly perhaps with other work including Altman 1993; Anderson et al. 2010; Butler 1997; Langton 1993; McGowan 2009; Maitra 2012; Matsuda et al. 1993; Schwartzman 2002; Tirrell 2012. To consider a performative aspect to hate speech is not to be guilty of 'febrile theorizing', as some have suggested (Heinze 2016, 75, 167), nor to deify the hate speaker, as Butler suggests (1997); see also Langton 2009.

Oxford Studies in Philosophy of Law Volume 3. John Gardner, Leslie Green, and Brian Leiter (eds)
This chapter © Rae Langton 2018. First published in 2018 by Oxford University Press

to all such, they are things, not persons'.[3] The law turned people into property that could be bought and sold, like things, and sent to jail, like rational human beings. The harm in slave law depended, in part, on its authority. This illustrates Catharine MacKinnon's observation:

> Together with all its material supports, authoritatively saying someone is inferior is largely how structures of status and differential treatment are demarcated and actualized. Words and images are how people are placed in hierarchies, how social stratification is made to seem inevitable and right, how feelings of inferiority and superiority are engendered, and how indifference to violence against those on the bottom is rationalized and normalized.[4]

Certain authoritative sayings can subordinate social groups, placing people in hierarchies, depriving them of powers and rights, and legitimating certain treatment of them. Such harms are achieved, in part, through the authority of the saying.[5]

If a law could subordinate by 'authoritatively saying someone is inferior', could hate speech ever do likewise? Hate speech often says that 'someone is inferior', whether authoritatively or not. One form of hate speech is assaultive, its addressee being the target of hatred. These are 'words that wound', as Richard Delgado puts it. They convey, according to Mari Matsuda, a 'message of inferiority', 'directed against a historically oppressed group', that is 'persecutory, hateful and degrading'.[6] Another form of hate speech is propaganda, its addressee being the recruit to hatred. Such propaganda attempts to 'justify or promote racial hatred and discrimination', as the 1965 UN Convention puts it, based on 'ideas or theories of superiority of one race or group of persons of one colour or ethnic origin'; to incite 'racial discrimination', or 'acts of violence...against any race or group of persons of another colour or ethnic origin'.[7] (An utterance of hate speech might have both roles, addressing targets and recruits.)

---

[3] Catterall 1926, 247; discussed also in Anderson et al. 2012. Not all speech acts, or 'illocutionary acts' are performative, but I do not do justice to those distinctions here.

[4] MacKinnon 1993, 31.

[5] This understanding of subordination is proposed in Langton 1993; 2009. Given our focus on bad authority structures, we shall not here be unpacking authority in terms of 'reasons'.

[6] Delgado 1993; Matsuda 1993, 36.

[7] United Nations 1965. 'Incitement' deserves more attention than I give it here, but I would interpret it as a kind of directive, rather than the (perlocutionary) production of certain effects.

It is worth observing that the Alabama slave law meets both those descriptions of hate speech, though it would not be normally be described as assaultive or propagandizing. Yet the slave law matches Matsuda's description: it conveyed a message of inferiority, directed against a historically oppressed group, that was persecutory, hateful, and degrading; and it would be an understatement to say these were 'words that wound'. It matches the UN description: the slave law was based on an ideas or theories of superiority of one race or group of persons of one colour or ethnic origin, and attempted to justify and promote racial discrimination. Our question here is not whether a law could be hate speech, however. It is whether hate speech could be like a law: whether hate speech could have authority, and if so, of what kind, and from what source.

Hate speech can have authority, I shall argue. I begin with a sketch (Section 2), and then fill in the detail. We shall need to pull authority down from its ivory tower, to confront non-ideal circumstances (Section 3), and bring out the relativity of authority to a subject domain, to a jurisdiction, and to rival authorities (Section 4). To treat authority in a non-ideal and relative way is not to oust the topic of 'legitimate' authority, only its exclusive demand on our attention. If authority is 'a feature of roles embedded in practices', as Scott Hershowitz has said, then whether some authority is justified will depend on whether the practice is justified.[8] We may need to bear in mind the less ideal and the more, to capture the harm in hate speech, and see how actual authority patterns fail by the light of something better.

Hate speech can have epistemic and practical authority: its words can be verdicts that tell someone how things are, and directives that tell someone what to do (Section 5). 'Epistemic authority' is authority for belief, including 'theoretical authority' or expertise; and also credibility.[9] Its characteristic speech act is a 'verdictive', a judgement that something is so. 'Practical authority' is authority for action, and its characteristic speech act is an 'exercitive': a directive, or an enactment of status—'a

---

[8] Hershovitz 2011, 11, 18. This applies *mutatis mutandis* to authority not based on roles.
[9] Besides expertise and credibility, I take epistemic authority to include certain knowledge-related skills, intellectual, perceptual, and imaginative. Since epistemic authority includes factors other than mastery of theory, I find 'theoretical' a misnomer (cf. Enoch 2012; Green 1989; Raz 1979, 2009).

decision that something is to be so, as distinct from a judgement that it is so', as Austin put it.[10]

The law is a paradigm practical authority, and commands are its paradigm speech acts. Yet the slave law was doing several things with words. It was indeed an exercise of practical authority, a decision that 'something was to be so', creating legal fact: that slaves counted as 'things', that they were required to be so treated. It was also an exercise of epistemic authority, a judgement that 'something was so', reporting an independent fact, that slaves were 'rational human beings'.

Practical and epistemic authority are distinguished by Joseph Raz, who calls the latter 'theoretical authority', and offers a methodological desideratum:

An analysis maximizing the similarities between authority for action and authority for belief is, other things being equal, preferable.[11]

We shall, at least, fulfil this desideratum. Epistemic authority can be practical, as we shall see, and hate speech can direct action with its authority for belief.[12] Moreover, epistemic and practical authority can have a common source.

There are many sources of authority, formal and informal, but I want to focus on authority gained, informally, by default. Authority can be obtained by *accommodation*, a default adjustment that occurs, without fuss, when hearers take on board what speakers presuppose (Section 6). Presupposition accommodation is a familiar phenomenon. Someone says 'Even George could win', presupposing that George is an unpromising candidate. No-one interrupts with a 'Whadda ya mean, "even"?' and the presupposition is taken on board. David Lewis used this example to suggest that conversation, unlike baseball, tends to evolve in a way that makes what is done count as 'correct play'. Acting as if it is your turn in baseball will not make it correct play, if you have just hit three strikes. But acting as if something is correct play in a conversation tends to make

---

[10] Austin 1962, 154, but exercitives need not be decisions in my view. For important work on exercitives and their ubiquity, see McGowan 2003, 2004, though she is interested in permissibility shifts that do not require speaker authority.

[11] Raz 2009, 8.

[12] Slurs and metaphors (e.g. of 'vermin') ease a transition from belief to action. As Lynne Tirrell argues in her study of hate speech in Rwanda, the 'action-engendering' uses of certain slurs—*inyenzi* (cockroach), *inzoka* (snake), in combination with other material social factors, helped, over time, to license non-verbal behaviour and violence (Tirrell 2012).

it correct play, if nobody stops you. Hearers routinely accommodate what speakers presuppose, and the hearer's omission is a quiet engine of the speaker's success.[13]

This applies to authority. Sometimes a speaker will presuppose their authority, and get what they presuppose. Perhaps they start bossing people around, and no-one objects. The hearers' omission need not be *consent* to the authority, though it may be.[14] Whether the hearer's silence is consent or no, a speaker, even a hate speaker, can sometimes acquire authority by presupposing their authority, and their speech act powers can shift accordingly. Accommodation supplies a straightforward way for hate speech to gain authority.

My essay ends with that conclusion, and some remarks (Section 7), but there is unfinished business. Presupposition accommodation contributes to the pragmatics of hate speech in several other ways, besides the endowment of authority.

It enables hate speech to convey implicit content about its targets, as Jason Stanley shows in his study of 'not-at-issue' content in propaganda, looking at how words like 'welfare' or 'inner city' manage to convey 'black'. Hate speech also exploits accommodation in its use of race categories that presuppose natural kinds; its use of unquantified generics that presuppose a shared essence; its use of slurs, metaphors, and thick concepts that presuppose a derogatory evaluation beneath a descriptive shell.[15]

It enables hate speech to normalize hatred or hierarchy, as MacKinnon implied, legitimizing it by presupposing that it is 'normal', in normative and descriptive senses of that term. A hate speaker who 'normalizes' something will often, in effect, 'outsource' the authority to a larger group: to 'the done thing', a supposedly shared social practice, for its practical authority; and to 'the known thing', a supposedly shared common knowledge, for its epistemic authority.[16]

---

[13] Langton 2012; Langton and West 1999; Lewis 1979.

[14] See Langton 2006; Swanson 2017.

[15] Stanley 2015; Langton and West 1999; Langton 2012. I treat these as tools for 'back door speech acts', e.g. of ranking and testimony: see Langton 2018 and forthcoming. See Sbisà 1999 on why presupposition is apt for conveying ideology; on generics, Haslanger 2010, 2014; Leslie 2017; on slurs e.g. Camp 2013; Hom 2008; Hornsby 2001; Swanson forthcoming; Tirrell 2012. I do not do justice to the question whether it is presupposition, conversational implicature, or some other implicit mechanism.

[16] See Langton 2015, 2018, and forthcoming. See Tirrell 2012; Swanson forthcoming; compare McGowan 2012 on how norms get 'triggered' by utterances. See Green 2013 on how the law can itself normalize, i.e. shape, social norms.

It enables hate speech to normalize *itself.* In using hate speech a speaker tends to presuppose it is acceptable to speak about people a certain way.[17] This can be accommodated, and become true, if nobody objects. As hate speech becomes more normal, it gains the informal authority of a social practice, rather than of an individual speaker or institution. The point is familiar to those who have been targets of hate speech. Gina Miller recently wrote:

Over the last year, as the hatred flooded into my inbox, I've watched as perpetrators have discovered a new boldness. They no longer hide under anonymity but openly sign their name. They no longer linger alone in their rooms, or at the end of some bar in a pub; social media amplify their vile voices and create echo chambers that reinforce their views [...] But we must not normalise hatred and intimidation.

She mentions, in this connection, an 'old saying':

Lines of decency are being violated, and as the old saying goes, bad things happen when good people do nothing.[18]

The 'saying' goes back to J.S. Mill that what it takes for evil to succeed is for others to 'look on and do nothing'.[19] It points to the role of omissions, in giving strength to 'evil' norms and authority structures, including this capacity for hate speech to normalize itself. To 'do nothing' can be to accommodate a presupposition of normality, and help build a new normal.

Accommodation enables hate speech to damage justice in other ways: as an agent of testimonial injustice, undermining the credibility of its targets; as an agent of silencing, undermining the speech powers of its targets; and as an agent of doubt, undermining their assurance of justice.[20] But these large topics I leave untouched.

---

[17] Swanson 2017; Tirrell 2012, make versions of this point, Tirrell in terms of an inference that is licensed, Swanson in terms of an acceptability implicature.

[18] Gina Miller, a UK citizen from a Guyanan family, led a successful legal challenge against the UK government's attempt to bypass Parliament in their plans for triggering Brexit. She became the target of a barrage of race and gender hatred, including death threats (Miller 2017).

[19] Mill 1867, 37. Similar sayings have been attributed to Edmund Burke, Abraham Lincoln, and many others.

[20] There is a large literature on these, but see e.g. Fricker 2007 on testimonial injustice; Langton 1993, Hornsby and Langton 1998 on silencing; and Waldron 2012, Langton 2016 on destruction of assurance.

I leave equally untouched the topic of current law and hate speech: whether the law would be justified in restricting, or zoning, hate speech, or giving substantial support for counter-speech.[21] This too is unfinished business; but I offer a brief, inconclusive reflection. The Alabama law would not itself be protected speech, the reason being not (or not only) because it conflicts with equality, but because it is not the relevant sort of speech. Directives, whether legal or informal, are not the sort of speech a free speech principle protects. It is not a free speech right you exercise when you order someone to close the door. A free speech principle does not cover 'situational altering' or 'obligation enacting' utterances, which, to a significant degree, alter someone's obligations or institutional status, or so it has been argued by Kent Greenawalt, Ishani Maitra, and Mary Kate McGowan.[22] My conclusion bears on that debate. If directives are not covered by a free speech principle, there is a question whether hate propaganda is covered, considering not only whether it conflicts with equality, but whether it is the relevant sort of speech in the first place.

These topics are postponed, with the excuse that the present argument is part of a larger one. What happens with the authority of hate speech is part of a broader pattern, the theme of my John Locke Lectures, in which unjust norms and authority structures are built by everyday speech acts, accommodated by everyday hearers and bystanders. Fortunately, better ones are built that way too, but they sometimes need some help.[23]

2. A SKETCH, WITH A REMINDER

Few would deny that hate speech has had authority in the past, even if the authority of hate speech and slave law are not the same. The UN Convention was drafted in recognition of the danger posed by the authority of some hate speech. Julius Streicher advocated a 'Holy Hate'

---

[21] See e.g. Gelber 2003 on state support for counter-speech; on zoning, see Langton 2009 (Introduction), and 2010.

[22] A free speech principle does not cover 'dominantly and substantially situation altering utterances' (Greenawalt 1989) or 'significantly obligation enacting utterances' (Maitra and McGowan 2007). There are important differences between their views. I do not mean to suggest that these authors would endorse the conclusion that hate speech would, for this reason, not be covered.

[23] Langton 2018 and forthcoming.

in *Der Stürmer* over many years, and published an essay with that title in 1943:

If we do not oppose the Jews with the entire energy of our people, we are lost. But if we can use the full force of our soul that has been released by the National Socialist revolution, we need not fear the future. The devilish hatred of the Jews plunged the world into war, need and misery. Our holy hate will bring us victory and save all of mankind.[24]

The harm in Streicher's hate speech was held to be a capital offence at the Nuremberg trials, and the Convention's commitments were informed by the gravity of that harm.

Streicher published a series of works directed to, and sometimes authored by, children. He loaned his state-sponsored megaphone to a child's school 'composition' in 1935. The child wrote:

The Jews are our misfortune. Regrettably, there are still many people today who say: Even the Jews are creatures of God. Therefore you must respect them. But we say: Vermin are animals too, but we exterminate them just the same. The Jew is a mongrel. He has hereditary tendencies from Aryans, Asiatics, Negroes, and from the Mongolians. Evil always preponderates in the case of a mongrel.[25]

Streicher urged young readers to mistrust their Jewish neighbours, in a rhyming title of 1935/6:

> *Trau keinem Fuchs auf grüner Heid*
> *Und keinem Jud bei seinem Eid*

('Don't trust a fox in a green meadow or the word of a Jew'.) The booklet went to seven editions, with a hundred thousand copies in circulation. A 1934 issue of *Der Stürmer* published a drawing of Jews extracting blood from childish corpses, one of a series which propagated the 'blood libel' that Christian children were ongoing targets of ritual murder. In *Der Giftpilz* (1938), the title story depicts a mother and son looking for mushrooms in the forest:

Just as it is often hard to tell a toadstool from an edible mushroom, so too it is often very hard to recognize the Jew as a swindler and a criminal.

---

[24] Streicher 1943; see also Bytwerk 1983. (The essay was written by Ernst Hiemer.) For an insightful philosophical examination of some of this material and its impact, see Altman 2012.
[25] Cited in Mann 1938.

In other stories, Hans and Else are offered sweets by an ominous hooked-nosed stranger, and virtuous Inge is assaulted by a leering Jewish doctor. Streicher compared 'the Jew' to a mongrel dog, a supplanting cuckoo, a hyena, a deceptive chameleon, a blood-sucking bedbug, a poisonous snake, a tapeworm, and a deadly bacterium.[26]

I begin this sketch with a historic reminder, to recall the point of thinking about the authority of hate speech. I focus on Streicher's publications because they seem a clear case of hate speech that had, at one time, authority. There is a more cowardly reason: their historic role, and the sheer passing of time, have made them an object of scholarship, and somehow easier to discuss than contemporary manifestations of hate speech. In this section we shall take a first look at how hate speech could have or acquire practical and epistemic authority, aided by the acts and omissions of hearers who themselves have, or lack, authority; and how omissions, in particular, aid the acquisition of authority, through presupposition accommodation.

Der Stürmer was an exercise of epistemic authority, since it had local credibility, even if it lacked expertise. Its role was, in the first instance, epistemic: its masthead proclaimed its dedication to 'the fight for truth'.[27] By contrast, the Alabama slave law was, mostly, an exercise of practical authority.

Yet hate propaganda is practical too, which is no surprise. *Authority for belief may be practical*, as Raz observes. A doctor has an ability to prescribe, based on his epistemic authority, which includes expertise and credibility.[28] We can add that a *quack* doctor's ability to prescribe is likewise based on his epistemic authority, in this case his credibility alone. This has implications for hate speech, whose force can depend on a comparable relationship between practical and epistemic authority. *Der Stürmer* tells its readers what to believe, and what to do: 'the Jew is untrustworthy' was diagnosis *and* prescription—'don't trust the Jew!'

While we are tracking similarities, as Raz advised, we can note that *practical and epistemic authority can have the same source*. Practical and epistemic authority, construed as credibility, may be acquired through

---

[26] Streicher 1938.
[27] 'Wochenblatt zum Kampfe um die Wahrheit', see e.g. Bytwerk 1983, 79; it did not gain Nazi support immediately; the story of its acquisition of authority is a complex one, more complex than I do justice to here.
[28] Raz 2009, 8.

the acts or omissions of other parties, from those who have authority, and from those who lack it. Here is where accommodation comes in.

To illustrate I borrow, and adapt, a series of vignettes from Ishani Maitra. Suppose a teacher decrees a pupil to be 'in charge' of the class, or to be 'the expert' of the class; or simply turns a blind eye to her bossy or know-it-all activities. In such a case the pupil's authority, practical or epistemic, is 'derived', she says, from the acts or omissions of someone who has special authority. Or suppose a pupil takes herself to be 'in charge', or to be 'the expert', and other pupils go along with it, in the absence of a teacher. In such a case the pupil's authority, practical or epistemic, is 'licensed', she says, by the acts or omissions of someone who lacks special authority.

I adapt Maitra's examples to include epistemic authority, and this needs comment. Acquiring the role of 'the expert' is not enough, of course, for *being* an expert. The examples of epistemic authority are about credibility, not expertise. By contrast, being put 'in charge' may be enough for being in charge. Notwithstanding these differences, for the student to be 'the expert', or to be 'in charge', is, I take it, for her to acquire authority, via the acts or omissions of others, to perform speech acts she would not otherwise have been able to perform.

Maitra draws conclusions for hate speech.[29] Suppose a black family wakes to find a burning cross on their lawn, and the culprits are unknown. Suppose the community leaders fail to denounce this action, and fail to express sympathy for the family. The cross-burning acquires, she says, a 'derived' practical authority. Just as the teacher confers derived authority on the bossy pupil, when she turns a blind eye, so these leaders, through their omissions, confer derived authority on the burners of the cross.

Or suppose, on a New Jersey subway, an Arab woman is addressed by an older white man with a string of abuse: 'F***in' terrorist, go home. We don't need your kind here.' Other passengers don't intervene. In this case, there is no role-based institutional authority in the picture, as there was the teacher, or the community leaders. Yet the racist speaker—like the

---

[29] Maitra 2012. She concludes that hate speech can therefore subordinate. Besides extending to epistemic authority I have altered her example of 'licensed' authority to make it a version of the classroom scene. For an insightful discussion of the omissions in her examples, and their possible force, see Swanson 2017.

bossy pupil when her peers do not object—acquires, to a certain degree, a 'licensed' practical authority, in virtue of the passengers' omissions.[30]

Maitra's examples (and my adaptations) bring out a contrast between derived or licensed authority, which accrues to a speaker from the contributions of authoritative or non-authoritative hearers, respectively; and they illustrate a role for omissions in supplying authority, both practical and epistemic.

The teacher's explicit decree, endowing the pupil with authority, would be an old-fashioned Austinian performative. Austin had much to say about the conferral and removal of authority via more or less ceremonial speech acts: performances of marriage, knighting, and coronation confer it, performances of firing and condemning to penal servitude remove it. By such explicit decrees a racist legal system could gain practical authority, or a racist propaganda machine could gain epistemic authority. But what of authority acquired by *omission*, for example, of the teacher or the students, of the city council or the fellow passengers. Do these 'eloquent silences' in informal contexts amount to speech acts that *authorize* certain speakers?[31]

If the silences were to express consent, that would be a familiar mode of authorizing a speaker. For many hearers of hate speech, that will more or less fit the case. For many recruits, hate speech will receive an enthusiastic welcome, with its flattering incentives to join the tribe of superiors, the tribe of us-against-them, the tribe of the knowing initiates, the tribe of the sainted martyrs. Propagandistic hate speech aggrandizes the hearer, often, as well as the speaker. Propaganda's message of *their* '*inferiority*' described by Matsuda and the 1965 UN Convention is also a message of '*our' superiority*, the superiority of a 'we' that includes both speaker and hearer. Such hearers quickly become fellow speakers, whose response is no longer silence, but a thumbs-up 'Like', an instant 'Share', expanding exponentially the initial weight of authority, as Miller described. Hate speech, for some, will not be an alien imposition like the law, but more like pornography, an ecstasy of loathing eagerly sought

---

[30] I have adapted her example—see note 29. Maitra uses other examples to illustrate licensed authority: a hike planner (comparable to Thomason's restaurant planner), and a driver who takes the initiative to direct traffic around a crash. Maitra does not take her examples to illustrate accommodation (personal correspondence).

[31] Langton 2006; Swanson 2017. One question here is whether the omission functions as default uptake, or as itself performative.

out, a Trojan Horse dragged willingly through the doorways of the mind.[32] Such hearers ardently crown hate speech with authority, avidly form part of its jurisdiction, and zealously seek to increase it.

The examples just considered, however, are not like this. The omissions described do not express consent, nor need they be read as speech acts at all. The teacher and the civic leaders turn a blind eye, the passengers listen to a racist tirade in uncertain, or appalled, silence. Nevertheless authority accrues to the speaker, to some degree. How? Not, I think, because silence counts as, or appears to be, consent, in such a context; but because authority is accrued simply through the omission.[33] The omission, whatever its motive, is a *failure to block* what is presupposed. The authority, in the omissive examples, is gained through accommodation.

This would be an instance of a more general phenomenon: within limits, a speaker tends to get what they presuppose, if nobody stops them. Richmond Thomason illustrates accommodation with a comparable example, in the context of indecision about dinner plans:

Someone takes charge, asks for suggestions about restaurants, decides on one, and asks someone to get two cabs while she calls to make reservations. When no one objects to this arrangement, she became the group leader, and obtained a certain authority. She did this by acting as if she had the authority.

The leader 'obtained' a certain authority, by acting 'as if' she had it: she presupposed her authority, and when nobody blocked that presupposition, she obtained authority via accommodation. The social world, unlike the inanimate world, can be accommodating.

Acting as if we don't have a flat tire won't repair the flat; acting as if we know the way to our destination won't get us there. Unless we believe in magic, the inanimate world is not accommodating. But people can be accommodating, and in fact there are many social situations in which the best way to get what we want is to act as if we already had it.[34]

The social world can sometimes be accommodating, especially when helped along by background expectations. There is a familiar connection

See Langton 2017 for discussion of this aspect of pornography.

[33] On illocutionary force of silences, and how they themselves can be silenced, see Langton 2006; Pettit 1994; Swanson 2017.

[34] Thomason 1990, 342; cf. von Fintel 2008. The inanimate world *can* sometimes be accommodating, contrary to Thomason, but that is another topic.

between social hierarchy, and the presuppositions that speakers introduce, and that hearers accommodate. One speaker might bring 'a sense of entitlement', another is 'to the manner born'. Getting 'what we want' by acting 'as if we already had it' is a fair description of much that is good and bad in social life, from the building of friendship and intimacy, to the building of privilege. It is also, I suggest, a fair description of the building of authority, in some circumstances, for hate speech.[35]

We shall take a closer look at this in a moment, but we need to address a more basic question. Some readers might wonder whether this deserves the name 'authority' at all.

3. AUTHORITY FOR 'LOW TYPES' AND NON-IDEAL CONTEXTS

The suggestion that hate speech could have authority may seem absurd for two reasons. The first concerns the nature of authority. You might think that the slave law itself had no genuine practical authority. The slave law falsely claimed authority, and was falsely taken to have it. The law possessed merely 'effective' or de facto authority, so that slaves were never really things to be bought and sold. The law lacked legitimacy, so it lacked authority, in the proper *de jure* sense of that term. Extending this thought, *Der Stürmer* likewise had no genuine epistemic authority, though it purported to have it. In reality it likewise possessed merely 'effective' or de facto epistemic authority, if we may describe epistemic authority in such terms.

We can give this response its due. In some ultimate sense, the law lacked authority, and so did *Der Stürmer*, but that is not the sense we are after. With regard to epistemic authority, we are focusing on *credibility*, which *Der Stürmer* possessed, despite its lack of knowledge or expertise; and as for practical authority, we are not setting our sights very high.

We are not pursuing, here, an ideal theory of authority, investigating what is required for ultimate legitimacy. If we regard authority as a noble source of distinctive reasons, hate speech will never fit the bill. If we place authority on a pedestal, and hate speech in the gutter, our question—'Can hate speech have authority?'—will get an easy, and negative, answer.

---

[35] See von Fintel 2008 on the accommodation of intimacy, especially in languages where it is mediated by the familiar second person pronoun such as 'tu' or 'du'. William James comments in similar vein on love and friendship (James 1896). See also Langton forthcoming.

But that would be too hasty. As Charles Mills has argued, ideal theories can obscure injustice; and this applies to authority, as to much else.[36] Authority is often 'a feature of roles embedded in practices', in Hershovitz's phrase, and those practices will not always be good ones. Our topic is not idealized authority, but something closer to home: structures of social authority, relative to practices, which enable the enactment of norms and hierarchies that are socially real—whether or not they exist in Plato's heaven, or the better neighbourhoods of Earth.[37]

The second reason concerns the nature of hate speech. You might allow that a slave law could have authority, but hate speech could not. The hate speaker lacks the requisite role or stature. The hate speaker is in this sense like Austin's 'low type', in his story about the naming of a ship. The authorized official waits, champagne in hand, ready to name the ship 'The Queen Elizabeth'. All of a sudden, a low type rushes up, grabs the bottle, and smashes it, shouting 'I hereby name this ship "The Generalissimo Stalin"'. We would all agree, said Austin, that it would be 'an infernal shame'—and that the low type had not named the ship.

The hate speaker may seem a low type, if anyone does, when we bear in mind the anonymous graffitist who sprays on a New Jersey wall, 'Muslims and 9/11! Don't serve them, don't speak to them, and don't let them in!';[38] the anonymous Twitter user who sends rape threats to classicist Mary Beard, and splices pornography onto images of her face;[39] the sorry character who writes a poisonous letter to baseball star Hank Aaron:

Dear N—Henry, You are [not] going to break this record [for home runs] established by the great Babe Ruth if you can help it [...] Whites are far more superior than jungle bunnies [...] My gun is watching your every black move.[40]

It is routine to assume that hate speakers lack authority. Waldron's study, for all its sympathy to hate speech legislation, casts the hate speaker as a detested lone wolf, an exception to the rule of a happy and shared egalitarian commitment. Judith Butler ridicules the idea that hate speech could have authority, suggesting it attributes a quasi-divine power to the

---

[36] Mills 2005, building on O'Neill 1987. He rejects the 'ideal' as a model, holding on to the 'ideal' as normative.
[37] Hershovitz 2011, 11, writing of the role-based authority an individual may have.
[38] Waldron 2012.
[39] Beard 2014.
[40] Kennedy 2002.

hate speaker.[41] It is tempting to regard hate speakers as embittered, marginal figures, who reach for the 'words that wound', precisely because they lack authority. On this picture, a comparison between hate speech and racist law could never be apt.

We can give this response its due as well. There are stark limits to the comparison. The authority of hate speech is unlike the law in kind and degree, and it would be grotesque to suggest otherwise. We may consider parallels with hate speech without questioning the unique gravity of slave law. Moreover, unlike the law, certain features of hate speech may allow it to wound *even without authority*. This would not render our inquiry otiose, if authority would aggravate its wounds.

Hate speech might wound without authority, because other factors contribute to its force: the oppressive history of slurs, and the power of words to invoke and retrieve that history;[42] the 'truthiness' of danger and conspiracy claims, got from a seeming-truth of the content, not the seeming-trustworthiness of the speaker;[43] the attention-grabbing, evidence-resisting power of lurid rumours, whatever their source;[44] the word-transcending power of graphic images to shape attitudes; the ambiguity of unquantified generics, reifying danger or inferiority, tarring too many with a too-sweeping brush.[45] Hate speech may work to alter perception itself, so that we literally come to see our fellows as dehumanized or animal-like, literally hear them as shifty, contemptible, or dangerous.[46] Unlike the law, the harm in hate speech dwells partly in factors independent of its authority.

Hate speech is unlike the law in a further respect. Hate speech is about *hate*, and this makes it gut-wrenchingly different to the cool discriminatory speech of a legal enactment.[47] It involves the feelings of speaker, and of hearer. It expresses a speaker's emotions and attitudes, so vividly

---

[41] Butler 1997; for response Langton 2009.

[42] McGowan 2012; Matsuda 1993; Tirrell 2012. There is a large philosophical literature on slurs, but hate speech need not be slurring. See Anderson et al. 2012.

[43] Langton, forthcoming.

[44] There is a large social science literature but see Berinsky 2017 for a recent study of how attempts to scotch rumours backfire, with further references. (Note also the 'Streisand effect', Simpson in progress).

[45] Anderson et al. 2012; Haslanger 2011, 2014; Langton 2012; Leslie 2017.

[46] See Siegel 2017 on 'hijacked perception', of which this would be an instance (she discusses racially biased perception of an item as a gun).

[47] For an attempt to do justice to the appeals of hate speech to emotion and desire, as opposed to belief, see Langton 2012.

indeed that it may seem that this is *all* it does.[48] Besides expressing
feelings, hate speech *provokes* feelings. It invites an emotional response,
as well as a cognitive and practical one. It tells someone what to feel, as
well as what to believe, and what to do. Its effects—its perlocutionary
goals, in Austin's terms—include hatred, for some hearers, pain and fear
for others. Hate speech harnesses horror and disgust in ways that go
beyond our topic, and beyond simple hierarchy. How the harnessing of
emotion can help enact inequality is a large question, and I shall not
offer adequate answers.

Such problems are independent of authority: but authority would
surely exacerbate them. A vicious slur, a 'truthy' rumour, a misleading
generic, a hate-filled tirade—these will be all the more wounding.
Whatever else 'the harm in hate speech', it will be the worse when hate
speech has authority. So let us proceed, insisting that authority matters
still, even if other things matter too.

4. AUTHORITY AS RELATIVE

There is a relativity to authority, thus conceived. Practical and epistemic
authority are relative, on three dimensions: to a subject domain, to a
jurisdiction, and to comparative rivals.[49] The slave law had practical
authority on these three dimensions. Its authority was relative to a certain domain or subject matter: it was about a group of people, and how
they should be treated. It had a certain jurisdiction: it was binding in
Alabama, at a certain time in history. And its authority was strong, in
comparison to rival authorities: it was more binding than, say, the rules
of a club or church.

Nazi propaganda had epistemic authority, on these three dimensions.
It was relative to a certain domain or subject matter: it was about a
group of people, and what they were like. Its Nazi endorsement enabled
it to masquerade as testimony, conveying expert knowledge of a Jewish
menace. It had a certain jurisdiction: it was credible for certain readers,

---

[48] Hence the focus of philosophical attention on the expressive function of slurs; again, I do
not do justice to the large literature on this: see Anderson et al. 2012.

[49] For relativity of authority to jurisdiction, see Green 1998; Hornsby and Langton 1998;
for its relativity to domain, jurisdiction, and contrast class, see Langton 2017. Such relativity
would not imply subjectivism or anti-realism (any more than would a comparable relativity in
baseball).

and not others, aiming especially at the young. And its authority was strong, in comparison to rival authorities: it was more credible than alternatives, in part because there were not many alternatives.

This pattern of relative authority is familiar in philosophical debate about pornography. In response to some who doubt that pornography could have authority, it has been argued that pornography has authority relative to a certain domain, the topic of sex; to a certain jurisdiction, for example, its adolescent consumers; and to rival authorities, where the field may be entirely empty.[50]

The relativity to jurisdiction is important, because it explains how there could be a local jurisdiction in which hate speech has authority, which is smaller than a nation state. Within 'longstanding', 'stable', and 'prosperous' democracies, where democratic norms are supported, and acts of violence and discrimination policed, there may be a microcosm where the reverse is true. According to Eric Heinze, laws banning hate speech may be justified when support or policing of democratic norms is inadequate. He assumes adequate support, and concludes that such laws are *un*justified. But if there were a smaller jurisdiction without such support, then, by his own lights, his permissive conclusion would be wrong.

The relativity to jurisdiction is also important because it explains how a low type relative to one hierarchy could be, so to speak, a high type relative to another. That might be because being higher in the one system *makes* you lower in the other, and vice versa.[51] One would expect this to hold especially in contexts of conflict, and polarized hatred. Austin's low type, who tries to name the ship after Stalin, may be a leader among his fellow revolutionaries. The 'marginal' figures despised by the majority may, for that reason, be esteemed figures among the minority. The higher one's credibility in the fraternity of doctors, the lower one's credibility in the fraternity of quack doctors, and vice versa. The lower one's standing in the eyes of The Great Satan, the higher one's standing on the side of the angels. So a speaker may have authority relative to one jurisdiction, and not to another, and their authority may, for this reason, be invisible to those on the other side.

---

[50] Green 1998; Hornsby and Langton 1998; Langton 1993, 2017. The argument of the present essay applies to pornography, as well as to hate speech, with certain amendments.

[51] I thank Amanda Greene for bringing out this point for me, in conversation.

The relativity to comparative rivals is important, because it reminds us that a low type may be all one has, when it comes to authority. 'In the land of the blind, the one-eyed man is king', as the unreconstructed proverb has it.[52] If hate speakers are the *only* local voices, whether because of state-imposed restrictions, or technology-imposed echo-chambers, then hate speakers will have the authority of a monopoly.[53] So a speaker may have authority relative to one field, where there are no rivals, but not to another, where there are many rivals; and for this reason too, the speaker's authority may be invisible to those looking from outside the bubble.

In taking the relativity of authority seriously, we are departing again from Raz, who says:

> What one ought to do depends on who has authority in a non-relativized sense. That a person has authority according to some system of rules is, in itself, of no practical relevance.[54]

On the contrary, it seems of immense practical relevance whether someone has relative authority, if for example, you happen to live within a slave code's jurisdiction, or among the readership of *Der Stürmer*. Such authority is relevant, even if not, thankfully, the final arbiter.

Raz also argues for the conceptual and methodological primacy of *legitimate* authority:

> A common factor in all kinds of effective authority is that they involve a belief by some that the person concerned has legitimate authority. Therefore, the explanation of effective authority presupposes that of legitimate authority.[55]

(I take it he would think the relative authority I describe to be at best 'effective' authority.) Here too we must disagree, not only because authority need not involve belief, but because there is no threat of vicious circularity.

Two somewhat different analogies will bring this out. A theorist may propose an understanding of *money*, in a way that is relativized to a practice: something is money if sufficiently many people treat it a certain way, and believe it to be valuable. Such a theorist may also hold

---

[52] The proverb is attributed to the collection in *The Adages*, Erasmus 1500.
[53] The structural problems for counter-speech are pressing, and described in Sunstein 2001.
[54] Raz 2009, 10.
[55] Raz 2009, 29.

a normative view that something *should* only be money if it conforms to the Gold Standard, for only then would it really have value; and they might wish the practice would so conform. They could still do their social ontology of money, without needing to first substantiate their theory about the Gold Standard. Or a theorist may propose an understanding of *cool*, in a way that is relativized to a practice: something is cool if sufficiently many people treat it a certain way, and believe it to be intrinsically cool. Relativized 'coolness' would then depend in part on beliefs about 'intrinsic coolness'. But the theorist could again do their social ontology of coolness without needing to first substantiate some theory of intrinsic coolness (there may, in that case, be none). So whether or not participants in a practice, or the theorist of the practice, hold a non-relativized view, there is scope for a relativized understanding of authority.[56]

Let us move on now to consider more closely the interaction of epistemic and practical authority in hate speech; and the accrual of authority to hate speech through accommodation.

5. AUTHORITY AS EPISTEMIC AND PRACTICAL

The distinction between practical and epistemic authority is reflected, as we saw, in two broadly distinct ways of 'authoritatively saying someone is inferior', returning to MacKinnon's phrase. The Alabama slave law had, primarily, practical authority, and its saying so was exercitive, enacting the status of slaves, and associated permissions and obligations. The Nazi propaganda had epistemic authority, and its saying so was verdictive, authoritatively describing the nature, motives, and social status of Jews.

But as we have seen, the propaganda was not purely an exercise of epistemic authority. It was an exercise of practical authority as well. It enacted, as well as described, the inferior standing of Jews. It told its readers what to do, as well as telling them how things were. Practical and epistemic authority interact, as Raz pointed out. Your doctor's orders have their status as directives, in part because of what your doctor knows,

---

[56] My thoughts on intrinsic coolness have been influenced by Haslanger 1995, whose work on concepts and what we want them for is also highly relevant (Haslanger 2012). Compare also the philosophical literature on response dependent properties: 'x is *red* iff most observers under standard conditions judge it to be *red*'.

or is taken to know: his practical authority has its source in his epistemic, or 'theoretical', authority. As Raz remarks,

> There are practical authorities whose authority is based entirely on their being theoretical [i.e. epistemic] authorities: an expert doctor is an authority not only on the causes of illness but also on their cures.[57]

The doctor is able, as we say, to *prescribe*.

A caveat, to be repeated, is that Raz is talking about expertise, rather than credibility, while we are focusing on credibility alone. Yet what Raz says about epistemic authority, construed as expertise, applies also to epistemic authority, construed as credibility. It applies to the quack doctor, as well as to the doctor, in our non-ideal and relativized sense of authority. The credible quack doctor is an authority, for his gullible patients, not only on the causes of illness but also on their cures.

The interaction of epistemic and practical authority is reflected in the speech acts available to the doctor, or indeed the quack doctor. Suppose your doctor says, looking sadly at your file, 'Sorry, cigarettes are *out*.' That would exemplify, perhaps, a mix of speech act types, drawing on his epistemic *and* practical authority: a verdictive, ranking cigarettes as unhealthy; an exercitive, making it count as an inferior option, in this context; and a directive, ordering you not to smoke. A comparable interaction of epistemic and practical authority is reflected in the speech acts available to a hate speaker who has authority. Waldron has suggested that a basic message of hate speech is one of exclusion, '*Out!*' This could be read as a like exercise of epistemic and practical authority: as a credible verdictive, ranking Jews as outsiders; an exercitive making Jews count as outsiders; and a directive, saying that Jews should act and be treated accordingly. One difference is that the directives of hate speech extend beyond its hearers, including its recruits, and also its targets: Jews are described as out, count as out, should be treated as out, and should *get out*.

Hate speech, like the speech of the doctor or the quack doctor, can thus be an exercise of practical, as well as epistemic, authority. For *Der Stürmer*, the authority came via official Nazi endorsement, backed up by money, and by public postings in town squares that made it available,

---

[57] Raz 2009, 8. He says they have authority even when totally unrecognized. I accept this, since expertise is a kind of authority, but would say their speech acts will not *count as* verdictives or directives unless the speaker is also *taken* to have authority.

gratis, to any reader.[58] By contrast the anonymous contributors to hate sites, the anonymous scrawlers on sidewalks, do not have support of that order. They seem to possess neither practical nor epistemic authority: their words are not the edicts of a legislator, nor the pronouncements of a credible expert. We are looking here at something more informal.

6. ACCOMMODATION AS A SOURCE OF AUTHORITY

Sometimes you get the authority you presuppose, if nobody blocks you. With that suggestion, Thomason illustrates the phenomenon of presupposition accommodation, which is itself more general. Roughly, and within limits, you get what you presuppose, *whatever* it may be, if nobody blocks you. The main task for accommodation among philosophers of language has been to explain how presuppositions can be informative. Instead of breaking down when a speaker introduces a previously unshared presupposition, the conversation simply adjusts, accommodates it without fuss, to take it on board, and make it shared.

Conversations tend to follow a rule of accommodation, said Lewis, and like a baseball game, they have a 'score': an abstract structure comparable to the score of a game, which tracks what has been done at a given point, and what it is legitimate to do thereafter.[59] But unlike a baseball game, a conversation follows a 'rule of accommodation': if at a given time something is said that requires a component of conversational score to be a certain way, in order for what is said to be 'correct play', e.g. true, or otherwise acceptable; and if that component of score is not that way beforehand; and if certain further conditions hold; then, at that time, that component of score changes in the required way, to make what is said 'correct play', e.g. true, or otherwise acceptable.[60]

Accommodation can make a presupposition acceptable. To return to Lewis's example, when someone says 'even George could win', they introduce a novel presupposition, 'George is an unpromising candidate'. When no one blocks the presupposition by saying 'Whadda ya mean, "even"?'

---

[58] Altman 2012; Bytwerk 1983. There was additional support from a zealous readership, it seems.
[59] Lewis 1979. See also Atlas 2004; McGowan 2012; Roberts 2015; Stalnaker 2002; von Fintel 2008. I distinguish score from common ground: Langton 2012, 2018, and forthcoming.
[60] Lewis 1979; see also Atlas 2004; Stalnaker 2002; von Fintel 2008.

the novel presupposition, 'that George is an unpromising candidate' is then 'correct play'—it is acceptable. The speaker's presupposition is accommodated, added to the conversation's score, and from then on it is appropriate for participants to continue with that presupposition in place.

Accommodation can make a presupposition true. According to Thomason, the presupposition 'the speaker has authority' becomes true, not just acceptable. Authority's existence comes into being through accommodation, not only its acceptability. In an insightful study, Maciej Witek draws a similar conclusion:

the speaker's power to give the hearer felicitous directives is established by a mechanism akin to what Lewis calls presupposition accommodation.

On his proposal:

in some cases... the authority automatically becomes an element of the objective context of interaction provided the speaker's utterance is taken up, by default, to be a binding order.[61]

A presupposition about the restaurant organizer's authority can be made *true*, through accommodation; a presupposition that George is an unpromising candidate is made *acceptable*, but not true, through accommodation.[62] This difference needs more investigation, but the explanation surely lies in the fact that actual authority can be constituted by actual acceptability, unlike George's actual incompetence.

Consider the implications for a speaker's speech act, in such a situation. The speaker acquires the 'power to give the hearer felicitous directives', as Witek puts it. Presupposition accommodation supplies a speaker with practical authority, and this authority is a felicity condition for the speaker's directive speech act. Presupposition accommodation therefore has the power to alter the illocutionary force of an utterance. The acquisition of authority, by accommodation, supplies what is needed for

---

[61] Witek 2013, 8. I was delighted to learn of Witek's work on this topic when the present essay was in draft form. Witek distinguishes objective 'Austinian' from subjective 'Stalnakerian' presuppositions, and uses the accommodation of 'Austinian' presuppositions, such as authority, to address a regress problem about the origin of deontic powers. He observes that sometimes it is the speaker who is invited to 'accommodate' to the authoritative role attributed to the speaker *by the hearer*, the reverse of the usual pattern.

[62] Notice that the presupposition could in fact be made true causally, over time, by various social looping effects, as when an otherwise promising candidate falters, because of low expectations. This causal self-fulfilment is a topic of Langton 2009.

a directive. The getting of authority, and the altering of permissibility facts, go hand in hand.

This pattern of accommodation applies to Maitra's examples of practical authority acquired through omission: to the 'derived' authority of the bossy pupil who gets authority when the teacher turns a blind eye; and to the 'licensed' authority acquired by a bossy pupil from his peers, in the teacher's absence. It applies also to Maitra's examples of hate speech, where authority is licensed by hearers and bystanders: the hate speaker on the subway, whose tirade acquires greater force from the passivity of other passengers; the cross burning, which acquires greater force through the passivity of city leaders.

Although Thomason, Witek, and Maitra are dealing with practical authority, we have seen that the pattern can extend to epistemic authority, construed as credibility. Like practical authority, the credibility of a pupil could be derived from the omissions of a teacher, or licensed by the omissions of fellow pupils, in the teacher's absence. The credibility of *Der Stürmer* could likewise have been derived from the mere omissions of the Nazi Party, if it had merely turned a blind eye; or licensed by its readers, in the Party's absence.

Once a presupposition of authority has been accommodated, it can be strengthened by other factors, including confirmation bias. Dan Sperber has described what he calls 'the guru effect'—a 'runaway phenomenon' of 'credibility inflation', which occurs when hearers credit a would-be guru with authority, and find ever more persuasive evidence in favour of that hypothesis.[63]

Some hate speakers are likely to be gurus, in something like Sperber's sense: individuals for whom official endorsement, informal presupposition accommodation, and confirmation bias all play a mutually reinforcing part in a speaker's getting or keeping of authority.[64] Some hate speech, including perhaps *Der Stürmer*, could likewise benefit from 'the guru effect', and encounter a comparable credibility inflation, again with the

---

[63] In Sperber's examples, obscurity and uncertainty play a role. For hate speech, other factors may play a role, among which flattery and tribalism have already mentioned. Confirmation bias may help in a different way, assisting initial accommodation. Background patterns of prejudice will help some speakers, and hinder others, giving asymmetric capacities to have one's presuppositions of authority accommodated, an aspect of testimonial injustice in Fricker's (2007) sense.
[64] Sperber 2010.

same mutually reinforcing mix of official endorsement, presupposition accommodation, and confirmation bias. Note that the authority of the *endorser* might get reinforced that way too: the authority of the Nazi Party itself increased, because of the authority acquired by *Der Stürmer*.[65] We can add, finally, that a guru, like a doctor, can be a practical authority, on account of being an epistemic authority: so a runaway phenomenon of credibility inflation in hate speech may, at the same time, be an inflation of its practical authority as well.

7. CONCLUSION

There is something artificial about setting aside the venom in hate speech, and asking about its authority, neglecting the material persecution and physical violence targeted on actual human beings as its result. Hate speech has dimensions I have barely touched upon. Nevertheless the authority of hate speech matters, since authority makes a difference to what hate speech can do with words.

I have argued that hate speech can have epistemic and practical authority, when these are understood in a socially situated and non-idealized way. This enables it to be speech that does practical things with words, when it authoritatively says a group of people is inferior. Having practical authority may enable it to subordinate, to the extent that subordination involves directives that legitimate discrimination, or exercitives that deprive people of powers and rights.

I have pursued parallels between practical and epistemic authority, which hold when we focus on the credibility aspect of epistemic authority. On this picture, authority is relative, whether it is practical, or epistemic: relative to a subject domain, to a jurisdiction, and to its comparative rivals. This is important to keep in mind, when it looks as though a speaker of hate speech must surely be a 'low type', who lacks what it takes to perform authoritative speech acts. Given the relativity of authority, a speaker may be low relative to one structure, and high relative to another.

We asked about the origins of authority, and I argued that hate speech could sometimes acquire authority via presupposition accommodation: a default process of adjustment, dependent on hearers and bystanders,

---

[65] Bytwerk 1983.

that has been neglected in political philosophy, despite its familiarity to philosophers of language. We can build on work from Lewis, Witek, Thomason, and Maitra to suggest that authority itself can follow a rule of accommodation. You can get the authority you presuppose, if relevant hearers do not block that presupposition. Such authority can be epistemic, or practical, both of which alter speech act powers, and the illocutionary force of a speaker's utterance. Accommodation is only a tendency, as Lewis said. It does not always work, and whether it works is itself sensitive to background social hierarchies. But authority's genesis in accommodation is an application of a familiar social magic whereby, in the words of William James, 'faith in a fact can help create a fact', for good or ill.[66]

We can update Austin's ceremonial picture of authoritative speech acts, and the ceremonial conferring and removal of authority, to show how what we do, as speakers, depends in certain ways upon our audiences; and that hate speakers can exploit ignorant, polite, or passive hearers to shore up existing distributions of authority and hierarchy, and build new ones.

There are wider implications. When hate speech has authority, it can be harder to answer with 'more speech'. Hate speech can acquire strength: its force can go further than the expression of unpleasant ideas, or the wounding of sensitive feelings, to which an adequate response might be a counter-argument, or a deaf ear, or a thick skin. But hate speech can also lose strength. On this picture, the force of hate speech is partly hostage to the responses of hearers and bystanders, and this leaves a point of vulnerability. Hate speech can be hard to answer, but an active and fortunate hearer might manage to defuse it without arguing—by blocking its authority, and thus removing a condition of its success. The unnoticed strength of hate speech, which has been our topic, therefore goes hand in hand with an unnoticed weakness.[67]

Finally, if authority can emerge through accommodation, there may be implications for responsibility. Does a bystander, silent in the presence of a racist tirade, confer 'licensed' authority on its speaker? That is Maitra's case of the subway abuser, who gains default authority through the passivity of the other passengers. Does a law that merely tolerates

---

[66] James 1896, 25.
[67] Langton 2018.

hate speech nonetheless confer 'derived' authority on it? That would be like Maitra's case of the burning cross, which gains default authority through the passivity of community leaders. We postpone these hard questions. But if the answers are affirmative, the harm in hate speech may be the doing, not only of the low types we have considered, but also of an innocent law, and of innocent others who merely stand by.

BIBLIOGRAPHY

Altman, Andrew. 1993. 'Liberalism and Campus Hate Speech: A Philosophical Examination', *Ethics* 103: 302–17.

Altman, Andrew. 2012. 'Freedom of Expression and Human Rights Law: The Case of Holocaust Denial', in I. Maitra and M.K. McGowan (eds.), *Speech and Harm: Controversies over Free Speech* (Oxford: Oxford University Press), 24–49.

Anderson, Luvell, Sally Haslanger, and Rae Langton. 2012. 'Language and Race', in Delia Graff Fara and Gillian Russell (eds.), *The Routledge Companion to the Philosophy of Language* (New York: Routledge), 753–66.

Atlas, Jay David. 2004. 'Presupposition', in Laurence R. Horn and Gregory L. Ward (eds.), *The Handbook of Pragmatics* (Malden, MA: Wiley Blackwell), 29–52.

Austin, J.L. 1962. *How to Do Things with Words* (Oxford: Oxford University Press).

Beard, Mary. 2014. 'The Public Voice of Women', *London Review of Books* 36: 11–14.

Berinsky, Adam. 2017. 'Rumors and Health Care Reform: Experiments in Political Misinformation', *The British Journal of Political Science* 47: 241–62.

Butler, Judith, 1997. *Excitable Speech: A Politics of the Performative* (New York and London: Routledge).

Bytwerk, Randall. 1983. *Julius Streicher* (New York: Dorset Press).

Camp, Elisabeth. 2013. 'Slurring Perspectives', *Analytic Philosophy* 54: 330–49.

Catterall, Helen T. (ed.) 1926. *Judicial Cases Concerning Slavery and the Negro* (Washington, DC: Carnegie Institute).

Delgado, Richard. 1993. 'Words that Wound: A Tort Action for Racial Insults, Epithets and Name Calling', in K.W. Crenshaw et al., *Words that Wound: Critical Race Theory, Assaultive Speech, and the First Amendment* (Boulder, CO: Westview Press).

Enoch, David. 2012. 'Authority and reason-giving', *Philosophy and Phenomenological Research* 89: 296–332.

von Fintel, Kai. 2008. 'What is Presupposition Accommodation, Again?' *Philosophical Perspectives* 22: 137–70.

Fricker, Miranda. 2007. *Epistemic Injustice: Power and the Ethics of Knowing* (New York: Oxford University Press).

Gelber, Katherine. 2003. *Speaking Back: The Free Speech vs. Hate Speech Debate* (Amsterdam: John Benjamins).

Gilbert, G.M. *Nuremberg Diary* (Cambridge, MA and New York: De Capo Press, 1995).

Green, Leslie. 1989. *The Authority of the State* (Oxford: Oxford University Press).

Green, Leslie. 1998. 'Pornographizing, Subordinating, Silencing', in Robert Post (ed.), *Censorship and Silencing: Practices of Cultural Regulation* (Los Angeles, CA: Getty Research Institute for the History of Art and the Humanities).

Green, Leslie. 2013. 'Should the Law Improve Morality?' *Criminal Law and Philosophy* 7: 473–94.

Greenawalt, Kent. 1989. *Speech, Crime, and the Uses of Language* (New York: Oxford University Press).

Haslanger, Sally. 1995. 'Ontology and Social Construction', *Philosophical Topics* 23: 95–125.

Haslanger, Sally. 2011. 'Ideology, Generics, and Common Ground', in Charlotte Witt (ed.), *Feminist Metaphysics: Explorations in the Ontology of Sex, Gender and the Self* (Dordrecht: Springer), 179–208.

Haslanger, Sally. 2012. *Resisting Reality: Social Construction and Social Critique* (Oxford: Oxford University Press).

Haslanger, Sally. 2014. 'The Normal, the Natural and the Good: Generics and Ideology', *Politica e Societa* 3: 365–92.

Heinze, Eric. 2016. *Hate Speech and Democratic Citizenship* (Oxford: Oxford University Press).

Hershovitz, Scott. 2011. 'The Role of Authority', *Philosopher's Imprint* 11: 1–19.

Hom, Christopher. 2008. 'The Semantics of Racial Epithets', *Journal of Philosophy* 105: 416–40.

Hornsby, Jennifer. 1994. 'Illocution and its Significance', in S.L. Tsohatzidis (ed.), *Foundations of Speech Act Theory* (London: Routledge).

Hornsby, Jennifer. 1995. 'Disempowered Speech', *Philosophical Topics* 23: 127–47, ed. Sally Haslanger.

Hornsby, Jennifer. 2001. 'Meaning and Uselessness: How to Think About Derogatory Words', *Midwest Studies in Philosophy* 25: 128–41.

Hornsby, Jennifer and Rae Langton. 1998. 'Free Speech and Illocution', *Journal of Legal Theory* 4: 21–37.

James, William. 1896. *The Will to Believe and Other Essays in Popular Philosophy* (Norwood, MA: Plimpton Press).

Kennedy, Randall. 2002. *Nigger: The Strange Career of a Troublesome Word* (New York: Pantheon Books).

Langton, Rae. 1993. 'Speech Acts and Unspeakable Acts', *Philosophy and Public Affairs* 22: 305–30.

Langton, Rae. 2006. 'Disenfranchised Silence', in G. Brennan, R. Goodin, F. Jackson, and M. Smith (eds.), *Common Minds: Themes from the Philosophy of Philip Pettit* (Oxford: Oxford University Press).

Langton, Rae. 2009. *Sexual Solipsism: Philosophical Essays on Pornography and Objectification* (Oxford: Oxford University Press).

Langton, Rae. 2010. 'Esteem in the Moral Economy of Oppression', in J. Hawthorne (ed.), *Philosophical Perspectives*, vol. 23, *Ethics* (Indianapolis, IN: Wiley), 273–91.

Langton, Rae. 2012. 'Beyond Belief: Pragmatics in Hate Speech and Pornography', in I. Maitra and M.K. McGowan (eds.), *Speech and Harm: Controversies over Free Speech* (Oxford: Oxford University Press), 72–93.

Langton, Rae. 2015. 'How to Get a Norm from a Speech Act', *The Amherst Lecture in Philosophy* 10: 1–33. http://www.amherstlecture.org/langton2015/.

Langton, Rae. 2016. 'Hate Speech and the Epistemology of Justice, Review of Jeremy Waldron: *The Harm in Hate Speech*', *Criminal Law and Philosophy* 10: 865–73.

Langton, Rae. 2017. 'Is Pornography like the Law?' in M. Mikkola (ed.), *Beyond Speech: Pornography and Analytic Feminist Philosophy* (Oxford: Oxford University Press).

Langton, Rae. 2018. 'Blocking as Counter-Speech', in D. Fogal, D. Harris, and M. Moss (eds.), *New Work on Speech Acts* (Oxford: Oxford University Press).

Langton, Rae. Forthcoming. *Accommodating Injustice: The John Locke Lectures 2015* (working title) (Oxford: Oxford University Press).

Langton, Rae and Caroline West. 1999. 'Scorekeeping in a Pornographic Language Game', *Australasian Journal of Philosophy* 77: 303–19.

Leslie, Sarah-Jane. 2017. 'The Original Sin of Cognition: Fear, Prejudice and Generalization', *Journal of Philosophy* 114(8): 393–421.

Lewis, David. 1979. 'Scorekeeping in a Language Game', *Journal of Philosophical Logic* 8: 339–59.

McGowan, Mary Kate. 2003. 'Conversational Exercitives and the Force of Pornography', *Philosophy and Public Affairs* 31: 155–89.

McGowan, Mary Kate. 2004. 'Conversational Exercitives: Something Else We Do With Our Words', *Linguistics and Philosophy* 27: 93–111.

McGowan, Mary Kate. 2009. 'Oppressive Speech', *Australasian Journal of Philosophy* 87: 389–407.

McGowan, Mary Kate. 2012. 'On "Whites Only" Signs and Racist Hate Speech: Verbal Acts of Racist Discrimination', in Ishani Maitra and Mary Kate McGowan (eds.), *Speech and Harm: Controversies over Free Speech* (Oxford: Oxford University Press), 121–47.

MacKinnon, Catharine. 1987. *Feminism Unmodified* (Cambridge, MA: Harvard University Press).

MacKinnon, Catharine. 1993. *Only Words* (Cambridge, MA: Harvard University Press).

Maitra, Ishani. 2012. 'Subordinating Speech', in I. Maitra and M.K. McGowan (eds.), *Speech and Harm: Controversies over Free Speech* (Oxford: Oxford University Press), 94–120.

Maitra, Ishani and Mary Kate McGowan. 2007. 'Limits of Free Speech: Pornography and the Question of Coverage', *Legal Theory* 13: 41–68.

Mann, Erika. 1938. *School for Barbarians* (New York: Modern Age Books).

Matsuda, Mari. 1993. 'Public Response to Racist Speech', in M. Matsuda et al., *Words that Wound* (Boulder, CO: Westview Press).

Matsuda, Mari, Charles R. Lawrence III, Richard Delgado, and Kimberlé Williams Crenshaw (eds.). 1993. *Words that Wound* (Boulder, CO: Westview Press).

Mill, John Stuart. 1867. *Inaugural Address Delivered to the University of St. Andrews, Feb. 1st 1867* (London: Longmans, Green, Reader, and Dyer).

Miller, Gina. 2017. 'Hate-filled abuse is poisoning Britain. I fought it, and ask you to do the same'. *The Guardian* (12 July): https://www.theguardian.com/commentisfree/2017/jul/12/hate-filled-abuse-poisoning-britain-i-fought-it-viscount-st-davids.

Mills, Charles. 2005. 'Ideal Theory as Ideology', *Hypatia* 20: 165–84.

O'Neill, Onora. 1987. 'Abstraction, Idealization and Ideology in Ethics', in J.D.G. Evans (ed.), *Moral Philosophy and Contemporary Problems* (Cambridge: Cambridge University Press).

Pettit, Philip. 1994. 'Enfranchising Silence: An Argument for Freedom of Speech', in Tom Campbell and Wojciech Sadurski (eds.), *Freedom of Communication* (Aldershot: Dartmouth), 45–55; reprinted in Pettit, *Rules, Reasons, and Norms* (Oxford: Oxford University Press, 2002).

Raz, Joseph. 1979. *The Authority of Law* (Oxford: Oxford University Press).

Raz, Joseph. 2009. *The Authority of Law: Essays on Authority and Law* (Oxford: Oxford University Press).

Roberts, Craige. 2015. 'Accommodation in a Language Game', in Barry Loewer and Jonathan Schaffer (eds.), *A Companion to David Lewis*, Blackwell Companions to Philosophy (Oxford: Blackwell), 345–66.

Sbisà, Marina. 1999. 'Ideology and the Persuasive Use of Presupposition', in J. Verschueren (ed.), *Language and Ideology* (Antwerp: International Pragmatics Association), 492–509.

Sbisà, Marina. Forthcoming. 'Varieties of Speech Act Norms', in Maciej Witek and Iwona Witczak-Plisiecka (eds.), *Dynamics and Varieties of Speech Actions: A Theme Issue of Poznan Studies in the Philosophy of the Sciences and the Humanities* (Leiden: Brill).

Schwartzman, Lisa H. 2002. 'Hate Speech, Illocution, and Social Context: A Critique of Judith Butler', *Journal of Social Philosophy* 33(3): 421–41.

Siegel, Susanna. 2017. *The Rationality of Perception* (Oxford: Oxford University Press).

Simpson, Robert. In progress. 'The "Streisand Effect" and the Pragmatics of Oppressive Speech'.

Sperber, Dan. 2010. 'The Guru Effect', *Review of Philosophy and Psychology* 1(4): 583–92.

Stalnaker, Robert. 2002. 'Common Ground', *Linguistics and Philosophy* 25: 701–21.

Stanley, Jason. 2015. *How Propaganda Works* (Princeton, NJ: Princeton University Press).

Streicher, Julius (ed.) 1938. *Der Giftpilz*, by Ernest Hiemer (Streicher Verlag); 1940, *Der Pudelmopsdachelpinscher* in *German Propaganda Archive*, trans. and ed. Randall Bytwerk: http://www.calvin.edu/academic/cas/gpa/ww2era. htm (accessed 3 June 2009).

Streicher, Julius (ed.) 1943. *Der Stürmer* (Streicher Verlag), from an essay 'The Holy Hate', by Ernest Hiemer, *German Propaganda Archive*, trans. and ed. Randall Bytwerk: http://www.calvin.edu/academic/cas/gpa/ww2era.htm (accessed 3 June 2009).

Sunstein, Cass. 2001. *Republic.com* (Princeton, NJ: Princeton University Press).

Swanson, Eric. 2017. 'Omissive Implicature', *Philosophical Topics* 45: 117–37.

Swanson, Eric. Forthcoming. 'Slurs and Ideologies', in R. Celikates, S. Haslanger, and J. Stanley (eds.), *Ideology* (Oxford: Oxford University Press).

Thomason, Richmond H. 1990. 'Accommodation, Meaning, and Implicature: Interdisciplinary Foundations for Pragmatics', in P.R. Cohen, J.L. Morgan, and M.E. Pollack (eds.), *Intentions in Communication* (Cambridge, MA: MIT Press).

Tirrell, Lynne. 2012. 'Genocidal Language Games', in I. Maitra and M.K. McGowan (eds.), *Speech and Harm: Controversies over Free Speech* (Oxford: Oxford University Press), 174–221.

United Nations, 1965. *International Convention on the Elimination of All Forms of Racial Discrimination*: http://www.hrcr.org/docs/CERD/cerd3. html, accessed 3 June 2009.

Waldron, Jeremy. 2012. *The Harm in Hate Speech* (Cambridge, MA: Harvard University Press).

Witek, Maciej. 2013. 'How to Establish Authority with Words: Imperative Utterances and Presupposition Accommodation', in A. Brożek (ed.), *Logic, Methodology and Philosophy of Science at Warsaw University* (Warsaw: Semper), 145–57.

5

An Instrumental Legal Moralism

JAMES EDWARDS

Many who write about the criminal law defend or attack what is nowadays known as legal moralism. As with so many philosophical labels, this label is not used to refer to a single view. There is, however, one thing on which defenders and attackers seem to agree. As formulated by Antony Duff, Joel Feinberg, H.L.A. Hart, Michael Moore, and others, legal moralism amounts to the following thesis: the fact that φing is morally wrong is a reason to criminalize φing.[1] This paper considers a different kind of legal moralism, which I call *instrumental legal moralism* (ILM). Section I distinguishes ILM from the *act-centred legal moralism* (ALM) debated by Duff, Feinberg, Hart, and Moore. It points out that ILM is itself a label which refers to a family of principles, and identifies one such principle—which I call (E)—for further discussion. Section II introduces two prominent arguments for versions of ALM: the *retributivist argument*, offered by Michael Moore, and the *answerability argument*, offered by Antony Duff. The section argues that if we endorse the premises on which these arguments depend, we should—via certain further premises—also endorse (E). In short, if the two arguments are sound, we should endorse ALM *and* ILM.

Section III argues that the two arguments are not sound. This is not because their premises are false, but because ALM does not follow from them.[2] What follows, I argue, is (E). Section IV considers a question left

---

[1] As we will see, there is disagreement about almost everything else, including (a) whether this is true of all moral wrongs, (b) what it is for something to be a moral wrong, and (c) the type of reason to which legal moralism refers. It is worth noting that some take legal moralism to encompass not only the thesis mentioned in the text, but also theses concerning the use of criminal law to perfect character, or preserve certain ways of life. I do not consider this broader reading here, restricting my discussion to what Feinberg calls 'legal moralism in the strict sense': see J. Feinberg, *Harmless Wrongdoing* (OUP 1988), 4.

[2] Which is not to say the premises are true. I leave this open.

Oxford Studies in Philosophy of Law Volume 3. John Gardner, Leslie Green, and Brian Leiter (eds)
This chapter © James Edwards 2018. First published in 2018 by Oxford University Press

over from earlier in the paper: if (E) is true, does it tell us that preventing all moral wrongs, or only some such wrongs, is a reason to criminalize? As we will see, it appears that the retributivist and answerability arguments only identify a reason to prevent certain *secondary* wrongs.[3] Section IV argues that this is not a plausible conclusion. If preventing certain secondary wrongs is a reason to criminalize, then preventing the corresponding primary wrongs is a reason to criminalize also. Though they are commonly thought to be arguments for ALM, it is to the resulting version of ILM that the retributivist and answerability arguments ultimately lead.

I

In *Harm to Others*, Joel Feinberg identifies the following principles:

(A)　'It can be morally legitimate to prohibit conduct on the ground that it is inherently immoral, even though it causes neither harm nor offence to the actor or to others.'[4]

(B)　'It is always a good reason in support of penal legislation that it would probably be effective in preventing (eliminating, reducing) harm to persons other than the actor (the one prohibited from acting) and there is probably no other means that is equally effective at no greater cost to other values.'[5]

(C)　'It is always a good reason in support of a proposed criminal prohibition that it is probably necessary to prevent serious offence to persons other than the actor and would probably be an effective means to that end if enacted.'[6]

Feinberg calls (A) *legal moralism*, (B) *the harm principle*, and (C) *the offence principle*.[7] (B) and (C) are both formulated instrumentally. Whether there is reason to criminalize an act-type depends, in (B) and (C), on the likely effects of the prohibition itself: unless that prohibition will probably be effective in preventing harm or serious offence to others, neither

---

[3] What counts as a secondary wrong, and which secondary wrongs law-makers have reason to prevent via criminalization, are questions discussed in Sections III and IV.
[4] J. Feinberg, *Harm to Others* (OUP 1984), 27.
[5] Ibid., 26.
[6] Ibid.
[7] These principles are not mutually exclusive. Each identifies a reason to criminalize, not a constraint on permissible criminalization.

(B) nor (C) identifies any reason to enact it.[8] (A) is different. (A) implies that there is reason to criminalize act-types because of a property which the tokens of that type share: it is the fact they are 'inherently immoral' that gives us reason to prohibit them, irrespective of the effects of creating the prohibition. (A) is thus what I will call an *act-centred principle*; (B) and (C) are *instrumental principles*.

Now consider (D):

(D)   It can be morally legitimate to prohibit conduct on the ground that the conduct causes harm to others.

Like (A), (D) is act-centred. (D) implies that the fact that tokens of some act-type are harmful to others is a reason to prohibit that act-type. This is so irrespective of the effects of creating the prohibition. This shows that we can formulate harm principles that are either act-centred *or* instrumental.[9] And the same is true of legal moralism. Consider (E):

(E)   It is always a good reason in support of criminalization that it would probably be effective in preventing (eliminating, reducing) moral wrongs, and there is probably no other means that is equally effective at a lesser cost to other values.[10]

Like (B) and (C), (E) is instrumental: unless the prohibition will probably be effective in preventing moral wrongdoing, (E) does not identify any reason to create it.

Feinberg is not alone in defining legal moralism in act-centred terms. In *Law, Liberty and Morality*, H.L.A. Hart identifies the question he will consider as follows: '[i]s the fact that certain conduct is by common standards immoral sufficient to justify making that conduct punishable by law?'[11] Those who answer affirmatively endorse legal moralism. And to give this answer is to endorse an act-centred principle: it is to claim that

---

[8]   Other principles may, of course, identify further such reasons.

[9]   Some criticisms of 'the harm principle' succeed only on the assumption that it is an act-centred principle. But there are many possible harm principles, including instrumental principles. For discussion, see J. Edwards, 'Harm Principles', *Legal Theory* 20 (2014): 253.

[10]   I here slightly modify what Feinberg calls the necessity clause of (B), according to which there is reason to criminalize only if 'there is probably no other means that is equally effective at no greater cost to other values'. Feinberg's formulation implies that there is *no* reason to criminalize if there probably *is* an equally effective means which comes at the *same* cost to other values. I do not see why. If the effectiveness and costliness of two measures is identical, then *ceteris paribus* we have reason to use either one.

[11]   H.L.A. Hart, *Law, Liberty and Morality* (Stanford 1963), 4.

the fact tokens of an act-type are immoral justifies their criminalization. More recent accounts of legal moralism are also act-centred. According to Michael Moore: the 'theory of legal moralism' holds that the fact 'an action is morally wrong is always a legitimate reason to prohibit it with criminal legislation'.[12] And according to Antony Duff, legal moralism 'holds that the wrongfulness of a type of conduct gives us positive reason to criminalize it'.[13]

There are important differences between these versions of legal moralism, to some of which we will return. But all amount to act-centred principles.[14] One might say that Patrick Devlin is one legal moralist who endorses an instrumental principle, at least on what H.L.A. Hart dubs the 'moderate' reading of his work.[15] On this reading, Devlin claims that *any* moral wrong could in principle be criminalized legitimately, because the widespread commission of any such wrong could threaten social order, and because criminalization might then be necessary to prevent the harm this disorder would cause.[16] It is true that when read in this way Devlin endorses an instrumental principle. But he endorses (B), not (E). What Devlin claims, in effect, is that there is reason to criminalize any act-type the criminalization of which is probably necessary to prevent

[12] M. Moore, *Placing Blame* (OUP 1997), 70.

[13] See R.A. Duff, 'Towards A Modest Legal Moralism', *Criminal Law and Philosophy* 8 (2014): 217, 218. As we will see, for Duff this is true only of those moral wrongs he calls *public* wrongs.

[14] For other discussions which treat legal moralism as act-centred, see J. Murphy, 'Another Look at Legal Moralism', *Ethics* 77 (1966): 50, 51 ("the legal moralist maintains that criminal sanctions are demanded even when no obvious harm to others occurs. The intrinsic heinousness of sexual deviation, for example, is sufficient to justify its prohibition"); L. Alexander, 'The Legal Enforcement of Morality', in R. Frey and C. Wellman (eds.), *A Companion to Applied Ethics* (Wiley 2003), 128, 129 ("the immorality of conduct is a sufficient condition for legal proscription"); A.P. Simester, 'Enforcing Morality', in A. Marmor (ed.), *The Routledge Companion to Philosophy of Law* (Routledge 2012), 481 ("according to a school of thought known as legal moralism, an action can warrant proscription simply on the ground of its moral wrongfulness"); D. Brink, 'Retributivism and Legal Moralism', *Ratio Juris* 25 (2012): 496, 504 ("Legal moralism is the thesis that the state can and should regulate immorality, as such"); D. Scoccia, 'In Defense of "Pure" Legal Moralism', *Criminal Law and Philosophy* 7 (2013): 513, 515 ("if critical morality judges some act-type to be harmlessly wrong, then it should be criminalized unless the prudential costs of doing so outweigh the moral benefits"); R. Arneson, 'The Enforcement of Morals Revisited', *Criminal Law and Philosophy* 7 (2013): 435, 439 ("criminal prohibition of a type of conduct can be justified by an appeal to the immorality of conduct of that type independently of whether or not prohibiting it would prevent harm to any individual persons or advance the welfare of any individual persons").

[15] Hart, *Law, Liberty and Morality*, 48.

[16] P. Devlin, *The Enforcement of Morals* (OUP 1965), 12–14.

harm to others. If this is our principle, he further claims, we cannot rule out the possibility that, at some time or other, any moral wrong might be on the list of act-types to which it applies. Note, though, that neither claim makes Devlin a legal moralist. The principle Devlin endorses, on this reading, is Feinberg's harm principle. True, that principle may tell us that there is reason to criminalize moral wrongs. But the significance given to moral wrongdoing is entirely derivative—it derives entirely from the fact that criminalizing wrongdoing is sometimes likely to prevent harm.[17]

This tells us something about what it is to endorse legal moralism. For the legal moralist, moral wrongdoing has a non-derivative significance. According to *act-centred legal moralism* (ALM):

ALM: the fact that φing is morally wrong is a reason to criminalize φing.

To endorse ALM is thus to identify a reason to criminalize that exists irrespective of whether criminalization has any further effects. According to *instrumental legal moralism* (ILM):

ILM: the fact that criminalizing φing will probably prevent moral wrongdoing is a reason to criminalize φing.[18]

To endorse ILM is thus to identify a reason to criminalize that exists precisely because criminalization has certain effects. But the effects that matter are not those that matter for (the moderately read) Devlin. For him, the fact that criminalizing φing would probably prevent wrongdoing is not itself a reason to criminalize anything. There is reason to criminalize φing only if—and in virtue of the fact that—doing so will probably prevent harm to others. So Devlin does not endorse ILM.[19]

---

[17] As Duff puts it, on Devlin's view 'what gives us reason to criminalize [some act-type] is not its (perceived) wrongfulness as such, but the harm that it might, if not criminalized, cause to the stability and cohesion of society'. Duff concludes that Devlin 'was no legal moralist'. See R.A. Duff, 'Towards a Theory of Criminal Law', *Aristotelian Society* 84, Supp. Vol. 1 (2010): 8, n.12.

[18] I here suppress an additional condition, which I built into (E) above, namely that, 'there is probably no other means that is equally effective at a lesser cost to other values'. I return to this condition below.

[19] This is to take issue with Joel Feinberg, who distinguishes between pure and impure versions of legal moralism and puts Devlin in the latter camp. It turns out, however, that the impure legal moralist is simply a defender of Feinberg's harm principle, who disagrees with Feinberg about the empirical question of what that principle permits—see Feinberg, *Harmless Wrongdoing*, 8. It is therefore confusing for Feinberg to *also* claim that liberals who think that

Is there any significant difference between ALM and ILM? One might doubt it. But there is no room for doubt.[20] Contrary to what is sometimes assumed, there is no reliable connection between criminalizing an activity and reducing its incidence. Consider pimping and drug pushing. Let's grant that these are both moral wrongs. If we endorse ILM, is that the slightest reason to criminalize them? No. Not only might this be unproductive, it might even be counterproductive. The activities in question might be driven underground where their excesses are much harder to detect and control, and where their potential tax-invisible profits increase their attractions to the least scrupulous. In such cases, while ALM supports criminalization, ILM does not. What's more, moral wrongs cannot only be prevented by criminalizing the wrongs themselves. We may better prevent pimping and drug-pushing by criminalizing various ancillary activities (such as paying for sex, or possessing and using drugs) than by criminalizing pimping or pushing alone. When these ancillary activities are not wrongs ALM does not support criminalization, but ILM does.[21]

We have seen that some prominent legal moralist principles are versions of ALM. In the next section, I begin to consider what might be said in favour of one version of ILM—what I above called principle (E). Before doing so, it is worth clarifying several aspects of the principle I will discuss. First, (E) identifies *only* the existence of *a* reason to criminalize. Some versions of ALM are much stronger than this. Recall that according to Hart, the legal moralist claims that the immorality of an act-type is 'sufficient to justify making that conduct punishable by law'.[22] Moore sometimes makes similar claims. He writes that on a legal moralist view,

the harm and offence principles (what I have called (B) and (C)) identify the *only* reasons to criminalize, also *deny* the truth of legal moralism—see Feinberg, *Harmless Wrongdoing*, 3. If this latter claim is right, impure legal moralism cannot be a type of legal moralism after all.

[20] This paragraph draws on J. Gardner and J. Edwards, 'Criminal Law', in H. LaFollette (ed.), *The International Encyclopedia of Ethics* (Wiley 2013).

[21] Many characterize the debate between legal moralists and their opponents as a debate about the 'enforcement' of morality. Hart and Devlin write in these terms, and the language can be found throughout the subsequent literature: see e.g. G. Dworkin, 'Devlin was Right: Law and the Enforcement of Morality', *William and Mary Law Review* 40 (1999): 927; S. Wall, 'Enforcing Morality', *Criminal Law and Philosophy* 7 (2013): 455; Arneson, 'The Enforcement of Morals Revisited'. Unfortunately, the language of enforcement is itself ambiguous between ALM and ILM. Do we enforce morality by criminalizing immoralities, or by criminalizing act-types criminalization of which will probably prevent those immoralities?

[22] Hart, *Law, Liberty and Morality*, 48.

'the immorality of behaviour' is a 'sufficient condition with which to justify criminal legislation'.[23] These claims should not be taken at face value. If immorality were a sufficient condition of the permissibility of criminalization, there could be no immoral act that it was impermissible to criminalize. This is not Moore's view, nor was it Devlin's. Moore is clear that some wrongdoing is 'immune to criminalization even according to a legal moralist view of the proper reach of criminal legislation'.[24] I have already claimed that on the 'moderate' reading of his work Devlin was not a legal moralist. But even on what Hart dubs an 'extreme' reading—one which has Devlin give immorality a non-derivative significance—Devlin still accepts that some immoralities cannot permissibly be criminalized. In some cases this would disproportionately invade people's privacy; in others it would be insufficiently tolerant of different ways of life.[25] Devlin claims one must 'balance' competing considerations. He does not claim that the case for criminalizing wrongdoing will never be outweighed.

It is more plausible to take Moore and Devlin to be making a more modest claim. They should be taken, I suggest, to be claiming that the fact an act-type is a moral wrong is a *defeasibly sufficient* reason to criminalize that act-type.[26] If some fact, *f*, is a defeasibly sufficient reason to do X, then it is true both (a) that it is not a necessary condition of the permissibility of doing X that there be any additional reason to do it, and (b) that *f* may be (and sometimes is) defeated by reasons not to do X. We have already seen that Moore and Devlin both endorse (b): our reasons to criminalize immoralities may be (and sometimes are) defeated by reasons to protect liberty or privacy. But the fact an act-type is a moral wrong is not, for them, a reason that necessarily requires supplementation. It is the denial of this thesis—of (a)—which Joel Feinberg eventually took to be definitive of his 'liberal' view of criminalization. Having claimed otherwise in *Harm to Others*, Feinberg had come to accept by the time he wrote *Harmless Wrongdoing* that the immorality of an act-type is *itself* a reason to criminalize it.[27] What he continued to deny was that

---

[23] Moore, *Placing Blame*, 645.

[24] Moore, 'A Tale of Two Theories', *Criminal Justice Ethics* 28 (2009): 27, 33. For discussion of various reasons not to criminalize wrongdoing, see Moore, *Placing Blame*, 661–5, 739–95.

[25] Devlin, *The Enforcement of Morals*, 16–19.

[26] Moore's reply to David Dolinko's criticism of his retributivist theory of punishment suggests that this reading is one that Moore would accept: see Moore, *Placing Blame*, 173–4.

[27] In *Harm to Others*, Feinberg defines liberalism as 'the view that the harm and offense principles, duly clarified and qualified, between them exhaust the class of morally relevant

this reason is sufficiently weighty on its own. For the liberal, he claimed, it must be supplemented by additional reasons to criminalize, specifically the fact that criminalizing an immorality will probably prevent harm or offence to others.[28] Not so, say Moore and Devlin: all we need show is that certain reasons *not* to criminalize—which would otherwise defeat our reasons to do so—are absent in the case of our proposed offence.

Though Moore and Devlin's views are weaker than they first appear, they remain stronger than (E). To repeat, (E) merely identifies *a* reason to criminalize. If this principle is sound, at least one version of ILM is sound. Because many prominent legal moralist principles are versions of ALM, this would not be an uninteresting conclusion. Perhaps preventing moral wrongs is *also* a defeasibly sufficient reason to criminalize. But the truth of this stronger claim is a matter for another day.

So much for the first clarification. Legal moralists also disagree about *which* immoralities provide reasons to criminalize. On what I will call an *unrestricted view*, all immoralities provide such reasons. This is the view taken by Moore. On a *restricted view*, this is only true of some immoralities. Duff endorses such a view. He argues that there is only reason to criminalize *public* wrongs, where a public wrong is a moral wrong which 'violates the polity's defining values' and thus becomes the 'business' of the wrongdoer's fellow citizens.[29] Strictly speaking, then, we should distinguish between (E^U) and (E^R), where the former refers to the prevention of any

reasons for criminal prohibitions. Paternalistic and moralistic considerations...have no weight at all'. See Feinberg, *Harm to Others*, 14–15. In *Harmless Wrongdoing*, Feinberg writes that this position is 'obviously too extreme', and that immorality 'of any description is at least some kind of reason' to criminalize. See Feinberg, *Harmless Wrongdoing*, 322.

[28] Feinberg calls this view 'bold liberalism'. On a more cautious view, by which Feinberg is at times tempted, the additional reasons are not always necessary. See Feinberg, *Harmless Wrongdoing*, 324–7. Andrew Simester and Andreas von Hirsch take a similar view to Feinberg. Though the wrongfulness of φing is, they claim, *a* reason to criminalize, this reason always requires supplementation by further such reasons, specifically the fact that criminalization will probably prevent harm. This is the effect of what the authors call the *non-qualifying thesis*: see A.P. Simester and A. von Hirsch, *Crimes, Harms and Wrongs* (Hart 1982/2011), 29.

[29] R.A. Duff, 'Responsibility, Citizenship and Criminal Law', in R.A. Duff and S. Green (eds.), *Philosophical Foundations of Criminal Law* (OUP 2011), 139. Duff has recently called his view a 'modest' legal moralism, because it is both (i) restricted, and (ii) 'holds only that we have reason to criminalize [public wrongs], whilst recognizing that we might have weightier countervailing reasons either for doing nothing formally, or for preferring legal mechanisms other than that of criminalization'—see Duff, 'Towards A Modest Legal Moralism', 230–1. Strictly speaking, (ii) is compatible with holding that the fact that an act-type is a public wrong is a defeasibly sufficient reason to criminalize that act-type. Elsewhere, however, Duff writes that this fact is only a 'relevant' reason, which is not in itself 'powerful' and only becomes a 'good reason' when further conditions are met. One such condition is that any response to the wrong ought to be one that condemns wrongdoers—see Duff, 'Towards a Theory of Criminal Law', 21.

moral wrongdoing, and the latter to the prevention of only certain moral wrongs. Later, we will have reason to distinguish between these two interpretations. For now, I will simply refer to (E), leaving open whether the best interpretation of (E) is or is not restricted.[30]

As I formulated it above, (E) is a principle that identifies reasons to *criminalize*. It is not entirely clear what this means. Feinberg's principles—(A), (B), and (C)—refer respectively to reasons to 'prohibit', to enact 'penal legislation', and to enact a 'criminal prohibition'. (A) thus seems to apply to a wider range of acts than (B) and (C). When I use the term *criminalize*, I am referring to all acts that make it a criminal offence to φ.[31] These may or may not be legislative acts. I will assume here that an act creates a criminal offence if it makes φers liable to conviction and punishment at the conclusion of a criminal process.[32] The reader will have her own views of what such a process amounts to, but nothing turns on this here.

A final clarification, which may by now seem long overdue. So far, I have referred indistinctly to immoralities and moral wrongs, and I have said nothing about what I take either term to mean. Here is a modest proposal: φing is immoral or morally wrong only if there is moral reason not to φ. While this is a plausible necessary condition, it is not plausibly sufficient. What additional properties must the aforementioned moral reasons possess? Consider three possibilities:

(F)   Those reasons defeat any reasons to φ;
(G)   Those reasons add up to a moral duty not to φ;
(H)   Those reasons add up to a moral duty not to φ, and are such that φing is an unjustified and unexcused breach of that duty.

Some think that one has a duty not to φ only if at least one reason to φ is excluded.[33] If this is right, (F) and (G) do not refer to the same property. If the moral reasons not to φ outweigh any reasons to φ, without

If Duff's view is that this condition identifies an additional reason to criminalize that is necessary for permissibility, he denies that the reason mentioned in (ii) is defeasibly sufficient.

[30] Doesn't the possibility of restricted legal moralism convert (B) into a type of legal moralism after all? And doesn't this suggest that the opposition between the 'moderate' Devlin and legal moralism is a false opposition? It does not. Just as there can be harmless wrongdoing, there can be wrongless harmdoing. *Pace* Feinberg, (B) identifies a reason to prevent harms whether wrongfully inflicted or not, so (B) is not a type of legal moralism.

[31] I am thus referring to what Lacey calls 'formal' criminalization. See N. Lacey, 'Historicising Criminalisation: Conceptual and Empirical Issues', *Modern Law Review* 72 (2009): 936.

[32] If they have not successfully proved a defence.

[33] See J. Raz, 'Promises and Obligations', in P.M.S. Hacker and J. Raz (eds.), *Law, Morality, and Society* (OUP 1977).

excluding any of them, those reasons have the property mentioned in (F) but not that mentioned in (G). Some also think that one can have a duty not to φ even if φing is justified.[34] If this is right, (G) and (H) do not refer to the same property. Here I assume for the sake of argument that the aforementioned properties are indeed distinct. If the moral reasons not to φ possess the property referred to in (F) I will say that φing is *immoral*. If they possess the property referred to in (G) I will say that φing is a *moral wrong*.[35] If they possess the property referred to in (H) I will say that φing is a *culpable moral wrong*. This usage is stipulative,[36] but it will make clear which property I am referring to at any given point.

In what follows I will assume that (E) refers only to culpable moral wrongdoing. It is less clear that there is reason to criminalize whatever will probably prevent commission of *justified* moral wrongs. Take a case in which the only way to save five lives is for me to cut off your arm. Let's say I am justified in saving the five, but that when I do so I wrong you by cutting off your arm. Is there any reason for a third party to prevent me saving the five? Perhaps. Perhaps there is a reason to prevent me cutting off your arm, but this reason is defeated by the reasons to allow me to save five lives. Even if this is not so, it is plausible to think that there *is* reason to prevent circumstances arising in which this is the choice I face—in which I must choose between wronging you to save five lives and allowing the five to die. Much better if I could save the five without committing the wrong. And to make this option available, of course, is to simultaneously prevent any justified wrong from being committed.[37] I will not pursue this line of thought further here. It will be enough to consider whether the fact that criminalizing φing will likely prevent culpable wrongdoing is *itself* a reason to criminalize φing. Remember that to conclude that such a reason exists is not to conclude

---

[34] See J. Gardner, *Offences and Defences* (OUP 2007), chs. 4–5.

[35] This distinction between the immoral and the morally wrong is made in Simester, 'Enforcing Morality', 481, and J.R. Edwards and A.P. Simester, 'Wrongfulness and Prohibitions', *Criminal Law and Philosophy* 8 (2014): 171.

[36] I do not mean, in particular, to take a position in debates about the nature of culpability. For disagreement about whether committing a moral wrong without justification or excuse is necessarily culpable, see Gardner, *Offences and Defences*, 225–35; A.P. Simester, 'A Disintegrated Theory of Culpability', in D. Baker and J. Horder (eds.), *The Sanctity of Life and the Criminal Law: The Legacy of Glanville Williams* (CUP 2013), 178.

[37] The possibility of justified wrongdoing ceases to exist because I was justified in wronging you only when and because my one remaining option was to save the five. This is no longer the case.

that there is reason to criminalize culpable wrongs themselves. We may have no such reason. And we may have reason to criminalize other activities entirely. (E) is an instrumental not an act-centred principle.

It may be objected that I have omitted from consideration an important legal moralist view. According to that view, the concern of legal moralism is not with what we actually have moral reason not to do, but with what we have moral reason not to do *in the eyes of most members of our society*. This suggests that my modest proposal was already too immodest. I doubt this is correct. As Les Green remarks:

There is no guarantee that the requirements of social morality will not be repugnant, superstitious, absurd, confused, and so forth. We are morally fallible and so are all our customs and practices. Thus, to think that the fact social morality provides adequate warrant for its own enforcement is to think that there are features of social morality that justify enforcing it even when it is repugnant.[38]

Perhaps there are such features. Perhaps the fact that social morality requires us not to φ gives the state legitimate authority to prohibit φing. This is not, I think, a particularly plausible view of authority. But even if it is correct, it does not conflict with my modest proposal. If the state has legitimate authority to prohibit φing, then once it is prohibited we have moral reason—indeed, a moral duty—not to φ.[39] Violation of the requirements of social morality is then also a moral wrong. Things are different, of course, if those requirements generate no moral reasons for action at all. But why, then, would violation of those requirements, or its prevention, be any reason at all to criminalize?[40]

In the absence of a satisfactory answer I set this view aside. That said, the previous paragraph does help clarify an important point. A legal moralist need not claim that the question of whether φing is a moral wrong is one that must be answered prior to, or independently of, the law. It may be that φing is a moral wrong *partly because* it is a criminal offence. Once road traffic offences are created, reliance on those laws may make

---

[38] L. Green, 'Should Law Improve Morality?' *Criminal Law and Philosophy* 7 (2013): 473, 476.

[39] I assume here that to have legitimate authority is to have a normative power to, among other things, impose duties on those over whom one has authority.

[40] One might think, of course, that the fact there is widely thought to be moral reason not to φ establishes that there is moral reason not to φ. So be it. The modest proposal I made earlier takes no position on the nature of moral reasons, so there is no conflict here.

my offending acts especially dangerous. Those acts may then be moral wrongs—they may breach a moral duty I owe to other road-users—even though this would not have been so had the road traffic offences never come into existence. In cases like this, criminalization helps *make* some actions morally wrong.[41] When this is so, (E) holds that there is reason to criminalize φing if doing so will not only help create the wrong, but will also probably prevent culpable commission of it.

II

This section considers two prominent arguments for versions of ALM. The first, offered by Michael Moore, derives an act-centred legal moralism from a retributivist theory of punishment. I will call it the *retributivist argument*. The second, offered by Antony Duff, derives an act-centred legal moralism from an account of citizens' duties to answer to one another. I will call it the *answerability argument*. This section does not assess the soundness of either argument. Instead, it argues *from* premises on which the two arguments rely *to* the soundness of principle (E). This requires defence of certain further premises. But these premises seem to me to be eminently defensible. If I am right, those who endorse ALM because they endorse the retributivist or answerability arguments, should also endorse ILM in the form of (E).

Consider first the retributivist argument. 'The moral wrongness of any sort of behaviour', Moore writes, 'is always some reason to legislate against it in the criminal law'.[42] His argument for this thesis can be summarized as follows:

(1) Retributive justice is done when those who deserve to be punished are given the punishment they deserve;

(2) Society has a duty to make it the case that retributive justice is done;[43]

---

[41] For discussion of this possibility in the criminal law, see Simester and von Hirsch, *Crimes, Harms and Wrongs*, 24–9. For general discussion, see A.M. Honoré, 'The Dependence of Morality on Law', *Oxford Journal of Legal Studies* 13 (1993): 1.

[42] Moore, *Placing Blame*, 72. As he also puts it, 'the immorality of conduct, no matter how slight, constitutes a prima facie reason to criminalize the behaviour': ibid., 187.

[43] 'For a retributivist, the moral responsibility of an offender also gives society the *duty* to punish. Retributivism, in other words, is truly a theory of justice such that, if it is true, we have an obligation to set up institutions so that retribution is achieved': ibid., 91; see also 104, 154.

(3) Punishment is deserved by those who culpably commit moral wrongs;[44]

(4) Criminalizing moral wrongs can bring it about that those who culpably commit them are given the punishment they deserve;[45]

(5) Therefore, there is reason to criminalize φing if φing is a moral wrong.[46]

Consider second the answerability argument. According to Duff, the legal moralist holds that 'the wrongfulness of a given type of conduct is always a reason in favour of criminalizing it'.[47] A 'modest' legal moralist, however, claims only that this is true of some moral wrongs, and Duff claims only that it is true of *public* wrongs.[48] His argument can be summarized as follows:

(1) We are answerable to others for committing moral wrongs which are their 'business';[49]

(2) A moral wrong which 'violates the polity's defining values' is the 'business' of the wrongdoer's fellow citizens, and is therefore a *public* wrong;[50]

(3) Citizens have a duty to answer, and call one another to answer, for public wrongs;[51]

---

[44] For Moore, 'the desert that triggers retributive punishment is itself a product of the moral wrong(s) done by an individual, and the moral culpability with which he did those wrongs': ibid., 71.

[45] The achievement of retributive justice, Moore claims, is the criminal law's 'function', and we determine the function of a thing by identifying the goods it can bring about: ibid., 23–30. Note that criminalization also clears away an objection to the doing of retributive justice that would otherwise exist, namely the unfairness of punishing those whose actions were not prohibited at the time of acting: ibid., 71, 187.

[46] As we saw above, Moore claims that this reason is defeasibly sufficient.

[47] Duff, 'Towards A Modest Legal Moralism', 218.

[48] Ibid., 222.

[49] 'Retrospective responsibility is responsibility as answerability: to be held retrospectively responsible is to be called to answer for my actions, by those who have the standing to do so—to be called on to explain my actions, and if necessary to justify or excuse them, or accept censure for them. That is how we properly treat each other in extra-legal moral contexts: if another's wrongdoing is my business, I respond properly by calling her to answer for it': see Duff, 'Towards a Theory of Criminal Law', 16.

[50] A public wrong is 'one that is the business of the public—of all members of the polity in virtue simply of their membership as citizens': ibid., 9; a wrong is the business of the public when and because it 'violates the polity's defining values': see Duff, 'Responsibility, Citizenship and Criminal Law', 139. See also R.A. Duff, *Answering for Crime* (Hart 2007), 140ff.

[51] 'As citizens we have a special duty to attend to public wrongs committed within the polity: a duty to respond to such wrongs by calling the wrongdoer to public account which we

(4) Criminalizing public wrongs can bring it about that citizens answer, and are called to answer, for committing those wrongs;[52]

(5) Therefore, there is reason to criminalize φing if φing is a public wrong.[53]

There are important differences between these arguments. As I already mentioned, Duff's legal moralism is *restricted*. We can now see why. The reasons to criminalize identified by Duff are reasons citizens have in virtue of a particular type of community membership. To be a citizen, Duff claims, is to be a member of a political community which defines itself by reference to certain values;[54] as a member of that community one is answerable to one's fellow members for 'violating' those values— that is, for public wrongs. By calling members to answer, the criminal law sees that their duties to answer, and to call one another to answer, are duties to which those members conform. Moore's argument is very different. The reasons to criminalize identified by Moore derive from the value of retributive justice itself. That value generates a duty to punish deserving offenders. By bringing about said punishment, the criminal law sees that this duty is one to which society conforms. Because he claims that all culpable moral wrongdoing deserves punishment, Moore's legal moralism is *unrestricted*.

Assume that the premises of both these arguments are true. By taking some of these premises, and adding some further premises, we can construct two arguments for (E). Consider first the following argument, which builds on the retributivist argument:

---

owe to both victim and wrongdoer; a duty to answer to our fellows for our own commissions of such wrongs': see Duff, 'Responsibility, Citizenship and Criminal Law', 140.

[52] '[I]f another's wrongdoing is my business, I respond properly by calling her to answer for it; that is how I take both her and her wrongful conduct seriously. And *that is what the criminal law does in relation to public wrongdoing*: it calls alleged perpetrators of such wrongs to account, and holds them formally answerable for their commissions of such wrongs through the criminal trial': see Duff, 'Towards a Theory of Criminal Law', 16 (my emphasis).

[53] The argument relies on the assumption, made by Duff, that state officials—including those who create criminal offences—should act on behalf of the citizenry: the fact that those citizens have a duty to φ gives state officials reason to do what will help citizens conform to that duty. See Duff, *Answering for Crime*, 49. I do not challenge this assumption here.

[54] 'The polity is a distinct community, engaged in a distinctive enterprise of living together, structured by a set of values that help to define that enterprise, and by a distinction that any community must draw between what is "public" and what is "private"': see Duff, 'Towards a Theory of Criminal Law', 5.

(1) If there is reason for A to bring about x, and y is better than x, there is reason for A to bring about y;

(2) Officials have reason to give those who culpably commit moral wrongs the punishment they deserve;

(3) *Ceteris paribus*, it is better if instances of culpable moral wrongdoing do not occur than if those who culpably commit moral wrongs are given the punishment they deserve;

(4) Criminalizing φing will probably prevent culpable moral wrongdoing;

(5) Therefore—*ceteris paribus*—the fact that criminalizing φing will probably prevent culpable moral wrongdoing is a reason to criminalize φing.

Premise (2) of this argument is entailed by the retributivist argument.[55] I return to (1) in due course. To deny (3) is to claim that, all else being equal, it is no worse if people commit wrongs deserving of punishment and are then punished, than if they never commit such wrongs at all. This claim is hard to accept. Imagine that if Molly stays in tomorrow morning, she will not culpably commit a wrong. If she goes out, Molly will culpably commit the wrong and Alice will give Molly the punishment she deserves. *Ceteris paribus*, it seems obvious that it would be better if Molly stayed in tomorrow morning. We might explain this in two ways. According to a first explanation, the imposition of deserved punishment is intrinsically good.[56] But nothing counts as punishment if it does not make the person punished worse off.[57] So in addition to its intrinsic goodness, deserved punishment necessarily brings with it some countervailing badness. Culpable wrongdoing, on the other hand, does not necessarily bring with it anything good. And in addition to whatever impersonal badness it has, culpable wrongdoing is also bad *for people*. Some wrongs cannot be committed without damaging the lives of victims. And the culpable commission of any wrong damages the life of the

---

[55] If premises (1)–(3) of that argument are true, society has a duty to impose deserved punishments on culpable wrongdoers. It follows that officials have at least some reason to impose these punishments.

[56] This is Moore's view. For him, 'the good that punishment achieves is that someone who deserves it gets it. Punishment of the guilty is thus for the retributivist an *intrinsic* good.' See Moore, *Placing Blame*, 87–8.

[57] See e.g. D. Boonin, *The Problem of Punishment* (CUP 2011), 6–7.

wrongdoer herself.[58] Because all this damage will be done if Molly culpably commits a wrong, in addition to the damage done by deserved punishment itself, it would be better, *ceteris paribus*, if Molly stayed in and did not act wrongly.

Some would object to this first explanation for the following reason. According to the retributivist argument, to impose deserved punishment is to do a type of justice. But justice ought to be done, so the objection goes, not because of the good that doing justice brings into the world. Justice ought to be done irrespective of whether good is thereby brought into the world.[59] Even if we grant that this is true, it does not threaten (3). To see why, note that justice is not the only thing that ought to be done. It is also the case that each of us ought to refrain from culpably committing wrongs. Now return to the case in which staying in tomorrow morning will prevent Molly culpably committing a wrong. *Ceteris paribus*, if Molly stays in she will act as she ought to act by refraining from wrongdoing. If Molly goes out, Alice will act as she ought to act by imposing just punishment for Molly's wrong. It might thus seem that we should be indifferent as to where Molly spends her morning. But if she goes out, Molly will act as she ought *not* to act, by culpably committing a wrong.[60] *Ceteris paribus*, it would thus be better if Molly stayed in, and the culpable wrong did not occur. This gives us a second explanation of the truth of (3).

What other challenges might be made to the argument offered above? One possibility is that an objector might deny (4). They might deny, that is, that criminalization is capable of reducing the incidence of culpable wrongdoing. But it seems implausible to claim that criminalization could *never* have this effect,[61] and (E) applies only to cases where

---

[58] I do not mean that culpable wrongdoing damages lives because it has bad effects. I mean rather that culpable wrongdoing damages lives *in and of itself*—our lives go worse in virtue of our acting wrongly without justification or excuse. Why? Because it is worse for us, all else being equal, to live with reasons for regret, and culpable wrongdoing gives us such reasons. For further discussion, see J. Gardner, 'Wrongs and Faults', in A.P. Simester (ed.), *Appraising Strict Liability* (OUP 2005).

[59] For possible defences of this claim, see M. Berman, 'Two Kinds of Retributivism', in R.A. Duff and S. Green (eds.), *Philosophical Foundations of Criminal Law* (OUP 2011).

[60] Notice that it is *not* true that if Molly stays in, *Alice* will act as she ought not to act. This is not true because if Molly stays in, she will not culpably commit a wrong, and there will be no retributive justice for Alice to (fail to) do.

[61] And there is some empirical evidence that it can. This evidence suggests that criminalizing conduct which was permitted (as opposed to increasing the severity of the sentences on offer

it will probably do so. If there are few such cases, (E) will rarely support criminalization. But this does nothing to show that (E) is not a sound principle. Alternatively, one might object that even if criminalizing φing would probably reduce the incidence of culpable wrongdoing, there is only reason to criminalize φing if there is probably no other means that would be equally effective at a lesser cost to other values. If this is correct, (4) and (5) should be reformulated as follows:

(4a) Criminalizing φing will probably prevent culpable moral wrong-doing, and there is probably no other means that is equally effective at a lesser cost to other values;

(5a) Therefore—*ceteris paribus*—it is always a good reason in support of criminalization that it will probably be effective in preventing culpable moral wrongs, and there is probably no other means that is equally effective at a lesser cost to other values.

This is not a concession. Aside from the *ceteris paribus* clause, (5a) is simply (E) as I first formulated it in Section I.[62] The presence of this clause, however, suggests a further possible objection. One might object that when the better world mentioned in (3) is brought about via criminalization, all else is not equal, and that on closer inspection this world is not in fact better at all. Consider the following remarks:

there are two considerations that suggest that the only function of our criminal law is the achievement of retributive justice. One is the tension that exists between crime-prevention and retributive goals. This tension is due to retributivism's inability to share the stage with any other punishment goal. To achieve retributive justice, the punishment must be inflicted because the offender did the offence. To the extent that someone is punished for reasons other than that he deserves to be punished, retributive justice is not achieved.[63]

Moore's remarks suggest the following objection: even if it is a good thing that instances of culpable wrongdoing do not occur, things are worse (or no better) all-things-considered if those wrongdoers who remain will not face retributive justice; and when law-makers aim to prevent wrongdoing,

---

for conduct already criminalized) *can* reduce the incidence of that conduct: see e.g. A. von Hirsch, A. Bottoms, E. Burney, and P.-O. Wikstrom, *Criminal Deterrence and Sentencing Severity* (Hart 1999).

[62] The addition of the word 'culpable' is necessary in light of the text to n.37.

[63] Moore, *Placing Blame*, 27–8.

retributive justice will not be done. This argument, however, depends on a non sequitur. It assumes that the legitimate aims of those who criminalize and those who punish are identical, such that if law-makers criminalize φing in order to prevent some culpable wrong, judges may (or even must) punish offenders for those same reasons.[64] This assumption should be rejected. The act of criminalization is a very different act to that of punishment: to criminalizing φing is, inter alia, to make φers *liable* to punishment; but it is not to impose it. The two acts can thus be performed for different reasons. One can criminalize in order to prevent, without punishing in order to prevent. And one can punish in order to hand out just deserts, without criminalizing in order to hand out any deserts at all. To say that officials legitimately aim to prevent culpable wrongdoing when they criminalize, is thus to say nothing about the reasons for which officials legitimately act when they punish. The cost Moore identifies thus need not be borne by those who endorse (E).[65]

Moore's objection might also be rejected for a second reason. (E) identifies a particular reason to criminalize certain act-types. This is to say that it identifies a consideration that counts in favour of their criminalization.[66] It is not necessarily to say that legislators legitimately criminalize *for that very reason*. There is a difference, to put it another way, between normative and motivating reasons: between the considerations that count in favour of my doing something, and the considerations that motivate me in doing it. Not all considerations of the former kind ought to be considerations of the latter kind. It is those that should not which are *excluded* in Joseph Raz's sense of that word.[67] The point in the previous paragraph was that (E) is consistent with the exclusion, when it comes to punishment, of normative reasons to prevent wrongdoing. The point here is that (E) is also consistent with the exclusion of those reasons when it comes to legislation itself. I use the word 'may' here advisedly: (E) does not itself commit us either way. But this is enough

---

[64] It also assumes that retributive justice is only done if punishment is imposed for the reason that it is deserved. I grant this for the sake of argument.

[65] This argument is pursued at greater length in J.R. Edwards and A.P. Simester, 'Prevention with a Moral Voice', in A.P. Simester, A. Du-Bois Pedain, and U. Neumann, *Liberal Criminal Theory: Essays for Andreas von Hirsch* (Hart 2014).

[66] 'Any attempt to explain what it is to be a reason for something seems to me to lead back to the same idea: a consideration that counts in favor of it': see T.M. Scanlon, *What We Owe to Each Other* (Harvard University Press 1998), 17.

[67] On exclusion, see J. Raz, *Practical Reason and Norms* (OUP 1975), ch. 1.

to dispose of the Moore-inspired worry about (E)'s implications for the reasons for which sentencing officials may act. (E) has no such implications. So we are yet to see why the above argument for (E) does not go through. We are yet to see, in other words, why the world in which criminalization reduces the incidence of culpable wrongdoing is never a better world.[68]

Let us now turn to a second argument for (E),[69] which builds on some of the premises of the answerability argument:

(1) If there is reason for A to bring about x, and y is better than x, there is reason for A to bring about y;

(2) Citizens have reason to answer, and call one another to answer, for public wrongs;

(3) *Ceteris paribus*, it is better if instances of public wrongdoing do not occur than if those who commit such wrongs answer, and are called to answer, for their commission;

(4) Criminalizing φing can bring it about that there are fewer public wrongdoers;

(5) Therefore—*ceteris paribus*—that criminalizing φing will probably prevent public wrongdoing is a reason to criminalize φing.

(2) is entailed by the answerability argument.[70] I set aside (4), having already considered objections to the equivalent premise of the retributivist argument. One might deny (3). But we can again rely on the case of Molly and Alice. If all else is equal, it would be better if Molly stayed in tomorrow morning and did not commit a public wrong, than if Molly went out, committed the wrong and Alice called her to answer for doing so.[71] It might be argued that all else is *not* equal when prevention is achieved via criminalization. Perhaps those who criminalize in order to prevent culpable wrongdoing treat potential offenders with disrespect.

---

[68] Which is not to say that it always is. Hence the *ceteris paribus* clause in (5) and (5a).

[69] This second argument is an argument for a restricted version of (E), but as mentioned above I set aside for present purposes the question of whether the best version of (E) is or is not restricted.

[70] Premise (3) of the answerability argument states that citizens 'have a duty to answer, and call one another to answer, for public wrongs'. This entails that they have a reason to do so.

[71] In defending the equivalent premise of the previous argument I gave two explanations. Suffice it to say that similar explanations could be offered here.

Duff argues that when legislators have preventive aims, potential offenders face a criminal law that

creates a new reason—the threat of punishment—to make it in their interest to obey laws that they would otherwise have no such reason to obey. But this is no longer to address them as autonomous agents in a language to which they will listen. It is to seek to coerce their obedience by threats which treat them like 'dog[s] instead of with the freedom and respect due to [them]' as moral agents.[72]

Duff's remarks suggest the following possible objection: even if it is a good thing that culpable wrongs do not occur, things are worse (or no better) all-things-considered if the law achieves this by treating people disrespectfully; and when legislators aim to prevent wrongdoing (at least via the criminal law) this is just what they do. This objection fails.[73] We do not always treat others with disrespect by creating new reasons for action for them, even when we create those reasons in order to prevent them acting in some way. If you are about to attack me, I create a new reason for you to refrain if I am ready and willing to act in justified self-defence. Though you always had moral reasons not to attack me, you now have an additional prudential reason not to do so, a reason given by the injury I will inflict if you attack. Imagine I now warn you of my readiness to self-defend, in the hope that this will prevent your attack. It seems clear that I need not show you disrespect in doing this.[74] And the same, it seems, can be true of those who criminalize in order to prevent wrongs. When we criminalize φing we make it the case that those who φ are liable to punishment. Let's assume the punishments to which φers are made liable are morally justified, on whatever theory of morally justified punishment is correct. That judges are now ready to impose these punishments creates an additional prudential reason not to φ. If we criminalize in order to prevent wrongdoing, we warn potential φers that morally justified punishment may be imposed on them if they φ, in the hope that this will prevent them φing. Just as in the self-defence case, we are warning others that if they act in certain ways, we will do

---

[72] R.A. Duff, *Punishment, Communication, and Community* (OUP 2001), 85.

[73] We already saw that (E) does not itself tell us anything about the reasons for which law-makers legitimately act. But I set this reply aside here.

[74] In particular, it is hard to see why I am no longer addressing you as an 'autonomous agent'. Much depends, of course, on what is meant by autonomy. But it seems that my warning *assumes* you are autonomous in one sense—that you are capable of responding to the reasons to which the warning draws your attention. Why else bother issuing it?

what we are morally justified in doing, and we issue the warning to prevent them from acting in those ways. But if this does not show disrespect in the self-defence case, there is no reason to think it must show disrespect in the case of criminalization. If it does not, the cost identified by Duff need not be borne by those who endorse (E).[75]

The Duff-inspired objection might also be rejected for a second reason. According to the objection, it is disrespectful to assume that unless one creates prudential reasons for them not to φ, others will φ in violation of their moral duties. Yet, so the objection goes, this is precisely what one assumes when one criminalizes in order to prevent wrongs. If the previous paragraph is correct, there need be nothing disrespectful in what I have just described. We can now add that those who criminalize in order to prevent wrongs need not make the offending assumption. To see this, notice that in some cases we can prevent wrongs only if enough people contribute to the production of goods that help to prevent them;[76] yet each of us has a duty to make a contribution only if we can be assured that enough people will do the same. Such cases arise most commonly when the contribution is costly to make, such that we have a duty to make it only if this is likely to do a sufficient amount of good. Now imagine it is possible to provide the requisite assurance only by making it a crime to fail to contribute. Only the prospect of conviction and punishment is likely to get enough people to do their part.[77] In such a case, failure to contribute is criminalized in order to prevent wrongs, by getting enough people to contribute to the aforementioned goods. But the assumption is *not* that, absent criminalization, people will violate a moral duty to contribute. The assumption is rather that, absent criminalization, it is morally permissible *not* to contribute, but that

---

[75] For further discussion, see Edwards and Simester, 'Prevention with a Moral Voice'.

[76] The goods I have in mind include affordable housing, community centres, policing, schools, etc.

[77] Victor Tadros mentions taxation as one example. In some cases, 'tax avoidance is wrong only on condition that sufficient other people pay their taxes. If I pay my taxes and others do not do so, not only is my absolute level of wealth reduced for the sake of some goal, my *comparative* level of wealth is reduced. The value of the money that I have depends on how much others have. Their bargaining position becomes stronger if they have more than I, and that will increase the burden that I bear by paying taxes. For this reason it is often wrong to demand that citizens pay taxes unless sufficient assurance is given that others will pay. The threat of punishment is probably a necessary condition of ensuring that enough people pay their taxes to render all cases of tax evasion wrong.' See V. Tadros, 'Wrongness and Criminalisation', in A. Marmor (ed.), *The Routledge Companion to Philosophy of Law* (Routledge 2012), 171.

acting permissibly will produce an outcome that is bad for everyone. By criminalizing we prevent this bad outcome from coming about. The key point here is that those who criminalize in such cases do not show anyone disrespect: they do not make what I called above the offending assumption. So we are yet to see why the argument for (E) set out above does not go through.

Let us turn finally to (1). Some think that if some action is of value, that either is, or entails that there is, a reason to do it.[78] Duff denies this:

> I agree that values speak to us all, that they invite appropriate responses from us all, but I do not think that they always speak to us all as agents: sometimes the appropriate response to a value is a recognition with no practical implications, not because I am not well placed to help realize the value, but because it is not connected to me as an agent. The site of agency is not the whole world; my agency is grounded in the more limited, particular forms of life in which I function, and find my reasons for action.[79]

These remarks suggest a possible challenge to (1): even if y is better than x, and there is reason for A to bring about x, it may not follow that there is reason for A to bring about y. There will be no such reason if the value which makes y better is not 'connected to [A] as an agent'. Grant for the sake of argument that this is correct. In the argument under consideration, to bring about x is to bring it about that people answer, and are called to answer, for public wrongs; to bring about y is to bring it about that there are fewer such wrongs. But public wrongs *just are* wrongs which are the 'business' of the members of the political community. As Duff and Marshall put it, they are wrongs that are of 'concern' to the public at large.[80] So it cannot be said that those wrongs are not connected to citizens as agents. The challenge in question thus fails.

III

Section II considered two arguments for ALM: the retributivist argument and the answerability argument. It did not challenge the soundness of either argument, but contended that, with the addition of certain further

[78] See e.g. J. Raz, 'Facing Up: A Reply', *Southern California Law Review* 62 (1989): 1153, 1230.

[79] R.A. Duff, 'In Response', in R. Cruft, M. Kramer, and M. Reiff (eds.), *Crime, Punishment, and Responsibility: The Jurisprudence of Antony Duff* (OUP 2011), 351, 357–61.

[80] R.A. Duff and S.E. Marshall, 'Criminalization and Sharing Wrongs', *Canadian Journal of Law and Jurisprudence* 11 (1998): 7.

premises, these arguments also support (E) and thus support a version of ILM. In this section, I deny that the two arguments are sound arguments for ALM. My claim is not that they depend on false premises. It is rather that ALM does not follow from them. What does follow, I argue, is ILM in the form of (E). Properly understood, the conclusion of both arguments is that there is reason to criminalize φing in virtue of the fact that criminalizing φing will probably prevent certain wrongs. But neither argument supports the criminalization of moral wrongdoing in virtue of the fact that it is moral wrongdoing. So neither the retributivist nor the answerability argument supports ALM.

Recall the initial premises of the retributivist argument:

(1)   Retributive justice is done when those who deserve to be punished are given the punishment they deserve;

(2)   Society has a duty to make it the case that retributive justice is done;

(3)   Punishment is deserved by those who culpably commit moral wrongs.

Moore makes clear that when he claims a person deserves to be punished he is referring to a more general principle:

One more general principle that does not seem clouded in metaphor is a general principle of desert. Such a principle arises because of what might be called the 'secondary' moral rights and duties we all possess. I have a primary duty not to break (most of) my promises and another primary duty not to injure or kill (most of) my fellow persons. . . . I also have what I shall call secondary duties and rights—respectively, a duty either to perform my promise, even belatedly, or in some other way to put the promisee in as good a position as he would have been in had I kept my promise; a duty to correct the injustice that I have caused in injuring or killing another by making amends in whatever way I can, including compensation. . . . It is breach of these secondary duties that warrants the judgment that I ought to be made to keep my promise or pay its equivalent, or that I ought to be made to compensate the victims of my violence. . . . We idiomatically make this 'ought' judgment using the word 'desert'.[81]

To say that a culpable wrongdoer deserves punishment is to make use of this general principle:

The retributive principle—that offenders should be punished because and only because they have culpably done wrong—is an instance of this more general

---

[81] Moore, *Placing Blame*, 171.

principle of desert. We all have primary duties not to do the sort of acts that *malum in se* criminal statutes prohibit. We also have secondary duties to allow ourselves to be made to suffer if we have violated these primary duties. The trigger for these secondary duties is again our culpability in violating the primary duties that define wrongdoing.[82]

To say that A deserves to be punished is thus to say that A has a secondary duty to allow herself to be punished—a duty, as I will put it from now on, to 'take the punishment'. Retributive justice is done when the punishment imposed on A is the punishment A has a secondary duty to take. Premise (1) of the retributivist argument must be understood accordingly. We know from premise (3) that those who have the aforementioned secondary duty are culpable wrongdoers. Their secondary duty exists *because* they breached a primary duty—this is what makes them wrongdoers—and did so culpably. Premise (2) of the argument identifies a further duty: a duty to make it the case that retributively just punishments are imposed.

Consider now the remainder of the retributivist argument:

(4)   Criminalizing moral wrongs can bring it about that culpable wrongdoers are given the punishment they deserve;

(5)   Therefore, there is reason to criminalize φing if φing is a moral wrong.

Premise (4) is crucial. If criminalizing moral wrongs could not bring about deserved punishment, the retributivist argument would identify no reason to criminalize those wrongs. That it can bring about deserved punishment is a reason to criminalize because such punishments, premise (1) tells us, are retributively just, and because society, premise (3) tells us, has a duty to bring about retributive justice. What we now know is that to bring about retributive justice is to bring it about that culpable wrongdoers conform to their secondary duty to take the punishment.[83] We saw in Section II that to fail to conform to a moral duty is to commit a moral wrong. Are the aforementioned secondary duties also moral duties?

---

[82] Ibid., 172.

[83] It might be said that the duty to take the punishment is a duty not to resist or complain *if* one happens to be punished. On this interpretation, that duty is itself no reason to punish culpable wrongdoers. But this implies that the *desert* of culpable wrongdoers is also no reason to punish them: as we already saw, it is the secondary duty to take the punishment in which the desert of culpable wrongdoers consists. I assume in what follows that the duty to take the punishment is better understood in a different way: as a duty to which culpable wrongdoers conform if and only if they are punished.

It is plausible to think that they are.[84] If this is right, to bring about retributive justice is to prevent certain moral wrongs—the moral wrongs that would be committed were culpable wrongdoers to breach the secondary duties I just mentioned. To claim that bringing about retributively just punishment is a reason to criminalize φing—the claim on which, as we just saw, the retributivist argument depends—is thus to claim that preventing the aforementioned secondary wrongs is a reason to criminalize φing.

It is worth re-emphasizing at this point that criminalization is not punishment. True, when law-makers create a criminal offence they make offenders *liable* to punishment. But whether anyone is actually punished—let alone given the punishment they deserve—depends on the actions of private individuals (who may or may not offend) and various public officials (police officers, prosecutors, trial judges, sentencing judges, etc.). Strictly speaking, then, criminalization can at most make it highly likely that the wrongs identified in the previous paragraph will be prevented. The retributivist argument is thus best read as claiming that this likelihood is itself a reason to criminalize.[85]

Let us now return to (E). I pointed out earlier that both restricted and unrestricted versions of this principle are possible. According to what I called (E^R):

(E^R):   It is a good reason in support of criminalization that it would probably be effective in preventing (eliminating, reducing) certain moral wrongs, and there is probably no other means that is equally effective at a lesser cost to other values.

The last three paragraphs showed that the retributivist argument is *itself* an argument for one version of (E^R). Properly understood, that argument identifies a reason to criminalize φing when and because criminalizing φing will probably prevent certain *secondary* wrongs. It is true that in many legal systems, criminalizing moral wrongs *themselves* will probably

---

[84] If there really are principles of retributive justice, those principles are presumably moral principles, and the duty to take retributively just punishment is presumably a moral duty.

[85] It might be said in reply that even if criminalization is not likely to result in *more* retributive justice being done, there is still reason to do it because criminalization will make doing retributive justice *legitimate*. Whether or not we should accept this claim about legitimacy, the suggested reading of the retributivist argument does not make it any less instrumental. The fact that criminalization makes the doing of retributive justice legitimate is a reason to criminalize *only if* criminalization is likely to result in some retributive justice being done in the criminal courts.

prevent these wrongs: criminalizing murder, rape, and theft, for instance, will bring it about that deserved punishment is taken by murderers, rapists, and thieves. In those legal systems, the retributivist argument thus *does* identify a reason to criminalize the primary moral wrongs of murder, rape, and theft.[86] But like Devlin's argument, when given Hart's 'moderate' reading, the significance given to the fact that φing is a moral wrong is derivative—it derives from the fact that criminalizing φing will probably prevent secondary wrongs.[87] According to ALM, there is reason to criminalize moral wrongs irrespective of the effects of doing so, in virtue of the fact that they are moral wrongs. The retributivist argument does not support this claim. But unlike Devlin's argument, it does support (E^R): it identifies a reason to criminalize φing in virtue of the fact that doing so will probably prevent a particular secondary wrong: the wrong of failing to take the punishment, as committed by culpable wrongdoers.

Two further points are worth making at this stage. First, nothing in the previous paragraph rules out the possibility that a refusal to do one's secondary duty might sometimes be *justified*. Perhaps offenders are justified in resisting punishment if state officials have secured their presence in court only by breaking the law, or if the regime of which those officials are part lacks legitimacy.[88] Recall from Section I that, as interpreted here, (E)—and so (E^R)—states only that there is reason to prevent *culpable* moral wrongdoing: it does not identify a reason to prevent the *justified* commission of secondary wrongs. We can therefore accept that officials have no reason to impose punishment on those justified in resisting it. There is nothing in this acceptance which conflicts with (E^R).

Second, the argument of this section relies on Moore's claim that to deserve some punishment is to have a secondary duty to take it. Does it follow that if a rival understanding of desert were forthcoming—one

[86] It will also identify a reason to criminalize *other* actions if criminalizing those others actions is likely to bring about retributively just punishment. One might doubt that this could be the case. One might doubt it if one thinks that retributively just punishment must be imposed *for* culpable wrongdoing rather than for anything else. Doesn't criminalizing other actions mean that punishment will necessarily be imposed for those actions? It does not. Morally salient facts that do not show up in offence-definitions, and which thus are not grounds for conviction, may still be grounds for punishments imposed by the criminal courts. Those punishments may thus still be imposed for culpable commission of a wrong.

[87] Remember: if criminalizing φing will not bring about any retributive justice, the retributivist argument identifies no reason to criminalize.

[88] For discussion, see R.A. Duff, 'Blame, Moral Standing and Legitimacy of the Criminal Trial', *Ratio* 23 (2010): 123.

which does not cash out wrongdoers' deserts in terms of secondary duties—the retributivist argument would no longer be an argument for (E^R)? It does not. It is true, of course, that if culpable wrongdoers do not have a secondary duty to take the punishment, punishing them cannot prevent the secondary wrong of failing to take it. But this does not mean that the retributivist argument is no longer an argument for (E^R). According to the retributivist argument, there is reason to criminalize when and because criminalization can bring about deserved punishment (however desert is understood). The reason to bring about deserved punishment is that society thereby conforms to its duty to do retributive justice.[89] We already saw that failing to conform to a duty of justice is plausibly thought of as a moral wrong. If this is correct, the reason to criminalize identified by the retributivist argument is a reason to prevent society committing the moral wrong of failing to do retributive justice. It follows that the retributivist argument remains an argument for (E^R): it remains an argument that there is reason to criminalize in virtue of the fact that doing so will probably prevent a particular moral wrong.[90]

Let us now turn to the answerability argument. Recall premise (3) of that argument:

(3)   Citizens have a duty to answer, and call one another to answer, for public wrongs.

This premise identifies two duties of citizenship: a duty to answer to one's fellow citizens for one's own commission of public wrongs, and a duty to call other citizens who commit public wrongs to answer for doing so. Duff describes these duties in the following terms:

The criminal law gives institutional form to a particular subset of what we might call secondary associative obligations: associative because they are obligations we owe to our fellow citizens in virtue of our shared membership of the polity; secondary because they concern our civic response to breaches of the primary obligations that the criminal law presupposes—to commissions of the kind of wrongs with which the criminal law is concerned. As citizens we have a special duty to attend to public wrongs committed within the polity: a duty to respond to such wrongs by calling the wrongdoer to public account, which we owe to both

---

[89] Recall that according to premise (2), society has a duty to make it the case that retributive justice is done.

[90] Or its culpable commission—see the previous paragraph.

victim and wrongdoer; a duty to answer to our fellows for our own commissions of such wrongs, and to answer to any accusations of such wrongdoing that are reasonably brought against us.[91]

As this passage makes clear, the duty to answer for committing public wrongs is a *secondary* duty—a duty one has when and because one violates a primary duty and commits a public wrong. This is the first duty mentioned in (3)—a secondary duty of wrongdoers themselves. The other duty mentioned in (3) is a further secondary duty—a duty one has when and because *other* citizens have breached their primary duties and committed public wrongs.

Consider now the remainder of the answerability argument:

(4)   Criminalizing public wrongs can bring it about that citizens answer, and are called to answer, for committing those wrongs;

(5)   Therefore, there is reason to criminalize φing if φing is a public wrong.

Premise (4) is crucial. The answerability argument succeeds only if it identifies some fact that gives us reason to criminalize φing. (4) identifies that fact: that criminalizing φing can bring it about that citizens are called to answer for public wrongs. This fact is reason-giving precisely because of the secondary duties we just mentioned. When the criminal law brings it about that wrongdoers are called to answer for public wrongs, citizens conform to their secondary duty to so call them.[92] And by calling public wrongdoers to answer, one makes it more likely that they will give the answers they owe. When such answers are given, public wrongdoers conform to *their* secondary duties as wrongdoers. It follows that to bring it about that citizens are called to answer for public wrongs, just is to prevent certain moral wrongs—the moral wrongs which would be committed were offenders to fail to answer, and were citizens to fail to call them. When Duff claims that calling citizens to answer for public wrongs is a reason to criminalize—the claim on which, as we just saw, the answerability argument depends—he is thus claiming that preventing the aforementioned secondary wrongs is a reason to criminalize.

It is worth repeating that creating a criminal offence at most makes it highly likely that wrong-prevention of the kind discussed above will actually occur. This depends, again, on how potential offenders and various officials react to the new offence.[93] Properly understood, then, the answerability argument is another argument for (E^R). It identifies a reason to criminalize φing in virtue of the fact that criminalizing φing will probably prevent certain secondary wrongs.[94] It is true that in many legal systems, these wrongs probably *will* be prevented by criminalizing public wrongs themselves—this will likely result in public wrongdoers being called to answer, and in them offering the answers they owe. In those legal systems, the answerability argument *does* identify a reason to criminalize public wrongs. But as with the retributivist argument, the significance this gives to the fact that φing is a moral wrong is derivative—it derives entirely from the fact that criminalizing φing will prevent the secondary wrongs of failing to answer, and failing to call others to answer. And to repeat, ALM states that there is reason to criminalize moral wrongs irrespective of the effects of doing so, in virtue of the fact that they are moral wrongs. The answerability argument does not support this claim.[95]

IV

Section III concluded that the retributivist and answerability arguments are both arguments for (E^R). Both arguments identify a reason to criminalize φing in virtue of the fact that criminalization will probably prevent certain secondary wrongs. Both are thus arguments for ILM not ALM.

---

[93] As made clear in Section I, to criminalize φing, as the term is used here, is to make it a criminal offence to φ. There can be no guarantee that this will be followed up in any particular way.

[94] Or at least the culpable commission of them. As suggested above, we may sometimes be justified in breaching secondary duties. If criminalization would probably only prevent justified breaches, (E) would identify no reason to criminalize.

[95] It might be said in reply that a version of ALM can be defended in a different way, by reference to the intrinsic value of expressing disapproval of public wrongs. If this is intrinsically valuable, there appears to be a reason to criminalize such wrongs irrespective of whether this has any preventive effects (assuming, of course, that criminalization expresses disapproval). This argument warrants sustained attention that I cannot give it here. But it is worth noting that it is not clear that Duff accepts it. In his view, to express disapproval, then fail to do anything about violations of the polity's values, 'would be to betray those values, and would fail to do justice both to the victims and to the perpetrators of such violations'. This is particularly important for Duff, because for him our reasons to criminalize 'have to do ... with what it is for a polity to take its defining values seriously'. In his view a polity does this only if it calls public wrongdoers to answer. If this latter claim is correct, it seems there is only reason to criminalize public wrongs if doing so *would* probably result in public wrongdoers being called to answer: otherwise, criminalization would only amount to a betrayal of the very values the state should be taking seriously. See Duff, 'Towards a Theory of Criminal Law', 15–16.

The argument of the present section is as follows: if preventing *secondary* wrongs is a reason to criminalize, then preventing the corresponding *primary* wrongs is also such a reason. If getting people to take the punishment or answer for robbery is a reason to criminalize, then getting people not to rob is also such a reason. This matters because, as we saw in Section I,[96] reasons to prevent primary wrongs are often reasons to criminalize more than just the wrongs themselves. If I am right, endorsement of the retributivist or the answerability argument should also lead one to endorse the existence of such reasons.

To make the argument, I must say something about secondary wrongs. We already know that to commit a secondary wrong is to violate a secondary duty. What makes a duty secondary? Clearly the answer has something to do with its relationship to some other duty. Earlier I wrote that secondary duties exist when and because another duty—what I called a primary duty—has been breached. But this is little advance. John Gardner suggests that the answer is given by what he calls *the continuity thesis*. To understand Gardner's suggestion, we must distinguish between reasons and obligations. An obligation, of course, is itself a type of reason: if I have an obligation to pay you £5, I have a reason to do so. But while obligations 'are individuated according to the action that they make obligatory', each 'reason for action is potentially a reason for multiple actions'.[97] Let's say that having promised to take my daughter to the beach today, I have an obligation to take her.[98] It follows that I have a reason to take her. This reason is also a reason to do various other things that contribute to our going to the beach. It is a reason to clear enough time in my schedule, and to ensure we have enough petrol in the car. Now imagine I sleep all day and never make it to the beach. Clearly I cannot conform to my obligation—the action it made obligatory can no longer be performed. But it is plausible to think that I now have certain *other* obligations, to which I still can conform, and which are in some way related to my original obligation—an obligation to apologize,

---

[96] See text to n.21 above. It is worth repeating that it does not follow from the fact that there is *reason* to criminalize an activity that it is *permissible* to criminalize that activity. We often have reason to do what we are not permitted to do.

[97] J. Gardner, 'What is Tort Law For? Part 1: The Place of Corrective Justice', *Law and Philosophy* 30 (2011): 1, 29–31.

[98] I here adapt an example devised by Neil MacCormick, and also discussed by Gardner. See N. MacCormick, 'The Obligation of Reparation', in his *Legal Right and Social Democracy* (OUP 1982), 212; Gardner, 'What is Tort Law For?', 28ff.

to take my daughter somewhere tomorrow, or the next time I am free. Why think I have such obligations? In Gardner's words,

> Once the time for performance of a primary obligation is past, so that it can no longer be performed, one can often nevertheless still contribute to satisfaction of some or all of the reasons that added up to make the action obligatory. Those reasons, not having been satisfied by performance of the primary obligation, are still with us awaiting satisfaction and since they cannot now be satisfied by performance of that obligation, they call for satisfaction in some other way. They call for next-best satisfaction, the closest to full satisfaction that is still available. We need to know the rationale of the obligation, of course, so that we can work out what counts as next best. But once we have it we also have the rationale, all else being equal, for a secondary obligation, which is an obligation to do the next-best thing. If all else is equal, the reasons that were capable of justifying a primary obligation are also capable of justifying a secondary one.[99]

Gardner's point here is that when we have an obligation to act in some way, there will typically be various reasons which contribute to making that action obligatory. Among the reasons that contribute to my having an obligation to take my daughter to the beach, are reasons to make my daughter happy and not to disappoint her. When I can no longer conform to my obligation to take her today these reasons do not simply disappear. They continue to count in favour of various actions I can still perform— including taking my daughter somewhere tomorrow, or the next time I am free. They count in favour, we can say, of doing *the next-best thing*. And in some cases these reasons will add up to a new obligation—an obligation to do the next-best thing by, say, taking my daughter ice-skating tomorrow. It is obligations of this kind to which we refer when we talk of secondary duties.

The normative significance of secondary duties is not, of course, limited to duty-bearers themselves. Imagine I breach my primary duty not to injure you, and deliberately cut off your arm. It is plausible to think I have a secondary duty to pay you compensation. That duty is a reason for me to pay you compensation. It is also a reason for at least some other people to do what will contribute to my paying it. One such class of people is the class of public officials, who can so contribute by making compensatory damages available in the law of tort, and awarding you damages if you successfully make a claim. Those officials have reason to do what

---

[99] Gardner, 'What is Tort Law For?', 33.

will contribute to my paying compensation, because they have a reason to do what will contribute to my doing my secondary duty to pay it.

Section III showed us that the retributivist and answerability arguments are built on the same logic. According to both arguments, officials have reason to criminalize when and because criminalization is likely to get wrongdoers to do what they have secondary duties to do. Consider a case of robbery. The robber has breached a primary duty, and done so culpably. According to the retributivist argument, the robber has a secondary duty to take the punishment for robbery. Gardner's discussion helps us see that when we make this last claim, we claim that the continued application of the reasons not to commit robbery—which gave rise to the primary duty not to do so—now count in favour of the robber taking the punishment for robbery. Taking that punishment is (part of) doing the next-best thing.[100] The reason to criminalize identified by the retributivist argument is a reason for officials to do what will contribute to the robber doing (part of) that thing.[101]

The answerability argument identifies rather different secondary duties. Not only are they duties to do different things—to answer and call to answer—they are duties of a different kind. In Duff's words they are 'associative obligations': obligations 'we owe to our fellow citizens in virtue of our shared membership of the polity'.[102] Why think that answering for public wrongs, and calling others to answer for them, are among the associative obligations citizens have? To see Duff's answer, notice that when he discusses our reasons to criminalize, he writes that

the reasons that we have to criminalize such core wrongs as murder, rape and other attacks on the person do not depend on the contingency of whether criminalization will efficiently prevent them. Those reasons have to do, rather,

---

[100] Only part, because the robber may have other secondary duties, including those identified by the answerability argument.

[101] Could it be argued that even if secondary duties to *compensate* are duties to do the next best thing, other secondary duties, including duties to take the punishment, are not duties of this kind? I cannot rule this out here. Two comments, however, are worth making. First, we saw in Section III that in Moore's view duties to compensate *and* duties to take punishment are instances of the same 'general principle'. This suggests that for Moore they are not duties of different kinds. Second, the suggestion that secondary duties to take punishment are duties to do the next best thing is a suggestion that has been defended by others: see e.g. V. Tadros, *The Ends of Harm* (OUP 2011), ch. 12. It is true that Tadros and Moore disagree about the *content* of the relevant duties. But this is compatible with their disagreement being one about what the next-best thing really is.

[102] Duff, 'Responsibility, Citizenship and Criminal Law', 140.

with what it is for a polity to take its defining values seriously, and for its members to take each other seriously as participants in the shared way of life who are bound and protected by those values.[103]

If a polity is to do this—if it is not to 'betray its values'[104]—the members must call one another to answer for wrongs that violate them: for public wrongs. This suggests that citizens' duties to answer for such wrongs, and call each other to answer, exist because failing to do so would betray, or fail to take seriously, the values by which the polity defines itself. It suggests that we ultimately have reason to criminalize the wrongs Duff mentions, because doing so avoids this kind of self-betrayal. Whatever one thinks of this last claim,[105] the key point here is this: according to Duff, our duties to answer, and call others to answer, are secondary duties. On the view we borrowed from Gardner, they are thus duties to do the next-best thing. The reasons which add up to give us these duties—for Duff, reasons to do what will take the community's values seriously— are reasons to which we can no longer fully conform. Once the primary (public) wrong of murder, rape, or robbery has been committed, we conform as fully as we can by offering answers to our fellow citizens, and by calling others to answer too. The reason to criminalize identified by the answerability argument, is a reason for officials to do what will con- tribute to this next-best conformity.

Let us now return to (E^R):

(E^R):   It is a good reason in support of criminalization that it would probably be effective in preventing (eliminating, reducing) certain culpable moral wrongs, and there is probably no other means that is equally effective at a lesser cost to other values.

We have seen that for defenders of the retributivist and answerability arguments, the moral wrongs mentioned in (E^R) are certain secondary wrongs. To say that law-makers have reason to prevent such wrongs, is to say that law-makers have reason to bring it about that potential secondary wrongdoers conform to their secondary duties. Such duties, I have suggested, are duties to do the next-best thing. This raises an obvious

---

[103] Duff, 'Towards a Theory of Criminal Law', 15.
[104] Ibid.
[105] For criticism, see J.R. Edwards and A.P. Simester, 'What's Public About Crime?', *Oxford Journal of Legal Studies* 37 (2017): 105.

question: if law-makers have reason to bring it about that we do the next-best thing, why should they have no reason to bring it about that we do the best thing? Why, that is, should they have no reason to bring it about that we conform not just to our secondary duties, but to our primary duties too? Recall that when we commit wrongs, we have duties to do the next-best thing precisely because the reasons that gave us our now-violated primary duty continue to apply to us. If law-makers have reason to prevent our secondary wrongs—in virtue of their being secondary wrongs—the reasons that gave us those primary duties must be reasons not just for us, but for law-makers too. They must give law-makers reason to do what will contribute to our conformity. But if this is so, law-makers surely have reason to do not only that which will contribute to our conforming *imperfectly*, but also to do that which will contribute to our conforming *perfectly*. To conform perfectly is, of course, to conform to the primary duty to which the reasons in question initially gave rise. If law-makers have reason to bring about perfect conformity, they have reason to prevent commission of primary wrongs.

We can see the point another way by returning to our parental example. In that example, I have a primary duty to take my daughter to the beach today but fail to do so. Let's now add that I have a secondary duty to take her ice-skating tomorrow. We have seen that my reasons not to disappoint my daughter contribute to the existence of the primary duty, so they contribute to the existence of the secondary duty also. Now let's say my sister, who lives nearby, hears of my failure. She phones me and tries to persuade me to do my duty by taking my daughter skating tomorrow. Assuming she has a chance of persuading me, it seems clear that this is something my sister has reason to do. She has reason, to generalize, to do what will contribute to my conforming to my secondary duty. She has this reason because my daughter's disappointment is reason-giving for her too. But if this is so now, why not yesterday? Why wouldn't my daughter's disappointment also have given my sister a reason to phone me up yesterday, and try to persuade me to take my daughter to the beach? It doesn't seem plausible to think that this reason becomes a reason for my sister only after I've failed to conform to it, when I can only do so imperfectly. And if that's right, my sister has reason to get me to conform to my primary duty, which is to say that she has reason to prevent my commission of primary wrongs.

As for my sister, it seems to me, so for the criminal law. It is not plausible to think that the reasons that give us primary and secondary duties are reason-giving for law-makers only after the primary duties have been breached. And if they are not, those law-makers have reason to prevent not just secondary wrongs, but primary wrongs too. One might point out, of course, that just because law-makers have reason to prevent primary wrongs, it doesn't follow that they have reason to do so via criminal-ization. My sister has reason to phone me only if she has a chance of persuading me to go skating. And perhaps she has no reason to phone if there are equally effective ways of getting me to go which are less costly all-things-considered. So be it. The principle we are discussing builds in both these conditions. (E) states that there is reason to criminalize only if this will likely be effective, and there is probably no other means that would be equally effective at a lesser cost to other values. The argument here is that when these conditions are met, there is reason to criminalize that which will prevent primary wrongs, and, if this fails, secondary wrongs also. This, ultimately, is the position that supporters of the retributivist and answerability arguments should accept.

v

I began by distinguishing between two types of legal moralism—between ALM and ILM. I pointed out that many prominent formulations of legal moralism are act-centred. This is not to say that the writers in question reject ILM. The distinction between act-centred and instrumental prin-ciples is not widely appreciated. Perhaps some really mean to sign up to ILM, despite the way they often formulate their views.[106] This paper has argued that this is precisely what they should do. If I am right, two

---

[106] Feinberg, in particular, at times writes as though he endorses a version of ILM, despite consistently giving a canonical formulation of legal moralism in act-centred terms. In *Harmless Wrongdoing*, he writes that a presumptive case for legal moralism can be made by arguing that 'it is always right, other things being equal, to prevent evils; that the need to prevent evils of any description is a good kind of reason in support of a legal prohibition'. See Feinberg, *Harmless Wrongdoing*, 5. This is an argument for ILM, not ALM. Similarly, Richard Arneson writes that '[if] conduct of a certain type is conceded to be immoral, aren't we already conced-ing there is reason, though perhaps not conclusive reason, for prohibition?' He thinks the answer is affirmative because he accepts Gerald Dworkin's claim that, at least *ceteris paribus*, 'immoral conduct should be discouraged' by whoever is in a position to 'lower its incidence'. But if this is the thought, there is no reason at all to criminalize immoral conduct when doing so will not prevent it, and there is reason to prohibit ancillary activities when doing so will

prominent arguments for versions of ALM are themselves arguments that offer support for ILM. I showed this in two ways. First, by pointing out that even if both arguments are sound, their premises can also be used to construct plausible arguments for versions of ILM. Second, by showing that neither argument is in fact a sound argument for ALM: it is ILM, not ALM, which follows from their premises. One might doubt that all of this matters much. One might point to my own admission that the version of ILM supported by the retributivist and answerability arguments will very often identify a reason to criminalize primary moral wrongs themselves, because doing so will very often prevent (culpable commission of) secondary wrongs.[107] One might claim that this shows that ILM has the same implications for criminalization as ALM. But that is too quick. Section IV argued that we should reject a version of ILM restricted to the prevention of secondary wrongs. Once we accept that preventing (culpable commission of) primary wrongs is a reason to criminalize, we should also accept that there will sometimes be reason to criminalize more than the primary wrongs themselves.[108]

That there is reason to criminalize something does not, of course, entail that it is permissibly criminalized. Even if there is reason to criminalize conduct that is not morally wrong, there may be constraints that render it impermissible to do so. Nothing I have said here denies that this is so. But if my argument is correct, one shortcut to conclusions about permissible criminalization is unavailable. One cannot argue that because there is *no* reason to criminalize what is not wrong, it is only ever permissible to criminalize wrongs. One cannot argue, as do Antony Duff and Sandra Marshall, that because there is *only* reason to criminalize public wrongs, it is only ever permissible to criminalize such wrongs.[109] Instead, one must explain why, despite the existence of reasons to criminalize more

prevent immoral conduct. So while Arneson writes as if he means to defend ALM, he is really offering a defence of ILM. See Arneson, 'The Enforcement of Morals Revisited', 441.

[107] On the retributivist argument, the wrong of failing to take deserved punishment; on the answerability argument, the wrongs of failing to answer, and to call others to answer, for public wrongs.

[108] Assuming, of course, that there are no alternative ways of doing so which come at a lesser cost in other values.

[109] See Duff, 'Towards A Modest Legal Moralism', 217; Duff, 'Towards a Theory of Criminal Law', 9; R.A. Duff and S.E. Marshall, 'Public and Private Wrongs', in J. Chalmers, F. Leverick, and L. Farmer (eds.), *Essays in Criminal Law in Honour of Sir Gerald Gordon* (Edinburgh 2010), 75.

than the wrongs themselves, it is impermissible to do what those reasons count in favour of doing.[110] Whether such an explanation can be provided is a matter for another day. These remarks, however, should be enough to show that, *pace* my imagined doubter, the truth of ILM is not unimportant. Whether legal moralists should sign up, qua legal moralists, to act-centred or instrumental principles—the question this paper has begun to explore—is therefore a question worthy of further attention.[111]

---

[110] Arneson puts the challenge as follows: if 'immoral conduct should be discouraged, and in many circumstances criminal prohibition can discourage immoral conduct, lower its incidence… how can there be a bar of principle against legal moralism? Isn't this like proclaiming that there is a bar of principle against using a hammer for a certain type of job, no matter how useful or cost-effective, in given circumstances, using a hammer for that job would be?' See Arneson, 'The Enforcement of Morals Revisited', 441.

[111] Thanks to James Chalmers, Lindsay Farmer, José Manuel Fernández, John Gardner, Ambrose Lee, Fiona Leverick, Ezequiel Monti, Andrew Simester, Findlay Stark, and Patrick Tomlin for comments on earlier versions of this paper.

6

Crime as Prime

RICHARD HOLTON

According to a familiar picture, two elements are needed for guilt in most common law offences: the action, the *actus reus*, and the associated mental element, the *mens rea*. Neither is sufficient for the offence on its own. So a murder requires a killing—a homicide—and also an intention—*malice aforethought* as it is traditionally, and misleadingly, termed. And it is natural to think that these two elements can obtain independently. Thus there can be a killing that is not accompanied by the relevant intention—that is what happens in cases of accidental killing. Conversely, there can be an intention without a killing—that is what happens in attempted murder, and also in cases where so little is actually done that we do not even have an attempt.

Natural though this picture is, I think that we should reject it. I don't suggest that we should give up the notions of *actus reus* and *mens rea*. But I do suggest that we make the best sense of the law if we reject the idea that they are independent. The central idea I will develop here is that a crime like murder cannot be understood as the conjunction of a self-standing mental element and a self-standing physical element. Instead we should think of it as involving an intentional action—murder—which involves both elements inseparably intertwined.

My argument for this proceeds by way of an account of the puzzles that arise if we think of *mens rea* and *actus reus* as separable. One account concerns the notion just mentioned, that of attempt. Why is it—a much discussed question—that in many jurisdictions, attempt, even a completed attempt where the perpetrator thinks that they have done enough, is often punished less severely than success?[1] After all, if we have two independent

---

[1] See R.A. Duff, *Criminal Attempts* (Oxford: OUP 1997), ch. 4, for discussion both of how attempt is punished in various jurisdictions, and of possible justifications for it.

Oxford Studies in Philosophy of Law Volume 3. John Gardner, Leslie Green, and Brian Leiter (eds)
This chapter © Richard Holton 2018. First published in 2018 by Oxford University Press

elements, the *mens rea* and the *actus reus*, it might seem, whether from considerations of natural justice or of deterrence, that it is the *mens rea* that matters; whether the act is successful or not is just down to luck. But if the *mens rea* is the same in each case, then the punishment should be the same. Yet we are, I think, naturally resistant to that conclusion. It isn't just that this is what the law happens to be. We think that this is what the law *should* be. We think that successful offences should be punished more severely than mere attempts; we are more inclined to morally condemn those who succeed than those who merely attempt; we feel more guilty about our own immoral successes than our mere attempts, and so on.

A second problem concerns the nature of *mens rea*. I said before that the traditional characterization of the *mens rea* for murder as *malice aforethought* is highly misleading: it has long been accepted that, as one authority puts it 'the "malice" may have in it nothing really malicious; and need never be really "aforethought" '.[2] Less misleadingly the mental element is standardly thought of as an intention. But that too is far from a perfect characterization. In many crimes a person can be guilty even though they lack what we would normally think of as an intention to commit the crime. So, to continue with the example of murder, if the death of the victim is sufficiently clearly foreseen by the accused, that may be sufficient to constitute the *mens rea*.[3] Moreover, even if the accused does not expect the victim to die—if they would indeed be surprised by their death—an intention to inflict grievous bodily harm is sufficient for the *mens rea* for murder.[4] And for many other crimes, though not in England for murder, recklessness is sufficient. How should we understand this? One possibility is that these various different criteria have no real unity: they have just been put together for pragmatic expediency. But the arguments that courts have used have typically been couched in terms of something like the development of the true nature of the crime, and of what it is, not to have an intention to murder, but to murder intentionally. This is reflected too in a common understanding

---

[2] C.S. Kenny, in J.C. Smith, *Smith and Hogan, Criminal Law*, 9th edition (London: Butterworths, 1999), p. 348.

[3] Quite how likely it is foreseen as, and whether this should be a subjective or an objective standard, has been an issue of ongoing debate in the courts. Since *Woollin* [1989] AC82, [1998] Crim LR 890, the standard requirement in the UK is a subjective one of virtual certainty.

[4] Moloney [1985] 1 AER 1025.

of what it is to do something intentionally. If you ask ordinary people whether the foreseen consequences of an agent's acts are things that they do intentionally, in many circumstances they will say that they are; a point to which we shall return.

A third problem arises when we put these two issues together. Although, as we have seen, the expectation that the victim will die is enough for the *mens rea* of murder, if the victim doesn't in fact die, it is not enough for the *mens rea* of attempted murder. (At least, not in England, and in most US jurisdictions; Scottish law is rather different, as is that of the State of Colorado.) Similarly, whilst intending to cause grievous bodily harm is sufficient for the *mens rea* for murder, attempting to cause grievous bodily harm is not sufficient for the *mens rea* for attempted murder.[5] And whilst recklessness is sufficient for the *mens rea* of a crime like rape, it is not sufficient for attempted rape. Again, this might be thought to result from expediency. But again that doesn't seem quite right. Attempting to do something that one believes will result in a killing is not the same as intending to kill, and the law is right to treat them as different.[6]

So we are left with a puzzle. The idea I want to explore here is that we can make some progress on solving it by thinking of the relation between the *mens rea* and the *actus reus* in a very different way. Rather than conceiving of them as two independent elements which come together to constitute an offence, we should think of the offence as a single primitive notion, though one which entails (or presupposes) these two elements. Our way of understanding the *mens rea* involved in murder is as the mental state that is common to those who perpetrate it. The mental state of those guilty of attempted murder is a different thing, that of someone who unsuccessfully tries to kill.

---

[5] *Smith and Horgan, Criminal Law*, p. 307. See R.A. Duff, *Intention, Agency, and Criminal Liability* (Oxford: Blackwells, 1990) and Duff, *Criminal Attempts* for illuminating discussion. In many ways the argument of this paper can be seen as an attempt to provide a theoretical underpinning for the position defended there. I hope that the main argument of this paper is also consistent with the position taken by Gideon Yaffe in his *Attempts* (Oxford: OUP, 2010), although my own view on why we should not distinguish tryings from attempts is somewhat different (see n.20 below). Yaffe's subsequent 'Criminal Attempts', *Yale Law Journal* 124 (2014): 92–156, also traces many of the difficulties in standard discussions on criminal attempt to the view that *mens rea* and *actus reus* can be identified independently; see especially pp. 118–20.

[6] Though whether or not they should be punished in the same way, or indeed even subject to the same conviction, is a further question. See Yaffe, *Attempts*, pp. 119ff.

Such ideas may seem mysterious, but in suggesting this I am following a path that has become very familiar in many areas of philosophy. The main ideas have gone under various different names—'externalism', 'disjunctivism'—and have been proposed with various different emphases. Here I want to take as my model the 'Knowledge First' account offered by Timothy Williamson.[7] So I start by outlining that.

KNOWLEDGE

How should we conceive of knowledge? A traditional approach held it to be built out of the conjunction of three different elements: belief (something internal), truth (something external), and justification (either external or internal, depending on the account). But in a justly celebrated piece Gettier showed that this couldn't be right.[8] To use an example first offered by Russell: agents are surely justified in forming beliefs about the time by looking at a station clock. If the clock is telling the right time, they will have true justified beliefs. But suppose that the clock has, unprecedentedly, stopped, and someone glances at it exactly twelve hours after it stops, when it happens to be telling the right time. They will form a justified true belief that will not be knowledge.

Once we have the recipe other examples are easy to create. The initial response from philosophers was to try to give more conditions: knowledge is belief + truth + justification + something else. The outcome was not edifying. More complex accounts brought more complex counter-examples, until many began to doubt that an effective analysis would ever be given. Why should it? Analysis must stop somewhere. Why not think that the idea of knowledge, fundamental as it is, is primitive? It seems to be grasped by monkeys who cannot grasp the concept of belief.[9] Why not think that it is one of our cognitive starting points?

Williamson's *knowledge-first* account draws just such a conclusion. Knowledge should be taken as a starting point. Part of the justification for this is simple induction on the failure of attempted analyses. But that is a consideration in favour of thinking that knowledge is *unanalysable*.

---

[7] Timothy Williamson, *Knowledge and Its Limits* (Oxford: Clarendon Press, 2000), chs. 1–3.

[8] Edmund L. Gettier, 'Is Justified True Belief Knowledge?' *Analysis* 23 (1963): 121–3.

[9] Drew Marticorena et al., 'Monkeys Represent Others' Knowledge but not their Beliefs', *Developmental Science* 14 (2011): 1406–16. It used to be thought that the same was true of young children, but that is now in debate.

Here we are concerned with the rather different claim that it is *prime*. So let us first get clear on the difference between the two.

Neither notion is quite as straightforward as it might seem at first glance, and nor is their relation. Start with analysability. Take it as a two-place property and it's fairly clear: a notion is analysable iff it can be explained in some target vocabulary. That is what early proponents of the approach wanted to do: everything legitimate had to be analysed into the language of physics, or of sense-data or the like. But taken as a one-place property, and it is much less clear what constitutes a successful analysis. Everything can be analysed in terms of itself, so that is no good. There has to be some idea of a simpler vocabulary in which the analysis must be couched.

Now take primeness. Williamson introduced the term to this area, so he gets to say what it means. He defines prime conditions as those that are not composite; and composite conditions as those that consist of the conjunction of an internal condition with an external environmental condition. We can literally think of an internal condition as internal to the subject's skin. We could generalize the notion to say that a condition is composite relative to any two exclusive sets of conditions iff it is a conjunction of one drawn from each, but Williamson's initial characterization is good enough for us here.

Distinguish this account of primeness from the very different claim that prime concepts must provide the blocks from which all others are built. (Such a claim might perhaps be motivated by an over-literal parallel with the mathematical notion, and hence with the Fundamental Theorem of Arithmetic.) While it may be true that all analysable concepts are built out of unanalysable ones, there is no reason to think that prime concepts will be fundamental. I will make no such assumption.[10]

What is the relation between being prime and being unanalysable? It might seem that if something is not prime it will be analysable, since its decomposition will constitute an analysis. But that depends on whether the decomposition is sufficiently distinct from the target notion to count as one. Suppose that someone wanted to characterize being red in terms of reflecting a certain frequency of light and being judged to be red. Such a characterization is composite, but it is plausibly not an analysis

---

[10] Note that, despite the 'knowledge first' slogan, and his gloss of belief in terms of knowledge, Williamson himself offers no such analytic claim: "a full-blown exact conceptual analysis of believes in terms of knows is too much to expect" (*Knowledge and Its Limits*, p. 47).

since the internal condition, being judged to be red, itself makes reference to the very notion of being red.[11] Conversely a condition can be analysable but not prime: it may be that the analysis does not split into the conjunction of an internal and an external condition (causal accounts of knowledge are like that: we shall return to them shortly). Primeness and unanalysability are independent notions.

Williamson offers a general argument for thinking that knowledge is not prime using a mix-and-match strategy. If knowledge really could be factored into these two elements, then it should be possible to take any two cases in which a certain thing is known, and come up with a new case of knowledge by combining the internal element from one and the external from the other. Yet this cannot in general be done. So the two elements are not independent.

Here is an adaptation of one example from the many that Williamson offers:

First Case. Suppose that Judy wants to know whether a party she missed was crowded. She gets testimony from two informants, A and B. A is trustworthy and Judy trusts him. He tells her that the party was indeed crowded and she believes him. B in contrast is utterly untrustworthy and wisely Judy puts no store in his testimony, but for reasons of his own in this case he truthfully tells her that the party was crowded (perhaps he is trying to make her regret having missed it). Since A is trustworthy, and is speaking the truth, and Judy accepts his testimony and comes to believe that the party was crowded, Judy gains knowledge that it was.

Second Case. This is just like the first, except that the characteristics of A and B are reversed, as are Judy's attitudes to them. This time it is B who is trustworthy, and it is B whom Judy trusts. Again Judy gains knowledge, but this time from B.

Third case. This is constructed from the first two cases by taking the features internal to Judy from the first, and the features external to her

[11] See Christopher Peacocke, 'Colour Concepts and Colour Experience', *Synthese* 66 (1984): 365–81 and Michael Smith, 'Peacocke on Red and Red', *Synthese* 68 (1986): 559–76 for the genuine debate here. There the account of redness under discussion is simply in terms of being judged to be red. That too is composite, but trivially so, since it consists of the conjunction of the internal state with any external state whatsoever; I gave a non-trivially composite version to avoid muddying the waters.

from the second. So Judy trusts A and distrusts B; yet it is B who is trustworthy and A who is not. Once again Judy forms the true belief that the party was crowded, but this time, since her belief is formed on the testimony of an utterly untrustworthy informant, it isn't knowledge.[12]

The Gettier cases showed us that in cases of knowledge there is a connection between what is known and the state of mind of the knower—intuitively this is what fails in cases like that of the station clock where the true belief is formed by chance. The mix-and-match argument shows us just how intimate that connection is: we cannot factor knowledge into independent internal and external elements. Whether we have a case of knowledge depends on the relations between those elements. Knowledge is *prime*.

Once we accept that knowledge is prime, we have to give up the idea that it is simply the conjunction of belief and something external. However, we do not have to deny that knowing entails belief. Indeed Williamson suggests that we can use the notion of knowledge to provide a rough gloss on belief: to believe a proposition is to treat it as if one knew it. But we cannot build a case of knowledge by adding truth to belief. (Can we turn a case of knowledge into one of false belief by subtracting truth? Yes, but only if that is understood temporally, not modally. If knowledge exists it can be lost because the world changes. But we cannot arrive at a case of knowledge by taking a case of false belief and then supposing that the thing believed had been true all along.)

MURDER

Now we turn from knowledge to criminal guilt. I suggest that the two are very similar. In particular, the relation between the *mens rea* and the *actus reus* in a crime like murder is much the same as that between the internal and the external elements in a case of knowledge. To see this, start by considering something like a Gettier case for murder:

D intends to kill V with poisonous tablets. The police have been watching; they remove the tablets and substitute some others that are apparently harmless. It turns out though that they contain a food colouring, to which V is, remarkably, and unknown to them, highly allergic. D gives them to V, who takes them and dies.

[12] Williamson, *Knowledge and Its Limits*, p. 72.

Is D intuitively guilty of murder? I can find no actual cases of quite this form.[13] However, variations on such cases are standard in law exams, and those who mark them tell me that the expected answer is 'No'. The gap between D's intention and the actual killing is too great and too accidental; in this it resembles the case of the stopped station clock.[14] D may be guilty of attempted murder, but not of murder.

Working backwards, we can construct from this a Williamson-style mix-and-match sequence:

First Case.   D intends to kill with his own poisonous tablets; the police do not intervene; D gives V the tablets; V dies; D is guilty of murder. In this case, D is internally just like in the case we started with, but externally things are different.

Second Case.   D intends to kill V; but he believes that the police are watching, and that they plan to substitute tablets. He also believes that V is allergic to the tablets they would substitute. Thinking this the perfect way to avoid liability for murder he allows things to take their course, and gives the substituted tablets to V. V dies. D is guilty of murder (though it would be doubtless hard to convict). In this case D is internally different to the case we started with, but externally things are the same.[15]

Third Case.   The third case is just our original case, the same as the first case with respect to D's internal features, and the same as the second with respect to the features external to D. Yet here D is not guilty.

---

[13] There are some cases that involve examples of more or less deviant causal chains. In Thabo-Meli vs R [1954] 1 WLR the victim died from exposure having been rolled off a cliff after the defendants thought they had killed him; there the Privy Council reasonably ruled that it would be 'much too refined a ground of judgement' to distinguish the initial assault from the subsequent treatment of the victim (thanks to John Gardner for the reference). Nyuzi and Kudemera vs Republic (Malawi) [1967] African Law Reports 249 involves a case (discussed in A. Kenny, *Freewill and Responsibility* (London: Routledge & Kegan Paul, 1978), pp. 12–21) in which a 'trial by ordeal' using an apparently harmless potion led to the death of four people who had been suspected of witchcraft; but there the charge, of which the accused was found guilty, was of witchcraft, not of murder, so the issue of the deviant causal chain was not germane to the finding.

[14] The actual legal doctrine may be muddied by the doctrine of transferred intent (or transferred malice), although, since it is the same person involved, it should probably not be. Even if it were, I should be inclined to think that not so significant. In contrast to the other legal doctrines that we have been discussing, transferred intent is a doctrine that strikes many as artificial: Lord Mustill described it as 'useful enough to yield rough justice' while lacking 'any sound intellectual basis' [1998] 1 Cr App R 91 at 106.

[15] Why not say that D *knew* about V's allergy, and the police plan? I don't want to assume that there could be a difference in knowledge without a difference in the external circumstances (though I don't think that Williamson's position requires this).

Is this so surprising? After all, it is a standard position, both in action theory and in the law, that causation matters: the mental state must cause the behaviour in the right sort of way. Are we simply seeing that mixing and matching disrupts the causal relationships, giving rise to deviant causal chains? I think that this is to understate the force of the challenge. The deviant causal chain approach encourages the thought that if we could understand the causal relation properly we could go back to a more complex conjunctive account. Murder = *mens rea* + *actus reus* + the right causal relation between them. The parallel attempt to reductively analyse the right causal relation has been made in both epistemology and in action theory, and in both it has failed dismally. No one has been able to specify the right kind of relation except by saying that it is whatever is needed to give rise to cases of knowledge or of action, and there is no reason to think that we will do any better in the case of murder. However, the problem with such an approach is not simply that it fails to provide a reductive account. It is that once one says that the relation is whatever is needed for knowledge, or for action, it is far from obvious that there will be a *causal* relation, even a non-reductively characterized one, that does the job (in cases of knowledge within abstract domains like mathematics, it is highly implausible that there is). While, in cases of action at least, there must be causation involved—Davidson showed us that—there is no reason to think that the causal relations constitute an independent third factor, rather than simply being further implications. Indeed it is unclear that we must accept that there is a non-reductive *relation* of any kind that fills a third place. All we can be sure of, in the case of knowledge, is that there is a belief, and the content of the belief is true, and that this is a case of knowledge; and in the case of action, that there is an appropriate mental state, and an appropriate bodily movement, and that this is a case of action. The primeness account provides an explanation of why we should be sceptical of the whole approach, of constructions using three conjuncts as well as of two.

My conclusion then is that, as with knowledge, so with murder: it is prime. It cannot be factorized into internal and external elements. But in some ways the conclusion is even more radical than it is for knowledge. As we saw, the claim that knowledge is prime is consistent with the idea that knowledge entails belief; and if, as Williamson suggests, to believe a proposition is to treat it as if one knew it, we have an explanation for the entailment (to know a proposition is certainly to treat it as if one knew it). So both cases of knowledge and of false belief can be seen to have something—belief—in common. It seems unlikely that there is anything similar that can be said to unify cases of murder with cases of attempted murder. We cannot say in a parallel way that to attempt to murder someone is for it to be as if one actually murdered them. For attempts do not need to be completed attempts. And even apparently completed attempts will often differ from actual murders, since the latter will involve monitoring of how things are going, with a readiness to make further interventions if needed. Murder is an ongoing process. Even a frenzied attack typically takes time, involving different steps mediated by knowledge of what is happening—Is the victim escaping? Are they still moving? Is someone coming who can help them?—and finishing only when the victim is dead. An attempt to murder, even one that is in a sense complete, need not be like that.

Let me make one further clarification. In the Introduction to *Knowledge and Its Limits* Williamson pointed out a possible parallel between knowledge and desire; in subsequent work he has replaced talk of desire with talk of intention.[16] The idea there is that one can parallel the relation between knowing that p, believing that p, and p being true, with the relation between performing the action of φ-ing, intending to φ, and one's φ-ing being successful. That is not what is being proposed here. Williamson's parallel is between two sets of schemas, those on the knowledge side substituting a sentence for 'p', and those on the action side substituting a verb phrase for 'φ'. In contrast I am arguing for a parallel between the verb 'to know', and a variety of other action verbs, typified by 'to murder'. Mine is not a schematic proposal in the way that Williamson's is; it does not apply to each possible substitution for 'φ'. To see whether verbs have the similarities to 'to know' that I am interested in we need to examine them individually. Non-intentional verbs like 'to drop' and 'to kill' do not; we turn to this distinction next.

THE *MENS REA* FOR MURDER

My suggestion then is that in a case of murder the *mens rea* is essentially connected with the killing itself. It follows that the *mens rea* for murder, and the *mens rea* for attempted murder, are bound to be different. The issue

---

[16] Timothy Williamson, 'Acting on Knowledge', in J.A. Carter, E. Gordon, and B. Jarvis (eds.), *Knowledge First: Approaches in Epistemology and Mind* (Oxford: OUP, 2017). Yair Levy has developed similar ideas: see 'Intentional Action First', *Australasian Journal of Philosophy* 91 (2013): 705–18.

is thus not why they are different; it is why they take the particular different forms that they do. Let's turn to that.

I have talked so far about criminal guilt. But the discussion can equally—perhaps preferably—be rephrased in terms of *action*. There are certain action verbs which we can think of as essentially intentional, in that they are only applicable if the agent is in a certain state of mind. Those expressing what have historically been the central offences of the criminal law are like this—to murder, to steal, to rape, to assault, to defraud—as are many others that have little place in the law—to borrow, to lie, to compliment. But other action verbs are not: one can kill someone or cause their death, drop something, wound someone, damage something, without needing to be in any particular mental state. Some offences make use of these verbs: causing death by dangerous driving for instance. And there are some offences—most obviously those involving negligence where it is distinguished from recklessness—that presuppose the *absence* of certain states of mind (though I cannot think of any ordinary verbs of action that do).

As a first thought, we can distinguish the intentional verbs from the others by saying that they can't readily be modified by the adverbs 'unintentionally' or 'inadvertently'. One can unintentionally kill someone or drop something; but there isn't a straightforward way in which one can unintentionally murder or steal. (Of course, if someone were to say something like that, we'd make some sense of what they said; but things would have to be stretched.) It is a plausible thesis that all intentional action verbs are, like 'murder' prime, though I shan't defend that here. I'll keep the focus on murder.

Understanding murder as an action verb, what might the *mens rea* for it be? I said at the outset that talk of an intention to kill is too restrictive. Recent philosophical discussions of intentions have identified them with plans: to have an intention to do something is to structure one's activities to try to ensure that it comes about, modifying those activities, and perhaps one's plans, if need be. That leaves space for a foreseen but unintended outcome, an outcome that one is not trying to bring about—one would not restructure one's activities to ensure that it did—but that one nonetheless believes will result from one's actions. But as we have seen, one can be guilty of murder if the death of the victim is a suitably closely foreseen consequence of one's action; and that is quite compatible with one not having had an intention to kill. So the *mens rea* for murder cannot be the intention to kill. A fortiori, it cannot be the intention to murder.

Our earlier discussion of primeness should have shown that there is a general problem of understanding the *mens rea* as an intention. Intention is plausibly an internal state (at least, putting aside questions of the externality of referring terms and the like). But if murder cannot be factored into an internal and an external state, then in looking to intentions to characterize the *mens rea* we are looking at the wrong sort of thing.

Rather than trying to identify an independent mental state as the *mens rea*, we should focus on the action—and hence the crime—of murder. The *mens rea* just is whatever state of mind is entailed by that. As we refine our understanding of murder, so we refine our understanding of the *mens rea* involved. Of course most of the changes there have been driven by the courts; but then murder is a well-established notion, and most of the recent revisions have concerned relatively minor issues around the degree of foresight and the like. For an example that concerns much more general involvement, and rather less from the courts, consider sexual harassment. This is a relatively recent notion, dating to the early 1970s, and evolving considerably since then. What is the associated *mens rea*? That remains a matter of disagreement. Those who see it as a structural injustice tend to minimize the importance of the actor's attitudes, but even they are unlikely to discount them altogether: the difference between harassment and legitimate behaviour will have something to do with the state of mind of the actor.

The central idea here is of our moral and legal concepts evolving as we think more about them, and as circumstances change. We may be more or less objectivist about this process—may model it more or less closely on the process of discovering natural kinds in science. I will leave that issue unexplored. What is important for us is that the relevant *mens rea* and *actus reus* are driven by our conception of the crime, and not the other way around. We do not start with an independent conception of the wrongful intention and build the moral or legal concept from that.

To deny that the *mens rea* for an offence should be understood as an intention is not, however, to deny that we can characterize the action that constitutes the offence as intentional. Indeed, talk of intentional action brings the external dimension that talk of intentions lacks. Just as knowing something entails, or presupposes, that the thing known is true, so intentionally performing some action obviously entails or presupposes that one performs that action. This is more promising.

If we switch to intentional actions, then we have two natural candidates for the *mens rea*: intentionally killing, and intentionally murdering. But if I am right that 'murder' is an intentional verb, then the second of these is something of a pleonasm. So let us focus instead on the first.

It might be thought that once again talk of intentionally killing is too restrictive: if one merely foresees that an action will result in a killing, the killing is not intentional. But in a much discussed set of experiments, Joshua Knobe found that most people don't think that way, at least for closely related cases. Consider an executive who, motivated entirely by the goal of maximizing profit, embarks on a policy that he knows will also cause environmental damage. Does he intentionally harm the environment? Most people hold that he does. It seems likely then that they would say similar things about killing: that they would class a merely foreseen killing in such circumstances as intentional.[17]

Consider now the other half of Knobe's findings. When asked to think about an otherwise identical case in which an executive embarks on a policy whose side effects are *beneficial* to the environment, most people hold that the executive does not intentionally help the environment. So how do we explain this? An obvious first thought is that bad foreseen consequences are counted as intentionally performed, whereas good foreseen consequences are not. However, another of Knobe's experiments shows that that cannot be quite right either. A profit-driven executive whose actions have the side effect of violating a pernicious Nazi law—surely a good outcome in most subjects' eyes—is judged to have acted intentionally; whereas a similarly driven executive whose actions have the bad effect of fulfilling the requirements of that law is not judged to have acted intentionally.[18]

So how should we explain these results? Elsewhere I have suggested that the asymmetry stems from a basic asymmetry in how we think about norms.[19] On one side we are concerned with *violation* of a norm;

[17] Joshua Knobe, 'The Concept of Intentional Action: A Case Study in the Uses of Folk Psychology', *Philosophical Studies* 130 (2006): 203–31.

[18] Joshua Knobe, 'Reason Explanation in Folk Psychology', *Midwest Studies in Philosophy* 31 (2007): 90–107.

[19] Richard Holton, 'Norms and the Knobe Effect', *Analysis* 70 (2010): 417–24. For related ideas, see Philip Pettit, *The Robust Demands of the Good* (Oxford: OUP, 2015), ch. 6. For some

on the other with *following* it. When it comes to violation of a norm, our concern is with whether someone is prepared to knowingly violate it. Intentional violation amounts to just that: acting with disregard for the norm. In contrast, intentionally following a norm requires more. It requires that one's actions be guided by the norm. It is this asymmetry, I suggested, that explains Knobe's findings. It is sufficient for intentionally harming the environment that one intentionally—i.e. knowingly— violates a norm on harming it. But it is not sufficient for helping the environment that one merely acts in a way that conforms to a norm on helping it. To help it would require having one's behaviour guided by that norm, in a way that the executive's is not.[20]

Let us return to murder, for now we have the pieces needed for a more convincing account. If the norm is not to kill, then intentional killing results from knowingly violating that norm. And one can intentionally violate it either by acting on a successful intention to kill, or by acting in such a way that the killing is foreseen. Arguably one also violates it by behaving with insufficient care: by behaving recklessly, or by doing something else—inflicting grievous bodily harm, for instance—that brings a real risk of death. The arguments in the courts that have surrounded these issues reflect, I suggest, our disagreement here.

Looked at in this way, the conditions on the *mens rea* for murder look as though they might be captured in the intuitive idea of intentionally killing. However, I'm still not sure that this is right. For obvious reasons, not every case of intentionally killing is a case of murder: not if it is done in self-defence, in legitimate warfare, as a result of provocation, and so on. Even if we insisted that in these cases the norm against killing is not violated, we surely cannot deny that they involve intentional killing. Nor does it help to say that since the *mens rea* is merely a necessary condition for the crime, it need not concern itself with the existence of defences. That doesn't help because these defences incorporate mental elements themselves. Thus self-defence requires that the accused honestly

---

plausible revisions to the account I offered, though in ways that I think are still compatible with what is said here, see B. Robinson, P. Stey, and M. Alfano 'Reversing the Side-Effect Effect: The Power of Salient Norms', *Philosophical Studies* 172 (2015): 177–206.

[20] One issue that I failed to address in the earlier paper is whether, in order to act with disregard for a norm, one needs to be aware of it. In cases like killing it is inconceivable that a sane agent would not. A genuine failure to recognize the norm against killing would be grounds for an insanity defence.

thinks the force used is both necessary and reasonable.[21] The absence of such a belief is thus implicitly part of the *mens rea* for murder.

Perhaps then the best we can say is that the norm one violates is a norm against murder. Killings in legitimate warfare, in self-defence etc., don't look like violations of that. But then any attempt to understand murder in terms of something else has been lost. There is a general point here. It might be thought that any intentional verb can be analysed in terms of intentionally performing some non-intentional action. That thought could be maintained even given my earlier arguments that verbs like 'murder' are prime: it might be thought that the *mens rea* can't be characterized independently of the *actus reus*, but that the converse doesn't hold. So provided we can identify the *actus reus*, and then talk about performing it intentionally, we can give a non-composite, but nonetheless reductive, account of the crime. I suggest though that that thesis is false too. I see no way to analyse murder in general as the intentional performance of some action that can be characterized in non-intentional terms. And the same, I suggest, goes for other core criminal acts. Consider, for instance, how one would try to characterize the relevant unintentional action for theft: it is certainly not adequate to say that it is intentional permanent removal of the property of another without their consent (and even that involves intentional vocabulary in its talk of consent).

THE *MENS REA* FOR ATTEMPTED MURDER

Finally let us turn to the *mens rea* for attempted murder. I have argued that it cannot just be the *mens rea* for murder, since that cannot be disentangled from the *actus reus* of the killing. So we need to think of it as a self-standing thing. Now it would be possible to have an offence under which someone would be guilty if they either intended to kill, and acted on that intention, or if they intended to do some other thing, acted on that intention, and foresaw that a killing would result, or if they intended to inflict grievous bodily harm, and acted on that. But such an offence really would be a medley. In most jurisdictions, the legal doctrine of attempt is much more unified.[22]

---

[21] Williams (Gladstone) [1987] 78 Cr App R 276; Oatbridge [1984] 94 Cr App R 367.
[22] Colorado's might be an exception. For discussion, see Yaffe, *Attempts*, pp. 47ff.

If we cannot understand attempt in terms of a successful crime minus success, we have to think instead of it as more self-standing. To get a grip on what it is we should start in the obvious place, with the ordinary idea of an attempt, that is, the ordinary idea of *trying* to do something.[23] Here I think we do need the idea of an intention, understood, as sketched above, as a plan. When one attempts to do something, the thing that one is attempting to do is what one has the intention to do. The intention brings a commitment to a certain course of action; the attempt is an attempt to fulfil that commitment.[24] But then we can immediately see why mere foresight does not provide the *mens rea* for attempted murder, since mere foresight, whilst it might be enough for doing something intentionally, is not enough for an intention; one is not committed to bringing about what one merely foresees.[25] Similarly, intentionally causing grievous bodily harm is not enough for an intention to kill, so attempting to cause grievous bodily harm is not enough for attempted murder.

There is of course more to say. The mere possession of an intention is not enough, for the idea of attempt is essentially action involving: one does not have an attempt until the plan has been put into motion. And I suspect that once again we have the structure with which we have become familiar: attempt entails an intention, and it entails action, but it cannot be factored into those two elements, since each is too intimately involved with the other. We have, not just intention, but intention-in-action. Quite how far down the path of action someone needs to go

[23] See Yaffe, *Attempts*, ch. 3, and 'Criminal Attempts' for very helpful applications of the notion of trying to the doctrine of attempt. Note that Michael Bratman, *Intention, Plans and Practical Reason* (Cambridge, MA: Harvard University Press, 1987), pp. 113ff. denies that trying to do something entails intending to do it. Like Yaffe I find that implausible. My own reason for doing so is rather different to Yaffe's: I deny that forming inconsistent intentions has to be irrational. See my *Willing, Wanting, Waiting* (Oxford: Clarendon Press, 2009), ch. 2.

[24] See Yaffe, 'Criminal Attempts' for a sophisticated development of this idea. Yaffe there divides the relevant commitment into a commitment to promote, a commitment not to reconsider, and a commitment not to feel regret, which can hold independently. I'm not altogether convinced of the need for such sophistication—I suspect that even in the law we can get away with what Yaffe calls the 'narrow sense' of intention—but I shan't argue for this here.

[25] For the classic articulation of the distinction, see Bratman, *Intention, Plans and Practical Reason*, ch. 8. Note that while in the cases discussed above Knobe and others have found that ordinary subjects are prepared to say that agents who pollute with foresight pollute intentionally, they are much less ready to say that they have intentions to pollute; see H. McCann, 'Intentional Action and Intending: Recent Empirical Studies', *Philosophical Psychology* 18 (2005): 737–48.

before mere preparation turns into enough of an attempt to be actionable is doubtless vague; but it certainly requires more than the possession of the intention alone.[26]

Let me finish this section by asking why this matters. Suppose it is true that the idea of attempt in most jurisdictions is more unified than the medley offence that I described several paragraphs back, which tries to understand it in terms of the *mens rea* that would be present for the successful crime. What significance should we assign to that? What reason do we have to think that the law works with the more unified notions, and hence that an account in terms of such notions is more likely to be accurate? And more pressing still, even if it does, why should it?

Obviously these are big questions. My answer is that insofar as the law is genuinely trying for an offence of attempt, as we ordinarily understand it, this is what it needs to do. I have argued that the common law works with something like the moral equivalent of natural kinds. This is so for the substantial offences—murder, rape, theft, and so on, and it is equally true of the idea of attempt. We can work to understand those ideas, and to see how they fit together, which have priority, and so on. Sometimes we discover new ones (I have mentioned sexual harassment), and sometimes we come to think that those we have been using are mistaken (the idea of honour thankfully has a smaller role in our current thinking than it once did). But if the development of moral philosophy has shown us anything, it has shown us that attempts to throw out these categories and start afresh are hopeless. In this though, the law is no different to other kinds of thought. We are all in Neurath's boat.[27]

[26] Again, see Yaffe, 'Criminal Attempts', pp. 116–18 for discussion, and for a clear argument that to state an intention is not, in the relevant sense, to act on it.

[27] This paper was presented at the Human Rights and the Human Mind conference in Tel Aviv, January 2014; thanks to Amit Pundik, my commentator there, and the audience members. An early version was published in the proceedings of that conference in *Law and Ethics of Human Rights* 9 (2015): 181–93. The material was subsequently presented at the Intention workshop at Leeds in February 2014, at the Criminal Law's Person conference at York in December 2015, and at Yale in March 2017; thanks to Yair Levy, my commentator at Leeds, and the audience members on all those occasions. Special thanks to Tim Williamson for discussion and comments on the written version, Gideon Yaffe, Michael Moore, and the referees for *LEHR*.

7

Uncertainties of War

VICTOR TADROS

A theory of the permissibility of killing is central to the morality of war. There is some set of facts that, if D knows these facts, D is permitted to kill V. In such circumstances, D's killing of V is permissible both in the fact-relative and the evidence-relative sense.[1] What these facts are has been the subject of a great deal of critical scrutiny. However, even a complete account of these facts would provide only a part of a general theory of the permissibility of killing from the evidence-relative point of view. The reason is that the person deciding whether to kill is often, for good reason, uncertain whether the morally salient facts, whatever they are, obtain. Answers to questions about what to do in the face of uncertainty form a key part of a theory of evidence-relative permissibility.

Given that we can do no better than to act in the light of the evidence that we have, or can get access to, about the facts, a theory of evidence-relative permissibility is crucial. Such a theory provides a guide to agents in the condition that we all find ourselves—the condition of uncertainty. Uncertainty is a normal feature of everyday life, and in war combatants are typically uncertain about the most important facts that are salient in fact-relative morality, such as whether they face a threat; who is responsible for posing threats they face, and to what degree; whether those who pose them will succeed in executing them if nothing is done; what harm it is necessary to inflict on others to avert them; what the collateral damage of responding to threats will be; what contribution they will make to the overall war effort if they respond; and so on.

---

[1] I take it that the difference between fact-relative and evidence-relative permissibility is sufficiently clear and familiar that I need not spell it out again here. It is spelled out in D. Parfit, *On What Matters*, vol. 1 (Oxford: OUP, 2011), ch. 7.

Oxford Studies in Philosophy of Law Volume 3. John Gardner, Leslie Green, and Brian Leiter (eds)
This chapter © Victor Tadros 2018. First published in 2018 by Oxford University Press

A familiar complaint about work in just war theory is that judgements about what to do in war are made on the assumption that a certain set of facts obtain—for example facts about the justness of a war, or the liability of a person targeted, or the number of non-combatants who will be killed, or whether the acts performed will advance a just cause. But, the complainant argues, combatants cannot be expected know these facts. Acts of war are marred by uncertainty.

A radical conclusion is that there is no point in evaluating what combatants are permitted to do relative to the facts. However, the problem of uncertainty is not a reason to reject the relevance of fact-relative permissibility. That combatants are, for good reason, uncertain about many of the most important facts that determine whether killing is permissible presses us to develop an account of how to respond to uncertainty. And any such account depends on answers to questions about fact-relative permissibility. After all, we are interested in uncertainty about some fact only if there is a reason to care about whether that fact obtains. Our interest in uncertainty thus depends on answers to questions about the facts that we have reason to be interested in independently of our uncertainty about them.

Until recently, treatment of the problem of uncertainty in just war theory has mostly been restricted to answering the question whether uncertainty about the permissibility of wars yields the moral equality of combatants. It does not. Even if most combatants are justified in fighting wars from the evidence-relative point of view (which is doubtful), being justified from the fact-relative point of view makes a significant difference to one's moral status. It is normally permissible to harm a person at least to some degree to avert a threat that the person poses if that person is not fact-relative justified in posing the threat, even if that person reasonably believes that she is so justified. That will normally not be true if the person is both evidence-relative and fact-relative justified for posing the threat she poses.[2]

This problem, which has received a great deal of attention, is only a drop in an ocean of questions that uncertainty in war raises. This paper will only address a small part of the much wider problem of uncertainty.

---

[2] For further discussion, see J. McMahan, *Killing in War* (Oxford: OUP, 2009), 60–5. It may sometimes be permissible to harm a person to avert a threat she poses if she is fact-relative justified but evidence-relative unjustified in posing threats to others. See V. Tadros, *The Ends of Harm: The Moral Foundations of Criminal Law* (Oxford: OUP, 2011), 235–9.

It is focused on uncertainty about facts that are relevant to whether the person killed is liable to be killed. Suppose that D is deciding whether killing V is permissible. If V is liable to be killed, D's killing of V will not wrong V. Let us suppose, further, that there is nothing else that makes killing V wrong from either the fact-relative or the evidence-relative point of view. If V is liable, killing V will then be permissible all things considered from the fact-relative point of view. But now suppose that D is, for good reason, uncertain about whether some fact obtains, and V's liability depends on that fact obtaining. In such circumstances, when is it evidence-relative permissible for D to kill V?

I. PRELIMINARIES

Suppose there is good reason, given the evidence available to her, for a person to be uncertain about whether some fact, *f*, obtains. There is some rough probability that *f* is true and some rough probability that *f* is false. When I refer to probabilities, I mean by them epistemic probabilities—chances that certain propositions are true given the evidence available to a person. I leave aside the question whether there are non-epistemic probabilities.

Epistemic probabilities are often contrasted with objective probabilities, but epistemic probabilities are at least objective in this sense: the epistemic probability of *f* depends on the assessment that a person ought to make in the light of the evidence available to her, or that she ought to gather, and not the assessment she actually makes. Epistemic probabilities are relative to evidence available to a person, but they are not relative to the person's actual state of mind. Similarly, we are interested not in whether a combatant is uncertain about whether some fact obtains, but whether she has good reason to be uncertain about it. That depends on the availability of the evidence to her. I leave aside difficult questions about what it means for evidence to be 'available' to a person.[3]

As I have already noted, moral questions about uncertainty depend on answers to questions concerning fact-relative permissibility. Uncertainty about some proposition, *p*, is normally morally significant only if *p* makes a difference to the fact-relative permissibility of acting. That being said,

---

[3] I clarify problems of this kind in *The Ends of Harm*, ch. 10, without making substantial progress with solving them.

the relationship between evidence-relative and fact-relative permissibility is more complex than appears at first sight. We can see this by noticing there are some cases where I ought to act in a way that I know is fact-relative wrong rather than acting in a way that might be fact-relative permissible. This can be so if acting in a way that might be fact-relative permissible might also have very bad consequences.

Consider this familiar case:[4]

> *Miners*: Two mineshafts, A and B, are about to be flooded with water. Ten miners are trapped in one of the shafts but we don't know which. We have enough sandbags to block either shaft A (option A) or shaft B (option B) but not both. If we block A, B will fill completely with water and vice versa. If a shaft fills completely with water any miners in that shaft are certain to be killed. If we block neither shaft (option C), water will flow into both shafts and one miner, but only one miner, will certainly be killed.

Either option A or option B saves the most lives from the fact-relative point of view but we are, for good reason, uncertain which. However, the option in the A and B set that is not best is very bad. Option C certainly saves nine lives. From the evidence-relative point of view, we ought to select C, even though from the fact-relative point of view C is certainly wrong—were we to know all of the facts, it would be wrong not to block the shaft with the miners in it.

This case already shows that a tempting view about what we ought to do from the evidence-relative point of view is false. It is tempting to think that, from the evidence-relative point of view, we ought to maximize the probability of doing what we are required to do from the fact-relative point of view. However, in *Miners*, option C reduces the probability that we do what we ought to do from the fact-relative point of view to zero. Nevertheless, we ought to select C from the evidence-relative point of view.

In response to this case, it might be argued that we ought to minimize the probability of acting wrongly from the fact-relative point of view, weighted to take account of the gravity of wrongdoing. This view yields the right result in *Miners*. Compare options A and C. A has a 50 per cent

---

[4] I discuss this case in *The Ends of Harm*, 222. I did not know, when I wrote that book, that it originates in D. Regan, *Utilitarianism and Cooperation* (Oxford: OUP, 1980), 265, n.1.

chance of killing ten. C has a 100 per cent chance of killing one. As killing ten is much more gravely wrong than killing one, we ought to pick C, even though this is certain to be fact-relative wrong.

This view is also false, however. For example, it is sometimes permissible to do an act that is supererogatory from both the evidence-relative and fact-relative points of view, even though doing that act creates some probability of acting fact-relative wrongly. Consider:

Plane Crash: A plane is being flown at a building. There are fewer people in the building than passengers on the plane. However, it is 99 per cent certain that terrorists have killed all of the passengers on the plane. If they are still alive, though, there is a good chance they will overcome the terrorists and land the plane safely. I can crash my plane into this plane to save the people in the building, but doing this will kill me.

It is supererogatory, from the evidence-relative and fact-relative points of view, for me to give up my life for the people in the building (let us plausibly suppose). Hence, refraining from crashing into the plane is certainly permissible from both the evidence-relative and fact-relative points of view. Yet crashing my plane into this plane seems permissible. That is so even though there is some probability that doing this is fact-relative wrong—if the passengers on the plane are still alive.

This idea is also important in the case of war. It is often permissible not to shoot another person in self-defence when one is highly likely wrongly to be killed by that person if one refrains from shooting. If we were required to maximize the probability of not acting wrongly, weighted for gravity of wrongdoing, we would almost never be permitted to defend ourselves in these circumstances. There is always some probability that defending ourselves is unnecessary. Hence, harming others in self-defence always raises the probability that one will act fact-relative wrongly.

II. UNDERSTANDING LIABILITY

Although the relationship between fact-relative and evidence-relative wrongness and permissibility is not straightforward, before we address the question of uncertainty, we need a theory of the morally salient propositions that combatants might be uncertain about. We are interested, here, in facts that are relevant to determining whether a person is liable to be harmed.

There is little agreement about what these facts are, so my judgements about uncertainty will be more appealingly presented to some than to others. That being said, a theory of uncertainty can be to some degree ecumenical about fact-relative permissibility. I aim to show that the proper approach to take towards uncertainty depends upon what one is uncertain about and why. There is no simple one-size-fits-all approach to uncertainty. The epistemic standard that one must meet to justify inflicting harm on others varies depending on the facts that one is concerned with. Some of the considerations that justify the views that I defend on this are general.

My focus is on uncertainty about facts relevant to liability in the moral sense. Furthermore, my focus is on liability to be harmed. I understand the concept of liability to be harmed to avert a threat in the following way:

> *Liability*:   X is liable to be harmed to degree h by Y in order to avert some threat, t, if Y does not wrong X by harming X to degree t without X's consent in order avert t where it is necessary for Y to harm X to degree h to avert t.

This account of the concept of liability to be harmed is controversially broad: it includes those who lack rights both as a result of having forfeited rights they once had, and those who lack rights not to be harmed against their will for other reasons. If there is something morally special about forfeiture, we can distinguish classes of liability: one class for those who have forfeited their rights, another for those who have not.[5]

I rely on various assumptions about liability without defending those assumptions. I will assume that X's degree of moral responsibility for a threat is relevant to the magnitude of harm that he is liable to suffer to avert it. I will assume that X's degree of moral responsibility for a threat depends on facts about agency and facts about causation. And I will assume X is only liable to be harmed to avert this threat if harming X is necessary to avert the threat.[6] This last assumption is controversial—some

---

[5] See, further, V. Tadros, 'Orwell's Battle with Brittain: Vicarious Liability for Unjust Aggression', *Philosophy and Public Affairs* 42 (2014): 42, and 'Causation, Culpability, and Liability', in C. Coons and M. Weber, *The Ethics of Self-Defense* (Oxford: OUP, 2016).
[6] See McMahan, *Killing in War*, 8–9.

believe, in contrast, that necessity is external to liability.[7] I won't say anything to defend the internalist view here, though I will respond to one pressing concern about it.

III. RESPONSIBILITY FOR UNCERTAINTY

One general question about uncertainty concerning liability concerns the responsibility that the subject—the potentially liable person—might have for the uncertainty. Suppose that there is some person, X, where if that person has some property, l, X is liable to be harmed by Y to a certain degree. Y is uncertain whether X has l. The significance of Y's uncertainty for what Y is evidence-relative permitted to do to X depends on whether X is responsible for Y being uncertain about l.

This idea is very important in the case of war. Consider McMahan's familiar view that a person makes herself liable to be killed to avert a threat only if that person is responsible for posing an objectively unjust threat. One forceful complaint that Seth Lazar has mounted against this view draws on the idea that many combatants do not fire their weapons.[8] If they make no further contributions to unjust threats, it follows that many combatants do not fulfil McMahan's criteria for liability. It will also be very difficult to identify who, amongst a group of combatants, poses a threat and who does not. Now suppose that a combatant, Y, can kill a combatant on the opposing side, X, only if Y is reasonably confident that X is liable. Combatants on the just side cannot be confident that any person who is killed is liable. Where this is true, McMahan's view threatens to yield something close to pacifism in the real world.

One possibility that I will mostly leave aside is that combatants who do not fire their weapons may make other kinds of contributions to the presence of unjust threats. For example, their presence might provide moral support for combatants who do fire, they might load and maintain weapons, they might administer medical assistance on and off the battlefield, and so on. It is, of course, also true that many non-combatants make contributions to unjust threats. There is a range of complex issues here about how to measure a person's responsibility and degree of

---

[7] See, for example, J. Firth and J. Quong, 'Necessity, Moral Liability, and Defensive Harm', *Law and Philosophy* 31 (2012): 673; H. Frowe, *Defensive Killing* (Oxford: OUP, 2014), ch. 4.

[8] S. Lazar, 'The Responsibility Dilemma for *Killing in War*', *Philosophy and Public Affairs* 38 (2010): 180.

contribution, and the difference that these things make to liability.[9] Let us assume that the moral responsibility of combatants who do not fire their weapons is insufficient to make them liable to be killed. Does it then follow that combatants on the just side are not permitted to kill any combatants on the unjust side because they are uncertain whether the combatants they kill are liable to be killed?

(i) Responsibility for Appearing Threatening

One response to this argument draws on the idea that in donning uniforms and entering the battlefield, combatants on the unjust side who will not fire their weapons create the conditions under which it is impossible to distinguish between them and those combatants who will fire their weapons. As they are responsible for the inability of those on the just side to distinguish them from those who are liable because of posing threats to others, it is evidence-relative permissible to harm a combatant on the unjust side even if she lacks strong reasons to believe that the person she is firing at is liable to be killed.[10]

To see the force of this idea, compare:

> *Scream*:   A serial killer is in town, and has been stabbing many people to death with a serrated knife whilst wearing an Edvard Munch *Scream* mask. Knowing this, X goes around at night to scare people, donning a similar *Scream* mask and carrying a serrated knife. X, though, poses no threat to anyone. Y knows that X behaves this way. He comes across a person wearing a *Scream* mask, who appears to be about to stab V to death. Y can shoot this person, but is uncertain whether the person is the serial killer or X. There is no time to discover who this person is before any stabbing occurs.

Suppose that the person in the mask is X. Were Y to know this, it would be wrong for Y to shoot X. X poses no threat to anyone.

---

[9] For discussion, see N. Zohar, 'Innocent and Complex Threats: Upholding the War Ethic and the Condemnation of Terrorism', *Ethics* 114 (2004): 734; McMahan, *Killing in War*, ch. 5; S. Lazar 'The Responsibility Dilemma for *Killing in War*'; C. Fabre, 'Guns, Food, and Liability to Attack', *Ethics* 120 (2009): 36; H. Frowe, 'Self-Defence and the Principle of Non-Combatant Immunity', *Journal of Moral Philosophy* 8 (2011): 1; H. Frowe, 'Non-Combatant Liability in War', in H. Frowe and G. Lang, *How We Fight: Issues in Jus in Bello* (Oxford: OUP, 2014); V. Tadros, 'Causal Contributions and Liability', *Ethics* 128 (2018): 1.

[10] For a brief exploration of this idea, see J. McMahan, 'Who is Morally Liable to be Killed in War', *Analysis* 71 (2011): 544, 555.

X is responsible for the fact that Y is uncertain whether the person in the mask is X because X, for no good reason, creates the conditions under which it is impossible for Y to distinguish between X and the serial killer. This makes a significant difference to the permissibility of Y shooting the person in the mask. If the person in the mask is the serial killer, Y will have saved V's life. If the person is X, X will be responsible for his own death. For this reason, even if Y thinks that the person in the mask is probably X, it is evidence-relative permissible for Y to shoot the person in the mask.

This view can be defended more deeply as follows. Suppose that Y were not permitted to shoot the person in the mask because this person could be X. Such a prohibition would make it true that X, by mimicking the serial killer, has reduced Y's ability to protect V. V is less secure because of X's conduct, for Y cannot prevent V being exposed to a risk of being killed by the serial killer. For this reason, Y's evidence-relative permission to shoot the person in the mask is not prohibited—X has a duty to internalize the security costs of his own conduct, at least if there is no reason for him to behave in this way. This makes it easier to justify Y imposing heavy burdens on him to ensure that V is protected.

Now consider a tricky technical question. Earlier, I indicated that necessity, on my view, is internal to liability—if it is not necessary to harm a person to avert a threat that she poses, say because there is an easy escape route, harming that person wrongs her. What should we say, though, where harming X is necessary to protect V from a risk of harm, from the evidence-relative point of view, but not necessary, relative to the facts, because X poses no threat?

Some might claim that X is liable to be harmed, in this case, even though he poses no threat and hence that harming him is fact-relative unnecessary. Lazar seems to imply (albeit the text is not completely clear) that the permissibility of killing X in such cases turns on X being liable in this case, and then asks for an argument that he is.[11] He seems willing to concede that he might be at least if X is culpable for the mistake. Kim Ferzan has also argued that in at least some circumstances where one person is culpable for acting in a way that causes another person to make a mistake about whether she poses a threat, the first person is liable: where one person threatens another but

---

[11] Lazar, 'The Responsibility Dilemma for *Killing in War*', 192.

is bluffing, she argues, the bluffer is liable to be harmed even though she poses no threat.[12]

I think that we need not answer this technical question. Any dispute about the answer is merely verbal. We can agree (1) that the killing of X is distinctively regrettable given that he didn't actually pose a threat; (2) that Y would have wronged X by killing X had Y known the facts; (3) it would be permissible for third parties to harm Y to some degree to prevent him from killing X; but (4) the killing of X is X's responsibility, and hence his complaint about being killed is significantly weakened, because of his responsibility for Y's inability to distinguish him from the serial killer. Claim (4) draws us to the view that X is liable to be killed. However, claims (1)–(3) pull us in the other direction.

If we agree on these claims, there is little reason to determine whether the best theory of liability implies that X is liable, or rather that Y is permitted to treat the person who he has shot as though he is liable. In cases of verbal dispute of this kind, where we are concerned with substantive matters that we agree about but are unsure about how best to describe them, and especially where the meaning of a term is disputed and unclear, we are often best to eliminate the term under consideration.[13] We could, for example, claim that the person is 'liable*' to refer to such cases to mark the fact that these cases have important similarities to and differences from core cases of liability.

It is also worth noting, in response to Ferzan, that it is permissible for Y to kill the person who appears to pose a threat to him in *Scream* even if X is not culpable for appearing like the killer. Culpability doesn't even seem very important in these cases. What matters in *Scream* is not that X's conduct is either culpable or wrong. What matters is that it is easily avoidable. X's behaviour might be wrong in *Scream* because of the fear that he induces in others. But that is not what makes it permissible for Y to act. It would be equally permissible for Y to act if it was imprudent but not wrong for X to dress up like the killer.[14]

---

[12] K. Ferzan, 'The Bluff: The Power of Insincere Actions', *Legal Theory* 23 (217): 168.

[13] See D. Chalmers, 'Verbal Disputes', *Philosophical Review* 120 (2011): 515.

[14] I am not completely clear whether Ferzan and I disagree in substance, because although she puts a culpability condition on liability in such cases, she may not mean what we ordinarily mean by culpability. She may just mean that the person has a relevant mental state, such as intention, belief, or awareness of risk.

Finally, the probability that Y will do what he is permitted, or even required, to do from the fact-relative point of view is quite high in *Scream*. Some may think this crucial in making Y's act permissible from the evidence-relative point of view. However, Y's permission does not depend on this. Consider:

> *Scream II*: As *Scream* except Y is faced with two people wearing scream masks—the serial killer and X—and Y cannot tell which one is which. V will be killed if he does not kill the serial killer.

Y is permitted to shoot both mask wearers. This is so even though he is certain that he will intentionally kill a person who is not liable, and hence that he acts wrongly from the fact-relative point of view. Hence he is permitted to do what he knows will be fact-relative wrong. Given the analysis of *Miners* earlier, this implication is not troubling.

(ii) Combatants and Non-Combatants

Lazar might complain that there are important differences between *Scream* and combatants in war. True enough. Perhaps the most important difference is that it was very easy for X to avoid appearing like a killer in *Scream* whereas, for familiar reasons, it is much more difficult for combatants on the unjust side to avoid appearing as though they are posing unjust threats. Briefly, the main reasons are: they may have been conscripted; they may be subject to duress and peer-pressure; they may have made reasonable mistakes about the permissibility of joining unjust forces; they may have been indoctrinated during military training; and they may lack the educational and social skills necessary for them to be able accurately to assess the evidence they have.

These factors are all important in determining what combatants on the just side should do in the face of uncertainty about liability-relevant facts. However, whilst these considerations weaken the case that it is permissible to kill unjust combatants in the face of uncertainty, they are not always decisive. Combatants bear at least some responsibility for appearing as though they pose unjust threats. If it is not evidence-relative permissible to kill those who appear to be unjust combatants in conditions of uncertainty, the unjust side will secure its unjust aims. And if that is so, many other people will be killed whose opportunities to avoid being killed will typically have been even worse.

Lazar might also object that my claims about *Scream* have implausibly permissive implications for the killing of non-combatants. Some non-combatants are responsible for making causal contributions to unjust threats. Does it follow that it is permissible to kill non-combatants given uncertainty about whether such contributions are made?

I doubt that the distinction between combatants and non-combatants is as morally significant as people claim, irrespective of their causal contributions.[15] It is unfair sharply to discriminate between combatants and non-combatants. Those who believe that this distinction is very important fail adequately to value the lives of combatants, and to appreciate the importance of the relationships between combatants and non-combatants.[16]

Nevertheless, causal contributions of non-combatants to the threats that others pose make a difference to their degree of liability. It is often difficult to distinguish non-combatants who causally contribute to unjust threats and those who do not. Sometimes these difficulties will be the responsibility of the non-threatening non-combatants.

Where there is a group of non-combatants only some of whom will causally contribute to lethal threats, and non-threatening members are responsible for the inability of those on the just side to distinguish them from threatening members, killing the whole group will typically be permissible, at least if the number of non-threatening non-combatants killed is no greater than the expected number of lives saved (and perhaps even if the number is somewhat greater).

Consider:

Chips: Twenty workers work in a lab that produces technology that assists the weapons systems of advanced fighter jets for the unjust side in a war. There are two groups of ten workers, group A and group B. One group is working on real chips that will be used in the fighter jets. This will significantly increase the potency of the unjust side, leading to many civilian deaths. The other group is producing non-operational dummy chips that commanders on the unjust

---

[15] Lazar provides the deepest defence to date of the importance of the distinction in *Sparing Civilians* (Oxford: OUP, 2015). For some doubts about the success of this defence, see V. Tadros, 'The Moral Distinction between Combatants and Noncombatants: Vulnerable and Defenceless', *Law and Philosophy*, forthcoming.

[16] For the argument, see Tadros, 'Orwell's Battle with Brittain'.

side intend to be secretly supplied to the enemy to confound their operations. X, a secret agent who works for the just side, has infiltrated the lab. He has an opportunity to kill group A. X has discovered that dummy chips will be supplied and informed his superiors, so if these chips are supplied to the just side, they will have no effect. X cannot tell whether group A is producing the real chips or the dummy chips, and has no time to find out before the opportunity of killing group A is lost.

If X knew that group A was producing real chips, killing them would be permissible because doing so is necessary to prevent them causally contributing to unjust lethal threats. As X does not know that group A will make these contributions, killing them is more difficult to justify. However, given that group A is intending to participate in unjust hostilities, and their attempt to do this makes it impossible for X to tell whether they pose a threat, the prohibition on X killing group A is not very stringent.

Some might argue that, in contrast with ordinary combatants, those producing the dummy chips lack a reason to believe that their contributions will make it difficult for people in X's position to distinguish those who pose threats and those who don't, and hence that those producing the dummy chips cannot be held responsible for any such difficulties.

I agree that the fact that X's predicament was less likely to result from group A's conduct makes a difference to the permissibility of X acting. I doubt that this fact is decisive. Group A can avoid being killed simply by doing what was independently required of them. It is hard to believe that, through their wrongful actions of attempting to participate in hostilities, they can significantly limit X's ability to prevent unjust attacks.

We can also consider a variation on *Chips* in which X can kill both groups. As with the variation on *Scream*, although X is certain that he will intentionally kill some people who do not in fact pose threats, killing both groups is permissible on the grounds that the group producing the dummy chips must bear responsibility for trying to contribute to the unjust war, and as a result have made themselves indistinguishable from those who actually make such contributions. At least that is so if the number of people saved exceeds the number of people killed.

IV. UNCERTAINTY WITHOUT RESPONSIBILITY

Recall the problem that many combatants will make no contribution to unjust threats posed in war, and that those who will and those who won't cannot easily be distinguished. We have already considered one fact that might affect the permissibility of killing members of such groups—they are typically responsible for creating the conditions under which combatants on the just side cannot distinguish them from those who are liable. What if those who do not pose threats are not responsible for being indistinguishable from those who do?

As responsibility for the appearance that one poses a threat is pervasive in war, excluding considerations of responsibility from our hypothetical cases makes them more fabulous. Considering such fabulous cases is important if we are to investigate the issue at hand without our intuitions being coloured by questions of responsibility.

Consider:

Firing Squad: A firing squad is about to kill ten innocent people. There are ten members of the firing squad who are indistinguishable. Eight members culpably pose a threat to the ten. Two have been hypnotized against their will to participate in the firing squad. Those who have been hypnotized have unloaded weapons.

Let us assume the controversial claim that intentionally killing an innocent person is more difficult to justify than killing an innocent person as a side-effect. Let us consider different ways in which members of the firing squad might be killed.

(i) Killing in Sequence

Consider:

Firing Squad I: The pilot can be certain of saving the victims only by shooting each member of the firing squad in turn. The pilot can shoot any number of the group.

If he kills all ten people, the pilot is certain of intentionally killing two innocent people. Of course, the fact that the person is innocent does not figure in his intention. Nevertheless, he knows that he is certain that two of the people that he will intentionally kill are innocent. This, it might be argued, makes killing the whole group in *Firing Squad I* very difficult to justify.

Is killing the whole group one by one permissible? Killing the eight who wrongfully pose threats is clearly permissible. They are liable to be killed. Their deaths are not insignificant, but the significance of these deaths is heavily discounted. It would clearly be permissible to kill all eight of these people to avert the threats they pose to the ten. It might even be permissible to kill all eight of these people to avert a threat that they together pose to one of the ten. Let us suppose that this is right. Though this is not completely clear, the right question to ask is plausibly whether two innocent people can intentionally be killed to avert the threat posed to the remaining nine.

In order to evaluate this, we might compare the eliminative harming of non-responsible threats. In one way, the two are similar to non-responsible threats. If they are killed, they are killed as part of a plan to eliminate a threat that the other members of the squad pose. Furthermore, although they will be killed intentionally, they will not be used to avert a threat.[17] To see this, compare:

> *Boulders*:   I am about to be crushed by one of two boulders and I don't know which. I destroy both in turn.

Although I intentionally destroy the non-threatening boulder, I don't use it. Hence, the pilot also does not use the non-threatening members of the firing squad as a means if he intentionally kills them in *Firing Squad I*. Even though the innocents are not killed as a means, though, they are killed intentionally. It is plausible that non-manipulative intentional killing is more difficult to justify than killing as a side-effect.[18]

Some might conclude that if it is permissible intentionally to kill two non-responsible threats to eliminate a threat they pose to ten, it is permissible for the pilot to shoot each member of the group in turn in *Firing Squad I*. This conclusion is too quick. In non-responsible threat cases, it plausibly makes a significant difference that the non-responsible person is the source of the threat. Her duty to avert threats that she is causally involved in is more stringent than the duty of strangers to avert

---

[17] See also, McMahan, 'Who is Morally Liable to be Killed in War', 558. McMahan concludes that killing is permissible in this case, just as in side-effect cases.
[18] See, further, V. Tadros, 'Wrongful Intentions Without Closeness', *Philosophy and Public Affairs* 43 (2015): 52.

such threats. That makes a significant difference to the permissibility of killing such threats.[19]

The hypnotized members of the firing squad, in contrast, are not responsible for posing threats. This makes killing them more difficult to justify. However, there is a somewhat related consideration that might ameliorate the concern that those killed are not threats. If it is impermissible to kill the members of the firing squad in virtue of these people being present, these people's presence will have made the victims of the firing squad much worse off. It might be argued that it is permissible to kill all members of the firing squad because otherwise these two people will have prevented the pilot from saving the ten.[20]

Overall, I think that it is more difficult to justify killing these people than killing standard non-responsible threats. They do not causally contribute to a threat, but only to the pilot's uncertainty about who the threat is. I am uncertain whether it is permissible to kill all ten members of the firing squad to save the ten victims.

In *Firing Squad I*, the pilot also has the option of killing fewer than ten members of the firing squad. Some might argue that if the pilot is permitted to kill a member of the group, he is permitted to kill all such members. If the intentionally killing of innocents is sufficiently difficult to justify to prohibit killing the whole group, the pilot must refrain from killing. This is not clearly right, though.

First note that if the pilot kills all members of the firing squad bar two, he is not certain that he will intentionally kill an innocent person. Earlier, in analysing *Miners*, I suggested that it is sometimes permissible to perform an act that is certain to be wrong from the fact-relative point of view. Nevertheless, it might be thought that there is some reason against acting in such a way. If the pilot kills eight, his act is consistent with his

---

[19] For somewhat related views, see F.M. Kamm, *Creation and Abortion: A Study in Moral and Legal Philosophy* (Oxford: OUP, 1992), 47–50; Tadros, *The Ends of Harm*, ch. 11; Frowe, *Defensive Killing*, 67–70. I now doubt that it is permissible to kill a non-responsible threat to save one victim. See V. Tadros, 'Why It is Wrong to Kill Non-Responsible Threats' (unpublished ms.).

[20] Variations on this idea are found in A. Walen, 'Transcending the Means Principle', *Law and Philosophy* 33 (2014): 427 and G. Øverland, 'Moral Obstacles: An Alternative to the Doctrine of Double Effect', *Ethics* 124 (2014): 481. These authors conceive of the idea in this paragraph as supplanting the Doctrine of Double Effect and related principles such as the *means principle*. Whatever the significance of their idea, I doubt that this is right. It is better to see the idea as a supplement to the *means principle* than a replacement of it. See, further, V. Tadros, 'Responses', *Law and Philosophy* 32 (2013): 241, 289–92.

hoping that he has not acted wrongly from the fact-relative point of view. If he kills more than eight, there is no room for hope about this.

It might also be thought that risk distribution matters. Suppose that any member of the firing squad will kill all ten victims if he is not killed. The more members of the firing squad the pilot kills, the greater the chance that he will intentionally kill a person who is in fact innocent. However, the pilot can increase the chance of saving the victims if he kills eight or more members of the squad. If he kills eight members of the firing squad, there is a small chance that all ten victims are safe. This chance is equal to the chance that the two hypnotized members of the squad are safe. If he kills nine members of the firing squad, he significantly increases the chance that all ten victims are safe, but he will certainly intentionally kill one innocent person. If he kills all ten members of the firing squad he is certain to save all ten victims, but he is certain intentionally to kill two innocent people.

Killing eight members of the squad does not equalize the risk of each innocent person being killed. Innocent members of the firing squad have a greater chance of survival, for there are possible outcomes where a member of the firing squad survives but all the victims are killed. There are no possible outcomes where the victims survive but an innocent member of the firing squad is killed. Nevertheless, killing eight members of the firing squad comes closest to equalizing the risk of death that each person faces. If risk distribution is important over and above expected outcomes, there is some reason for the pilot to kill eight members of the firing squad.

This reason may be outweighed. The expected outcome is very substantially improved if a further member of the firing squad is killed. And it is still substantially improved if the last member of the firing squad is killed. There is a four in five chance that the last member poses a threat. The pilot could kill the last member because in doing so he has a four in five chance of saving ten and a one in five chance of killing a nonthreatening innocent.

(ii) Obliteration

Now compare:

> *Firing Squad II*: The pilot does not know who the innocent members of the firing squad are. He can either drop a bomb obliterating the whole group or do nothing.

Some might argue that *Firing Squad II* is just like *Firing Squad I*.[21] In *Firing Squad I*, if the pilot kills the members of the firing squad one by one, he intentionally kills each person. If he drops the bomb in *Firing Squad II*, he intentionally kills the whole group.

Some might doubt this conclusion, though. They might compare:

> *Firing Squad III*:   As *Firing Squad II*, but the pilot knows that it is A and B who have been hypnotized.

In *Firing Squad III* the pilot might argue as follows. He intends to kill those members of the squad who culpably pose threats to the innocent people. A and B will be killed as a side-effect of killing these people. However, it is permissible to kill two people as a side-effect of saving ten. Hence, it is permissible for him to kill all ten.

I think that there is no important moral difference between *Firing Squad II* and *Firing Squad III*. The difference between *Firing Squad II* and *Firing Squad III* is that in *Firing Squad II*, the pilot does not know the identity of the innocent people. However, he does know that there are some people who are in fact innocent. Hence, there is some fact that he does not know, and were he to know that fact, *whatever it is*, his case would be like *Firing Squad III*. Hence, he knows that there is some fact that, were he to know what that fact is, his case would be just like *Firing Squad III*. But, in consequence, *Firing Squad II* cannot be importantly different from *Firing Squad III*. For were it different, there would be some reason for him to find out what this fact is, even though the particular properties of this fact can make no difference to the permissibility of his conduct, which is hard to believe.

However, it might be doubted that the killings of the innocent people are like side-effect killings in *Firing Squad III*. This analysis makes *Firing Squad III* comparable to:

> *Firing Squad IV*:   The pilot can drop the bomb on the eight liable members of the firing squad, who he can identify. However, shrapnel from the bomb will kill A and B as a side-effect.

---

[21] See McMahan, 'Who is Morally Liable to be Killed in War'.

Here is a reason to distinguish *Firing Squad III* and *Firing Squad IV*. Intentions affect permissibility, we are supposing. But a person's intentions, for moral purposes, are not to be understood in the narrowest way possible. For moral purposes at least, I do not only intend to do the least significant thing that is necessary to achieve my purposes.

We see a similar idea in standard contexts. For example, if I crack an egg, I do not intend to cause only the smallest hole in the shell that would be sufficient to get the contents of the egg out. I intend to crack it in half, even though I would prefer it if I could make the smallest hole given that doing so would cause less mess.

Similarly, D cannot plausibly claim, in *Firing Squad III*, that he does not intend to kill A and B. Those who defend this view might compare:

Individual Obliteration: X is pointing a gun at D. X's degree of liability is sufficient that D could justify intentionally harming X, but not killing him. However, D could justify killing X as a side-effect of averting the threat he poses. If D could obliterate X's trigger finger, X's threat would be averted. However, X only has a bomb, and if D sets it off X would be obliterated. D obliterates X.

Some might argue that D cannot claim that he only intends to obliterate X's little finger, and to kill him as a side-effect of doing this. The claim that there is an important moral difference between D's act in *Individual Obliteration* and standard cases of intentional eliminative killing is implausible. If intentions are relevant to permissibility, it is implausible that D's intentions are unproblematic on the grounds that D needs only to obliterate X's finger to achieve his aim of averting X's threat. It might seem equally implausible to claim that intentions matter to permissibility, but deny that any such prohibition applies to the killing of A and B in *Firing Squad III*.

There are, though, some differences between the intentions in *Individual Obliteration* and *Firing Squad III*. In *Individual Obliteration*, D executes a narrowly construed intention to affect V, and executing this very intention causes V's death. In *Firing Squad III*, in contrast, D does not execute a narrowly construed intention to affect A and B at all. Nevertheless, I think it wrong to treat *Firing Squad III* as just like *Firing Squad IV*.

CONCLUSION

I have by no means exhausted questions of uncertainty, even as they apply to questions of liability. I have focused only on a small set of problems—those that arise when it is uncertain who poses a threat and who does not. Even these questions, we have seen, pose a range of difficult moral problems. They are only a small part of the more general problem of uncertainty in war.[22]

[22] Earlier versions of this paper were presented at an epistemology workshop at Edinburgh and the *Wrongs Across Borders* workshop at Osgoode Hall. I am grateful to the audiences, and especially to Rahul Kumar, my commentator at Osgoode Hall. I am also grateful to the Leverhulme Trust for a Major Research Fellowship, which afforded me the time to work on this piece.